Pyramids of the Giza Plateau
Pyramid Complexes of Khufu, Khafre, and Menkaure

Charles Rigano

authorHOUSE®

AuthorHouse™
1663 Liberty Drive
Bloomington, IN 47403
www.authorhouse.com
Phone: 1 (800) 839-8640

Published by AuthorHouse 05/14/2015

ISBN: 978-1-4969-5249-3 (sc)
ISBN: 978-1-4969-5248-6 (e)

Front Cover:Khufu's Great Pyramid at dusk as seen from near the Sphinx. Photo by the author.
Back Cover: Top - The three Giza Pyramid from closest to furtherest: Menkaure and subsidary pyramids, Khafre, and Khufu. Photo by author.
  Bottom - Author Charles Rigano with Menkaure's Pyramid in the background. Author's photo

Contents

Preface

I remember the moment in 1970 that my fascination for Ancient Egypt started. At work, someone left a book on the Great Pyramid sitting on a desk. I casually picked it up and leafed through the pages. I was immediately absorbed by the subject. I borrowed the book and studied it closely; then I read every book the library had on Ancient Egypt. I wanted to discuss what I was learning with someone, but there was no one around who shared my passion for the subject …until the internet took hold. Then there were many others with the common interest, all eager to "talk". Over the next 15 years, people who started as just words on a computer screen took on personalities and became friends. They possessed a wealth of knowledge and provided an opportunity to discuss and "argue" over Egyptian subjects – something we did daily.

During those early years, my interest was in general ancient Egyptian subjects, but I soon found myself gravitating towards the Old Kingdom and my passion for the period developed and solidified. I soon progressed beyond the popular books on the subject and began digging into the professional literature. Many of these books were rare and hard to obtain, but curiosity and the need to know more of the detail drove me onwards. The original reports from excavators along with those of early amateur travelers provided a fresh appreciation for the monuments and never failed to raise questions that spurred additional research. I was puzzled by differences among the published reports, intrigued by the alternative hypotheses proposed, and challenged by the unresolved mysteries.

It was 25 years before my first trip to Egypt and the start of my in-person discovery. The aftermath of each trip only raised more questions and the need for additional trips and on-site answers. Each trip was self-directed, comprising only two or three of us, a driver, a trained Egyptologist, and sometimes the excavators themselves.

People have been writing about the monuments of the Giza Plateau for over 2000 years. Herodotus, a Greek historian who visited Giza in 450 BC, was probably the earliest whose original work remains. His report has to be carefully evaluated, only his eyewitness accounts believed, and the stories told him by the locals discarded. The reports by medieval Arabs and early European travelers require equal skepticism since few of them were trained observers of archaeological detail. Only in 1800 AD with the work of Napoleon's trained "savants" do we begin to see reliable information. Their careful drawings are invaluable in showing details that have since disappeared. Similarly, the publications by Howard Vyse and John Perring following their work at Giza from 1837-40 contain important information. Vyse, a British army officer has been severely criticized for using gunpowder rather than a trowel as an excavation tool. But he made important discoveries documented daily in his diary-like book. Perring was a trained civil engineer, and his plans and drawings were based on careful measurements.

Pyramid-measuring became something of a fad in the 19th century as theories about the esoteric knowledge supposedly enshrined in the Great Pyramid became popular, but only with the arrival of Flinders Petrie at Giza in 1880 do we have reports that we feel can be relied on. Petrie went to Egypt with an "agenda," namely to verify and extend the work of Piazzi Smyth who was convinced of the sacred origin of the pyramids and the revelations contained within the Great Pyramid. But Petrie was an experienced surveyor and with the best instruments available, soon realized the errors in Smyth's ideas.

Petrie, along with other trained archaeologists who studied the Giza Plateau such as George Reisner and Hermann Junker, are important as much for their rigorous scientific approach as for their first-hand experience with practical excavation methods. I depended on their work and later investigators Selim Hassan, Mark Lehner, and Zahi Hawass for the basic data that went into this book. However, I owe the greatest debt to the Italian team of Vito Maragioglio and Celeste Rinaldi. They were artillery officer and architect, respectively. They accomplished a detailed architectural study of the Old Kingdom pyramids between 1963 and 1977 and published the results in seven volumes entitled, "L'Architettura delle Piramidi Menfite." Early in my research I found their work frequently referenced, but it was only on discovering a complete set that I realized their texts were in English as well as Italian and that they contained exceptional descriptions and over 100 large and incredibly detailed drawings.

While the Giza Plateau is possibly the most excavated site in Egypt, the most popular tourist destination, and the most debated location, the focus in generally available books is on the Great Pyramid. These books usually treat the Great Pyramid as a single achievement removed from the flow of history and to which amazing theories are attached. Little is written about the rest of Khufu's Mortuary Complex or the rest of the Plateau. And there are limited photographs available. I wanted, but could not find, a single readily available book which would provide a "feeling" for and a detail understanding of the three primary constructions of the Giza Plateau – Khufu's, Khafre's, and Menkaure's Mortuary Complexes. That situation led me to this book. I have tried to provide that "feeling" and understanding by filling this book with descriptions of what the early archaeologists found, what the later Egyptologists discovered, my own on-site observations, and ideas and theories, some of which are new. To give meaning to the text I have added many pictures and diagrams. To make the book more readable and for those who want more detail, I have placed dimensions and angles inside tables. The book can be read with or without the information in the tables.

As you will soon discover, this is not just a book about pyramids. The Great Pyramid at Giza built by Khufu has often been described and discussed in isolation, instead of as one element of Khufu's Mortuary Complex and separate from the other Giza mortuary complexes of Khafre and Menkaure. And these three complexes have also been separated from the flow of ancient Egyptian history and architectural developments. This isolation and separation have resulted in many misinterpretations. In this book the individual Giza complexes are set in context.

In addition to enthusiasm for the subject, I applied skills in analysis, synthesis, and critical evaluation that have been honed during a long professional career. I attempted to bring together scraps of information, some of them conflicting, to arrive at conclusions supported by a weight of evidence. I have also attempted to apply a critical eye to the evidence both for commonly accepted conclusions and those of a more speculative, even controversial, nature. I hope the reader who already has a general grasp of the topics treated here will enjoy knowing more about these issues.

There are many photographs in the book; most are mine. To provide scale, photographs often include a one foot black ruler; others purposely have people in them. Many times I asked a traveling companion to stand in my photograph explaining I was not taking a picture on them, they are just providing a useful relative measuring device.

For the spelling of Egyptian place names I have relied on "The Atlas of Ancient Egypt" by John Baines and Jaromir Malek and used "The Chronicle of the Pharaohs" by Peter Clayton as a standard for names and dates. All other sources are identified in Endnotes and the Bibliography. For consistency I have used the dimensions provided by Maragioglio and Rinaldi, except where other sources are indicated. Their metric lengths have been converted to English units using 1 m = 3.28 feet.

Libraries at the University of North Carolina at Chapel Hill and Duke University, the Wilbour Library of the Brooklyn Museum, and the Cairo Library of the American Research Center in Egypt were all instrumental in researching this book. And the Ohio Greene County Library went out and found the innumerable books I requested through interlibrary loan.

My work has been facilitated by the patience of my wife, Jo Ann Rigano, who never complained when I explained the need to go to Egypt just one more time...again..., or the countless weekends I disappeared into my office. For many years Andrew Bayuk and Brent Benjamin of Guardian's Egypt, and photographer and writer George Johnson, all of whom I met on the internet, provided support, great help, and companionship in Egypt. Before my first trip to Egypt when I was hungry for the detail, Larry Orcutt sent me a pile of photographs which I spent hours digesting – my first real window into the Giza Plateau. JD Degreff, another internet friend who I have never met, proofread the book and identified many needed corrections. Egyptologists Mohammed Shata and Mahmoud Khodair have guided, instructed, and befriended me as I explored their country's heritage in which they take great pride. I hope they find this book a fitting tribute to that great society.

But most of all I provide my thanks to Bonnie Sampsell. By her suggestion I started this book and through her encouragement I continued work on it. Over the years of its preparation, she listened to my theories and provided pertinent and knowledgeable feedback. When I was steering wrong, she often set me on a right track. She read each chapter and through her comments, made every one of them better. She provided me many sources, including the Maragioglio and Rinaldi volumes and drawings, which I would not have otherwise had access. Without her this book would not have been possible.

The Gizeh Plateau

The small piece of desert plateau opposite the village of Gizeh, though less than a mile across, may well claim to be the most remarkable piece of ground in the world. There may be seen the very beginning of architecture, the most enormous piles of buildings ever raised, the most accurate constructions known, the finest masonry, and the employment of the most ingenious tools; whilst among all the sculpture that we know, the largest figure–the Sphinx-and also the finest example of technical skill with artistic expression-the statue of Khafra-both belong to Gizeh. We shall look in vain for a more wonderful assemblage than the vast masses of the Pyramids, the ruddy walls and pillars of the granite temple, the titanic head of the Sphinx, the hundreds of tombs, and the shattered outlines of causeways, pavements, and walls, that cover this earliest field of man's labours.

But these remains have an additional though passing interest in the present day, owing to the many attempts that have been made to theorise on the motives of their origin and construction. The Great Pyramid has lent its name as a sort of by-word for paradoxes; and, as moths to a candle, so are theorizers attracted to it. The very fact that the subject was so generally familiar, and yet so little was accurately known about it, made it the more enticing; there were plenty of descriptions from which to choose, and yet most of them were so hazy that their support could be claimed for many varying theories.

W. M. Flinders Petrie
The Pyramids and Temples of Gizeh
1883

Area Surrounding the Giza Plateau

A satellite image of the Giza Plateau with the three pyramids and surrounding area. North is to the top, east is to the reader's right. The image is 1.9 miles east - west and 1.4 miles north – south. (Image: DigitalGlobe and Apollo Mapping Copyright 2014)

In most photographs the Giza pyramids appear to be far out in the desert, but that is not the case. The town of Nazlet el-Simman is at the foot of the Plateau to the east and the city of Giza is to the north. The Nile River is about 5 miles to the east. Near the image top the Avenue of the Pyramids curves downhill from the Great Pyramid to the north towards the famed Mena House, the horse shoe shaped building. Here you can sit in your room or eat in the dining room with a view of the Great Pyramid just outside the window. The Mena House golf course is also just north of the Great Pyramid. To the south of the Plateau is desert.

Giza Plateau Pyramid Complexes

A satellite image of the three pyramid complexes on the Giza Plateau. North is to the top, east is to the reader's right. The image is slightly more than three-quarters mile square. (Image: DigitalGlobe and Apollo Mapping Copyright 2014)

The Khufu, Khafre, and Menkaure mortuary complexes are from top right to lower left. The Sphinx is near the right hand side, just below center of the page. Most of the limestone forming the bulk of Khufu's and Khafre's pyramids came from quarries just north and just south of Khafre's Causeway which is angled from Khafre's Pyramid towards the Sphinx. The Plateau is not flat but rises from in front of the Sphinx about 130' in elevation to Khufu's Pyramid, 163' to Khafre's Pyramid, and 172' to Menkaure's Pyramid. A modern Muslim cemetery is at bottom right. The feather like surfaces west of the cemetery are sand and debris from excavations.

Chapter 1
The Giza Plateau

Long before our great World Wars, the revolutions which shaped the face of our modern world, the American Declaration of Independence, and England's Magna Carta; much earlier than knighthood and the Crusades; before Christ, Julius Caesar and Socrates; already ancient when visited by Tutankhamun and Ramesses II; before Chinese writing emerged, Hammurabi's Code of Laws, and Stonehenge -- stood the pyramids of the Giza Plateau.

Here, 4,500 years ago Egyptian god-kings built their mortuary complexes. Their tombs represent the zenith of the age which produced more than 100 pyramids built over 900 years.[1] Giza was not only a place of kings and gods, but of the royal court, bureaucrats, and common men. Their tombs range from enormous pyramids to pits in the ground; size and style representative of the individual's station in life. From king to commoner they were laid to rest at Giza with the expectation of being reborn into an eternal life.

The Giza Plateau is an Egyptian Old Kingdom, Dynasty IV necropolis; a large, ancient cemetery. The centerpieces are the three pyramids of Khufu, Khafre, and Menkaure. Surrounding each pyramid is a mortuary complex and the tombs of the king's family and the officials who served the king.

To the Giza Plateau

We arrive in Egypt at the Cairo International Airport on the northeast side of the City. From here, we travel west by taxi or tour bus. We pass first through the prosperous suburb of Heliopolis, the location of the ancient temples dedicated to the sun god Re. We pass the walls of the Citadel, an enormous fortress constructed in 1176 AD. Within the Citadel perched high on a hill we see the shining dome and minarets of the Mohammed Ali mosque built in 1824 AD. Passing through Old Cairo we see the Coptic Church built over the cave where the Holy Family was sheltered on their flight into Egypt. Nearby are the remains of the Roman fort called Babylon.

Cairo, an urban area of 15,000,000 people, was not a pharaonic city, but was founded by Muslim conquerors in 969 AD. Every street is crammed with traffic, flowing like a slow river between the curbs.

The Giza Pyramids at the desert edge 5 miles away. People worked these same fields when the pyramids were being built.

Unless you enjoy fear, the traffic is best ignored to be dealt with by the driver. The scenery is city buildings, the primary color is concrete. The heavy city traffic is left behind as our driver turns on to the Ring Road, a modern highway circling Cairo.

Once out of the city, the primary color turns to the beautiful deep green of the farms and palm trees. The driver points; at the end of his finger still many miles away over the fields and behind the low buildings, stand the three Giza pyramids. The ancient farmer toiled in these same fields with the symbols of the king's power always visible. As the drive continues, the growing pyramids dart in and out between buildings. Finally the ride nears our hotel, Khufu's Great Pyramid is in plain view sitting high at the edge of the Giza Plateau. The Pyramid dominates our view and it is hard to look at anything else. But as we force your eyes away from the gigantic edifice, hundreds of other structures appear. Men and women were brought here 4,500 years ago to be buried and live for an eternity.

Kingdoms and Dynasties

The ancient Egyptians had no concept of kingdoms or dynasties and did not place their rulers into any groupings. It was not until their time was nearing its end that in the 3rd Century BCE Manetho wrote "Aegyptiaca" (History of Egypt) in which he divided all the ancient rulers from Narmer or Menes in about 3150 BCE to the period of Persian rule in 343 BCE into 30 dynasties. Modern Egyptologists accepted this division and further group the dynasties into Egyptian periods of stability and prosperity called the Old, Middle, and New Kingdoms, and periods of unrest, disorganization, and invasion

Ancient Egyptian Timeline

Ancient Egyptian Period[3]	Dynasties	Number Years	Number of Kings
Early Dynastic	I - II	464	18
Old Kingdom	III - VI	502	32
First Intermediate	VII – X	144	135
Middle Kingdom	XI - XII	258	23
Second Intermediate	XIII - XVII	212	217
New Kingdom	XVIII - XX	500	33
Third Intermediate	XXI - XXVI	545	34
Late Dynastic	XXVII - XXX	193	16
Foreign Rule		302	21
	Total	3,120	529

known as the First, Second, and Third Intermediate Periods.[2] These 30 dynasties were followed by 300 years of foreign rule ending in 30 BCE with Cleopatra and her son Caesarion, the last pharaoh.

Memphite Necropolis

The Giza Plateau does not sit alone in the desert as the only example of an Old Kingdom necropolis. Ancient Memphis, just 12 miles south of Cairo, was the center of Old Kingdom Egypt and primary

Old and Middle Kingdom Pyramid Sites			
Location – Miles from Memphis	**King (Dynasty)**	**Location - Miles from Memphis**	**King (Dynasty)**
Abu Rawash – 16mi N	Djedefre (IV)	**Saqqara** - 2mi W	Djoser (III)
Giza - 11mi N	Khufu (IV)		Sekhemkhet (III)
	Khafre (IV)		Great Enclosure (III)
	Menkaure (IV)		Shepseskaf (IV)
Zawyet el'-Aryan - 8mi N	Khaba (III)		Userkaf (V)
	Baufre (IV)		Djedkare Isesi (V)
Abusir - 4mi N	Sahure (V)		Unas (V)
	Niuserre (V)		Teti (VI)
	Neferirkare (V)		Pepi I (VI)
	Raneferef (V)		Merenre (VI)
Dahshur - 5mi S	Snefru (IV)		Pepi II (VI)
	Senusret (XII)		Iby (VIII)
	Amenemhet II (XII)		Merykare (IX)
	Amenemhet III (XII)		Khendjer (XIII)
Maidum - 30mi S	Snefru (IV)	**el-Lisht** - 17mi S	Amenemhet I (XII)
Hawara - 42mi S	Amenemhet III (XII)		Senusret I (XII)
el-Lahun - 43mi S	Senusret I (XII)		

residence of its kings. While today's pyramid sites are named for nearby towns, the ancient Memphite Necropolis ran for 21 miles along the desert fringe to the west of Memphis, from Abu Rawash in the north to Dahshur in the south. The only Old Kingdom exception was Maidum further south. After the disruption caused by the First Intermediate Period, pyramid building resumed in the Middle Kingdom but the grander and quality of Old Kingdom construction was never again achieved.

Selection of each specific pyramid site was probably based on several factors: a location in proximity to the capital to permit ease of inspection by the King during construction, access by the court officials invested in the building process, and incorporation of the complex into ritualistic ceremonies before the King's death. Most of the sites are elevated, permitting the King's pyramid to stand above the rest of the population and be viewed for miles. But of prime importance was proximity to building material, primarily good quality limestone with which to build the pyramid cores.

Tomb Development

We can follow the evolution of burial architecture as it changed slowly over 1,000 years through the end of the Old Kingdom. The earliest pre-dynastic burials were simple pits in the sand; items were included for use by the deceased in the afterlife. This simple burial changed as mounds were placed over top and mud brick was added to give some permanence. Wooden beams or mud brick were placed around the inside of the pit to form a space which later grew into a walled chamber. During this early period and through Dynasty I and II, adding size and complexity resulted in large mastabas with multiple rooms cut into the bedrock. To protect the burial, stone slabs, called portcullises, were lowered from above to block the entrance passage. During Dynasty III, mud brick was replaced by stone and the mastaba built for

King Djoser was enlarged five times to become the first step pyramid. The two pyramids which followed, Khaba's and Sekhemket's, were both intended, but never completed, to be step pyramids with a large number of chambers cut into the bedrock.

At the start of Dynasty IV, Khufu's father Snefru introduced significant changes. He filled in the sides of his step pyramid at Maidum to form the first true pyramid. Also at Maidum, for the first time Snefru moved the main chamber from being cut into the bedrock to being built within the pyramid core. He topped the chamber with a corbelled ceiling to remove the pyramid weight from the top of the chamber. Snefru went on to build two additional massive pyramids, the Bent and the Red, with corbelled ceilings and chambers within the pyramid core. His builders changed the orientation of the core blocks from being angled inward towards the pyramid center to being laid flat. He standardized the mortuary complex to include an enclosure wall, subsidiary pyramid(s), mortuary and valley temples, and a causeway connecting the temples.

Khufu likely watched as his father's mortuary complexes were designed and erected. The same architects, planners, and builders who worked on the Maidum, Bent, and Red Pyramids brought their expertise in building massive pyramids and new ideas to Giza. Through each of the three Giza pyramids we can follow the continuance of previous design elements and the flow of new ideas, some of which were employed in later pyramids and some of which were abandoned.

Many books focus on the building and design of Khufu's Great Pyramid as a single event with little or no regard to the more than 100 other pyramids which were built both before and after the Great Pyramid. We have a different view and recognize the Great Pyramid and the Giza pyramids not as a single event but within the flow and context of ancient Egypt as burial requirements, architectural designs, and construction techniques evolved over hundreds of years.

Old Kingdom Pyramids King	Base (Feet)	Height (Feet)	Volume % of GP	Temple Area (Feet^2)
DYNASTY III				
Djoser	412 x 361	206	11%	
Sekhemkhet	395	------	------	--------
Khaba	257	------	------	-----
Snefru (Maidum)	473	302	25%	875
DYNASTY IV				
Snefru (Bent)	619	345	55%	1,330
Snefru (Red)	722	342	65%	NA
Khufu	756	481	100%	24,800
Djedefre	343	297	13%	17,800
Khafre	706	472	86%	55,400
Baufre	706	------	------	-----
Menkaure	344	215	9%	32,000
Shepseskaf	327 x 244	61	5%	10,500
DYNASTY V				
Userkaf	240	161	3%	37,100
Sahure	258	155	4%	42,000
Neferirkare	360	241	11%	34,200
Neuserre	258	165	4%	26,400
Djedkare Isesi	258	164	4%	35,400
Unas	189	141	2%	40,000
DYNASTY VI				
Teti	258	172	4%	54,000
Pepi I	258	172	4%	73,000
Merenre	258	172	4%	------
Pepi II	258	172	4%	55,000

Overview of the Giza Plateau

The mile square Plateau is usually thought of as being a product of Dynasty IV, but it has served many periods. The earliest known tomb is from the Dynasty I reign of King Wadj, about 3000 BC. The name of Dynasty II King Ninetjer was found on jar sealings from a tomb in south Giza. There are also Dynasty V and VI tombs, Dynasty XVIII temples, and later restorations. As the tombs were robbed and emptied, Greeks and Romans were buried in them. But dominating the Plateau are the pyramid complexes of Khufu, Khafre, and Menkaure.

These three Giza pyramids display a great diversity in their construction and the interior layout of the passages and chambers. It is clear there was no single plan used for the internal design or in placing the pyramids on the Plateau. The three pyramids were not built in succession. Khufu was followed by his son Djedefre, who chose a site high on a hill five miles northwest of Giza near Abu Rawash for his much smaller pyramid. Khafre followed and after his death there was a five year period during which Baufre, possibly a son of either Djedefre or Khafre, reigned long enough to start his pyramid at Zawyet el-Aryan, and Hordefef, Khufu's son, ruled for a short period and has a mastaba east of Khufu's Pyramid.[4] Then Menkaure returned to Giza to build his mortuary complex.

Khufu's Great Pyramid at dusk. Subsidiary pyramids to the right; white Boat Museum in the center of the lit face, Sphinx at bottom right.

Khufu's Great Pyramid incorporated previous design features and some design changes which were either incorporated or abandoned in following pyramids. The Ascending Passage leading to a Burial Chamber high in the pyramid core, the storage of plug blocks in a high ceiling gallery, relieving chambers above the burial chamber for weight dispersion, and air shafts, were all used for the first time in a major pyramid but were not used in later pyramids. Other features used for the first time which included a gabled ceiling formed by inclined beams as a weight relieving device for the Queen's Chamber, boat pits, and the increased prominence of the mortuary temple were incorporated in later pyramids.

Khufu's Pyramid Complex centers on the 45 story tall Great Pyramid. Mastabas surround the Pyramid on three sides. The original plan had 89 mastabas to the west of the Pyramid for high officials. To the east of the Pyramid are 4 subsidiary pyramids and 30 royal mastabas with 10 more mastabas south of the Pyramid.[5] These cemeteries continued in use down through the Roman period with hundreds of additional burials filling every available space around the original mastabas. The planned orderly rows and street-like spaces between the rows were turned into a chaotic arrangement of tombs as people wanted to be buried on this "sacred" ground.

To the east of the Great Pyramid are the remains of the black basalt floor of Khufu's Mortuary Temple, three boat pits, Queen Hetepheres (Khufu's mother) pit tomb, the "Trial Passages," and the remains of Khufu's Causeway. On the pyramid south side, a reconstructed 143 foot long solar boat sits in a museum built above the pit in which the disassembled pieces remained hidden for 4,500 years. A second boat pit with another dismantled boat is just west of the Museum.

Khafre's Pyramid is slightly less massive then Khufu's but since it sits 33' higher on the Plateau, appears just as impressive. The builders had to carry out extensive quarrying to reshape the sloping side of the Plateau into a flat base for the Pyramid. This quarry activity created a 25' high vertical wall on the north and west sides of the Pyramid. To the south of the Pyramid is the destroyed subsidiary pyramid. Khafre's massive Mortuary Temple on the west side is surrounded by six boat pits, two still covered but empty. A Causeway extends down the slope to the Valley Temple, next to which is the Sphinx and the Sphinx

Khafre's Pyramid with the casing still in place near the top. The quarry is in the foreground. Tombs were cut into the quarry walls.

Temple. To the south of the Causeway are a large number of rock cut tombs for Khafre's royal family and officials.

Further southwest is Menkaure's smaller pyramid but no less elaborate Pyramid Complex. The granite casing covering the pyramid lower 16 courses remains largely intact but is unfinished. To the south of the main pyramid, are three subsidiary pyramids. From the Mortuary Temple on the pyramid east side the Causeway runs due east to the Valley Temple which has disappeared under the sand; only a black smudge remains on the surface to mark its location. The complex was incomplete at Menkaure's death and his son and successor, Shepseskaf, had to simplify the original design so the complex could be completed quickly to prepare for Menkaure's burial Rock cut tombs for the royal family and officials are to the south of the Causeway.

Besides the three main complexes, there are other places of interest. To the north of Khafre's Causeway, just above the Sphinx is Campbell's Tombs, a very wide, deep shaft tomb cut into the rock. Queen Khentkawes' tomb was cut into a large limestone knoll left in the quarry. To the south of Khafre's Valley Temple is the mysterious Wall of the Crow, an extensive workman's cemetery, and what appears to be a large food preparation area. The Sphinx attracted kings to its side for more than a thousand years.

Menkaure's Pyramid and the three subsidiary pyramids

Among others, Tuthmosis IV erected a stele between the Sphinx paws, Amenhotep II built a temple just to the north of the Sphinx, and Tutankhamun built a rest house to the west.

1. Actually 921 years as measured from Dynasty III Djoser in 2668BCE to Dynasty XIII Khendjer ~1747BCE
2. David, Rosalie and Antony, *Biographical Dictionary of Ancient Egypt, pp 71-72.*
3. Gardiner, Sir Alan, *Egypt of the Pharaohs*, pp 430-453, and Clayton, Peter, *pp16-213.*
4. Maragioglio and Rinaldi, . *L'Architettura delle Piramidi Menfite, Parte VI: La Grande Fossa di Zauiet el Aryan, la Piramide di Micerino, il Mastabat Faraun, la Tomba di Khentkaus* op. cit., p6 and Fakhry, *The Pyramids*, p 126.
5. Reisner, G. A., *History of the Giza Necropolis Vol I,* pp 13-17, 83.

Khufu Pyramid Complex

Khufu's Pyramid Exterior

Khufu's Pyramid Interior

Khufu's Mortuary Complex

Khufu's Pyramid - Designing, Closing, and Opening

Khufu's full Pyramid Complex (left) with all of the surrounding cemeteries. A close up (right) of the eastern part which can be compared to the drawing at the beginning of Chapter 4 to identify specific features. North is to the right and east is to the bottom to match the orientation of the drawing. (Image: DigitalGlobe and Apollo Mapping Copyright 2014)

Chapter 2
Khufu's Pyramid Exterior

Khufu's Pyramid, also known as the Great Pyramid, sits at the northern edge of the Giza Plateau. As a symbol of the King's power, it dominated the ancient landscape. Today, even with the cities of Giza and Nazlet-el-Samman built to the Plateau edge, the Pyramid can be seen for miles. Millions of tourists visit Egypt each year; they all stop to see the Great Pyramid. The lucky ones who arrive early get one of the few tickets available each day to explore its internal passages and chambers.

When the massive structure was covered by a smooth white Tura limestone casing, it must have been the most awesome monument of the ancient world. Today with the casing gone and the underlying internal blocks forming a rough exterior skin, the Pyramid appearance has changed but it still remains one of the most striking monuments in the modern world.

The Great Pyramid (Khufu's Pyramid) as viewed from in front of the Sphinx. The Khufu Boat Museum is the white building to the left. Two of the subsidiary pyramids are to the right.

Just How Big Is It

It is difficult to appreciate the enormous size of this structure. The pyramid, sitting on a base of 13 acres, is composed of 3,900,000 blocks[1] averaging 1.5 tons each for a total weight of almost 6 million tons. These numbers are hard to translate into a picture and a feeling in our mind for its sheer size. Instead, think of the Great Pyramid this way:

- Each side is 2 ½ times as long as an American football field.
- Its base sits on a space as large as a major league baseball or professional football stadium - not just the field, the whole stadium. Next time you go to a big league game, look across the field to seats on the other side and picture the whole stadium filled with limestone blocks.
- The average size block weighs as much as a car. But think about trying to move the car lying on its roof.

- The Pyramid is as tall as a 45-story building. Unless you live in a large city, there is no building in your town as tall as this Pyramid.
- The Pyramid weighs as much as 60 large ocean liners.
- For 3,871 years Khufu's Pyramid was the tallest structure in the world until the Lincoln Cathedral in England was completed in 1311 AD at a height of 525'.

We are awed not just at its sheer size but at the precision with which it was built. Flinders Petrie measured the base at the casing and found the sides differed in length between the longest and shortest sides by only 1.8". The four sides are perpendicular to the car-

Khufu's Pyramid Dimensions			
	Petrie 1883[2]	**Cole 1925[3]**	**Architect[4]**
Side	755'8.8"	755'9.4"	756'0.8"
Height	481'4"	481'1"	481'2"
Side Angle	51°52'		51°50'36"

dinal points with the largest angular error being 3 minutes 57 seconds.[5] The corners were intended to be right angles and are almost exactly 90° with the greatest error only 3 minutes 33 seconds.[6] The foundation pavement surrounding the pyramid on which the lowest course of casing blocks was laid has a maximum difference in level of .8".[7]

The Pyramid Casing

The sides were originally smooth, covered with 144,000 blocks of finely finished white Tura limestone fit to high tolerances. All have been removed except 138 casing blocks found at the bottom course around the four pyramid sides.[8] In 1883 Petrie admired the workmanship of the ancient builders and

the precision with which they cut and fitted together these large casing blocks. He measured the mean thickness of the casing block joints at .02" which requires that each joined block surface be cut to a tolerance of .01" over a surface measuring 35 square feet.[9]

In 450 BCE Herodotus visited Giza and saw

Casing blocks remain in-situ. The blocks against the west face (left) are heavily eroded by wind carried sand. The casing at the center of the north face (right) is largely intact and the fine finish is still visible.

the Pyramid with the casing still in place. He wrote that it was *"built entirely of polished stone, fitted together with the utmost care."* He also described an inscription in Egyptian characters on the Pyramid which was translated by his guide as recording *"...the quantity of radishes, onions, and garlic consumed by the laborers who constructed it..."* and the 1600 talents of silver that were expended in the construction.[10] There is no evidence of inscriptions contemporary with pyramid construction on the casing blocks of Menkaure's, Snefru's Bent, and the Maidum Pyramids, all of which still have a significant portion of their original casing in-place; or on the intact casing on other pyramids; or on the casing fragments scattered in the rubble around pyramids. It is doubtful that whatever Herodotus saw was an original record. Most likely his guide mistranslated graffiti as even the locals today will do for unwary tourists.

In the early 13th century an Arab historian described Khufu's Pyramid as being in perfect condition except for the tunnel cut by Al Mamun's in 820 AD. Soon after this description was written, earthquakes devastated a great deal of northern Egypt. The Pyramid casing blocks were high quality and more readily available than quarrying new blocks. As a result, over several generations during the 14th century virtually the entire limestone casing was removed from the Giza pyramids and used for building projects.[11]

As the casing blocks were removed from the three Giza pyramids, a rubble of limestone chips formed against the pyramid sides, possibly high enough on Khufu's Pyramid to cover and hide the original entrance 55' above the base.[12] Several hundred years later the mounds against Khafre's and Menkaure's Pyramids would frustrate Giovanni Belzoni and Howard Vyse in their search for entrances. These mounds have now been removed from the sides of Khufu's and Khafre's Pyramids and largely removed from Menkaure's Pyramid.

The casing was laid on the finely leveled pavement blocks. The eroded surface shows the line of the missing casing.

Internal Blocks and Courses

Immediately behind the finely finished and precisely laid casing blocks are finished backing blocks, behind which rough core blocks compose the bulk of the pyramid. From a distance the pyramid sides appear rough; up close the stair step formation of the uncovered backing stones is apparent. The casing and backing blocks are set in horizontal courses, the height of each block in a course is constant. While the height remains constant, there is great variation in the other block dimensions and there was no standard "assembly line" sized blocks cut in the quarries. The visible backing blocks have generally squared corners and finished sides but not to the extent of the casing blocks and therefore they do not fit together with the same precision. The gaps between blocks were filled with mortar, the larger gaps with mortar, limestone chips, and flakes. Care was evident to offset rising joints from one course to the next higher so joints were not continuous for two successive courses.[13] The core blocks that can be seen near the surface are only roughly set in courses. Core blocks near the pyramid center can be inspected from a tunnel dug behind the niche in the Queen's Chamber. Here the core blocks are roughly dressed on the horizontal faces with large, unfilled vertical joints.[14]

While the builders leveled an apron around the pyramid, they left an interior knoll of limestone bedrock within the pyramid core. This knoll can be identified

The blocks at the northwest corner of the Great Pyramid form individual courses. While the blocks are of standard heights, the other dimensions vary. Khafre's Pyramid with the intact upper casing is in the background.

On the south side the bedrock raises to a height of two courses behind Charlie Rigano and forms part of the pyramid core. (left). The dark bedrock is visible at the pyramid northeast corner (right). The sign near the top says "No Climbing."

inside the pyramid where the Descending Passage and the Well Shaft penetrate the bedrock. In both places the bedrock surface is higher than the apron surrounding the pyramid (see description next chapter). Today the internal knoll is visible on all four sides of the pyramid and shaped in steps to accept blocks. At the northeast corner dark bedrock is exposed to a height of 6'. Along the south side near the southeast corner the bedrock raises two courses. At the northwest corner the bedrock forms parts of both the north and west sides.

The individual course heights were measured by M. M. le Pere and Colonel Coutelle who accompanied Napoleon to Egypt in 1801,[15] by Piazzi Smyth in 1865,[16] by Petrie in 1880 – 1982,[17] and by Georges Goyon in 1978.[18] All arrived at approximately the same results. Today several of the top courses are missing giving the Pyramid a blunted look. Likely, the idea of watching a block careen down the Pyramid side was irresistible for many people who climbed to the top.

As a general rule the taller, heavier blocks are near the bottom and the block size decreases with pyramid height. This arrangement strikes a balance between the manpower required to separate a block from the bedrock at the quarry and the manpower required to raise the block up the pyramid side. Larger

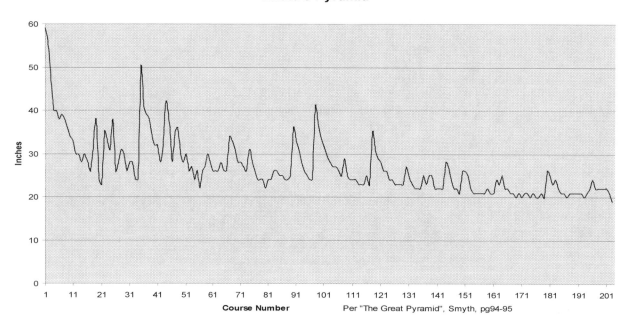

blocks could be quarried with fewer cuts than smaller blocks comprising the same volume but the larger blocks required more manpower to move and raise. The builders likely had to watch this balance closely to maximize workforce efficiency.

While the average block weighs 1 ½ tons, the blocks in the 58" tall first course weigh 8 to 10 tons each. Blocks on the top course measured by Piazzi Smith (course 203, which has since disappeared) were 19" tall and weighed about 600 pounds. While the larger blocks in the first course might take 20 to 30 men to transport on sleds from the quarry, the topmost blocks could be moved from the quarry by 2 men over level ground and by 3 men up a 9° ramp[19] which would be needed to bring the block from the bottom of the quarry up to the pyramid base. Though the general rule says "lower blocks larger, higher blocks smaller," there is a great deal of variability in course height and block size.

The graph, which plots Piazzi Smyth's data, shows that the course heights decrease from 58" at the bottom to 26" by course 17. But then there is a jump at course 19 to 38" high. Course 19 was the level of the original entrance and the jump in course height at this point was obviously part of the architect's plan to permit the entrance to occupy the height of one full course.[20] Continuing to follow the graph, there are a number of variations down to a course height of 24" at course 34. Surprisingly, then course 35 jumps to 50" high. We can follow the course heights on the graph, seeing peaks and valleys until course 125 where the variation dampens and the blocks remain relatively small.

Khufu's Pyramid today is 454' high[21] in 203 courses which means the top 27' is missing. We generally see estimates that this Pyramid originally had 210 courses,[22] but this would mean that each of the missing seven courses was 46" tall. A quick glance at the Course Heights graph will show this was obviously not the case. Based on the size of the courses near the top, there are about 15 missing courses for an original total of 218.[23] To approximate this missing height, in 1874 a wooden tripod was erected by the Transit of Venus Party to simulate the original peak.[24] They determined the position of this marker as latitude 29°58'44.38" north, longitude 31°07'02" east.[25] Using a GPS receiver, my readings were latitude 29°58'43" north, longitude 31°8'3" east.

Today, the Pyramid sides are not flat but display a hollowing at the center of each face. There is a famous 1940 aerial photograph which shows half the south face in shadow and half in sunlight that is credited with this discovery.[26] However, Petrie first identified the hollowing 55 years earlier which he determined to amount to 37". Given that the casing formed a straight line from corner to corner, he calculated that the casing at the corners was 33" thick while the casing at the center was 70" thick, accounting for the amount of the hollowing.[27] As a result, while the surface of the backing stones show the hollowing effect, the extra thickness of the casing would have resulted in a flat, non-hollowed, casing. Vito Maragioglio and Celeste Rinaldi found this same condition present in Menkaure's Pyramid. The builders may have intended that the deeper set center casing blocks would help bond the casing to the pyramid.

The Sockets

At each pyramid corner the builders cut a square socket in the bedrock with sides parallel to the Pyramid sides. We have looked at every other pyramid for similar constructions and only found them at the corners of the middle subsidiary pyramid to the east of Khufu's Pyramid – known as GI-b. Much has been made of these sockets and how they anchored the corners of the pyramid in place. Seeing them in person dispels this idea. Drawings show them to be square and deep; our examination showed them to be rectangular and shallow.

Socket Location	Dimensions	Current Depth
NW	87" by 150"	1" to 12"
NE	131.5" by 150"	0" to 2"
SE	86" by 57"	0" to 6"
SW	Too faint to measure	0" to 1"

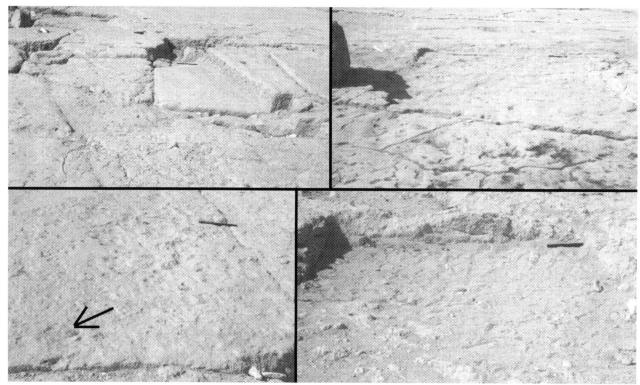

The four sockets: northwest (top left), northeast (top right), southeast (bottom right), and southwest (bottom left). The pyramid would be in the center. The survey marker (arrow) identifies the corner of the southwest socket. A black 1' ruler marks the northeast corner of each socket.

The socket at the northeast corner is the largest and reasonably well defined but is only 2" deep at the corner closest to the Pyramid and is almost level with the bedrock at the corner away from the Pyramid. The southeast socket is not well defined at the corner away from the Pyramid where it is essentially level with the surrounding bedrock. The southwest socket is not much more than a faint outline that is identifiable only because a survey marker is located in one corner. At the northwest corner the socket is difficult to identify from among a number of straight-sided cuttings. After much consideration we identified a rectangle as the socket with the corner away from the Pyramid only 1" deep. Based on the depths of the sockets, even allowing for erosion, they could not have negated any outward corner force produced by the pyramid mass. In any case, in examining the upper surface of the remaining casing blocks surrounding the pyramid, there is no evidence that the casing blocks were mechanically secured to the block above. Without some form of anchoring, placing the lowest casing block in a socket would not "lock in" the higher casing blocks or provide any stability to the pyramid.

When the sockets were uncovered in 1801 by Napoleon's savants, the impression was that the sockets identified the pyramid corners and the length of each side was measured between socket corners. However, Petrie proved the socket corners are outside the line of the casing blocks by 20" or 30" and that all the sockets are not at the same vertical level. Petrie determined that the lower the socket, the further it is from

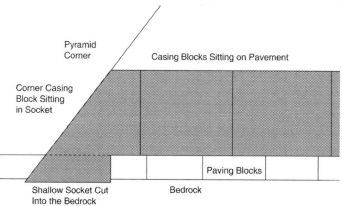

Paving blocks form a level surface around the pyramid. Casing blocks were laid on top of this pavement except the corner casing blocks which sit in the socket. From above, the corner casing blocks appeared to sit on the pavement.

the Pyramid center. We can see today that the bottom casing blocks along the Pyramid sides sit on the pavement blocks.[28] However, the corner casing blocks did not sit on the pavement but penetrated the pavement and instead sat in the socket 23" to 40" below the pavement. Because of the sloped side of the corner casing, the lower the socket the further the casing tip was from the pyramid center as Petrie observed. The pavement was built around the corner casing blocks giving the appearance to the ancient observer that the blocks sat on the pavement in line with the other casing stones.[29]

South Depression and a Piece of Iron

The north pyramid face is easily recognized by the depression in the center which surrounds the original entrance. A similar depression exists on the south face. In 1837 exploration of the ancient monuments was not as subtle or carefully approached as today. Instead of a trowel and brush, Colonel Howard Vyse used explosives to explore for a south entrance and left a 30' deep[30] depression in his failed search.

From Vyse's operations, came a mystery, actually an historic impossibility. On May 26, 1837, J. R. Hill, one of Vyse's associates, was blasting to remove blocks high on the south pyramid face near the mouth of the shaft from the King's Chamber. Hill found a flat iron plate 12" long, 4" wide, and 1/8" thick[31] in a location which he described as having no joint or opening to the point of discovery. If Hill's assertion was correct, the iron plate would date from the time the pyramid was constructed. Hill certified his find in a paper he sent to the British Museum with the iron piece. The paper read:

"This is to certify, that the piece of iron found by me near the mouth of the Air-passage, in the southern side of the Great Pyramid at Gizeh, on Friday, May 26th, was taken out by me from an inner point, after having removed by blasting the two tiers of the stones of the present surface of the Pyramid; and that no joint or opening of any sort was connected with the above mentioned joint, by which the iron could have been placed in it after the original building of the Pyramid. I also shewed the exact spot to Mr. Perring, on Saturday, June 24th."[32]

On June 25, 1837, John Shae Perring certified in writing that he saw the spot at the start of the blasting, and if the iron was found in the spot pointed out by Hill, then it was impossible that it could have been placed there since the building of the Pyramid. Two days later, Ed. S. Andrews and James Mash also certified in writing that they examined the spot and they were of the opinion that the iron had been left during construction of the Pyramid.[33]

A piece of the iron was submitted to analysis and determined to be smelted.[34] The problem here is that while wrought iron would be available about 500 years after the Pyramid was built, and smelted iron may have entered Egypt from other near eastern countries during the New Kingdom 1,000 years later, smelted iron was not common until the time of the Greeks, almost 2,000 years later.[35] This clearly produces a problem with the chronology of either the iron age or the age of Khufu's Pyramid. There does not seem to be a serious problem with either, so we should look for other solutions.

Depression in the center of the south face marks Vyse's exploration for a southern entrance. In-line and higher on the face, Perring found the iron plate. The white building is the Khufu Boat Museum.

The certifications by Perring, Andrews, and Mash only say that a month after the find they looked at the spot of the discovery. Since they really had no reliable information on what the spot looked like previous to the blasting, their certifications have no real meaning. In the case of Hill, he provided no before or after drawings of the location and his recollection of what the spot looked like beforehand may not have been accurate. While this may have passed for science in 1837, it falls short of a creditable account today.

When the casing was being stripped from the Pyramid, there were likely a large number of people working on the side of the Pyramid. Additionally, many thousands of people have climbed the Pyramid since. While we cannot be sure how the piece of iron was introduced, we can guess that it dropped behind some stones and was simply not retrievable, and nothing else.

Entrance

Since the pyramid north face is otherwise featureless, the shadows caused by the recess around the original entrance immediately call attention to the area. From the entrance, all of the Pyramid internal passages run north and south in a single plane while the three main chambers extent to the west from the passages. The entrance is located not in the center of the north pyramid face, but 287" (almost 24') east of the center.[36] The center line passes through the King's Chamber which contains the sarcophagus. The sarcophagus, which has been moved from its original location, is currently just 2' west of the center line. The architects may have placed the pyramid entrance east of center so that the center line would pass through the sarcophagus.

In describing the entrance as it appears today, we have to recognize that with the casing and the first 33' of the entrance passage missing, we are looking at the interior construction around the entrance passage. The original entrance was at course 19, 55' 8" above the pavement. The entrance today is at course 13, almost 41' horizontally inside the pyramid casing.

The architect took care in developing the entrance design which the missing casing allows us to examine closely. Sitting directly above the passage are two massive rectangular shaped blocks of 40 tons and 16 tons. Above these blocks are four remaining gable stones which average 7' high, 12' long, 33" thick and weigh 18 tons each. Angled at about 50°,[37] they meet in a vertical surface in the center, and to the outside rest against an inclined core surface. In this function we would expect a similar construction to continue above the length of the Descending Passage built within the pyramid core. But behind the exposed gables are only squared, closely fitting core blocks.

Looking over the roof of the Mena House (left) the pyramid entrance is easily identified on the north face. Imagine a line from the pyramid top down the center of the face; the entrance is east of center. A close-up view (right) clearly shows the gable stones, the entrance itself is not visible. To the right and below, tourists are entering Al Mamoun's Hole.

The gables continued above the passage as it rose to the pyramid surface. The remnants of two additional lower gable stones can be easily identified in line on the east side. Above these remnants are the inclined surfaces which supported the upper stones. On inclined surfaces over what would have been the passage rising to the original pyramid surface, there is space for at least two more sets of in-line gable stones between the existing partial stones and the original pyramid surface, for a total of five sets peaked over the passage.

While today these features are easily visible, they were originally hidden from view by the intact casing. Inclined stones are generally used as weight relieving mechanisms, however these were placed relatively close to the Pyramid surface and there was not enough weight pressing

The area around the entrance as drawn by Perring in 1837 and as it appears today.

Charlie Rigano stands on a small ledge (top left) just below the gable stones. The remains of two additional lower gable stones (bottom left) are in line with the existing gable. Behind the gable stones (bottom right) are blocks laid in horizontal courses. High on the right upper gable (top right) is Karl Richard Lepsius' inscription in hieroglyphics to mark his king's birthday.

down vertically to require that weight be removed from the Descending Passage ceiling here. Significant engineering planning and stone work went into this feature and it would not be without reason. However, the reason escapes us.

On the top west gable block is a rectangle with eleven rows of hieroglyphics neatly inscribed. We are first tempted to attribute them to an ancient Egyptian source, but this area was hidden within the pyramid and not exposed until the casing was removed well after the end of the ancient Egyptian civilization. This 4' high by 5' long inscription was cut in 1842 by Karl Richard Lepsius, an early Egyptologist, to mark the birthday of his patron, the King of Prussia. With Lepsius were several artists whom he mentions in the inscription.

"Thus speak the servants of the King, whose name is the Sun and Rock of Prussia, Lepsius the scribe, Erbkam the architect, the brothers Weidenbach the painters, Frey the painter, Franke the moulder, Bonomi the sculptor, Wild the architect: Hail to the Eagle, the Shelterer of the Cross, the King, the Sun and Rock of Prussia, to the son of the Sun, freer of the land, Frederick William the Fourth, the Philopater, his country's Father, the favourite of wisdom and history, the guardian of the Rhine stream, chosen by Germany, the giver of life. May the highest God grant the King and his wife, the Queen Elizabeth, the life-rich one, the Philometer, her country's Mother, the gracious, a fresh-springing life on earth for long, and a blessed habitation in heaven for ever. In the year of our Saviour, 1842, in the tenth month, on the fifteenth day on the seven and fortieth birthday of His Majesty, on the pyramid of King Cheops; in the third year, the fifth month, the ninth day of the Government of His Majesty; in the year 3164 from the commencement of the Sothis period under King Menepthes."

Petrie proposed a hinged stone door closed the original Pyramid entrance similar to the one he envisioned at the Bent Pyramid north entrance. His proposed door could swing to the outside to open and when closed would be flush with the pyramid casing, hiding the entrance. As proposed by Petrie, with the door in the open position, the space available to enter the Pyramid would have been reduced to half of the available passage height, about 19". This would seem to be a terribly bad design.

Strabo visited Giza in 24 BCE and described a removable stone covering the entrance which when in-place, was indistinguishable from the other casing stones. Strabo apparently saw the entrance since he also accurately described a sloping passage to the foundation.[38] We believe it unlikely that the pyramid architects would have limited access to the interior of the Pyramid by using a hinged stone. Petrie did not have available to him Ahmed Fakhry's work in 1951 at the Bent Pyramid. Fakhry discovered the Bent Pyramid west entrance closed by a casing block inserted in the passage, which from the outside was indistinguishable from the other casing blocks.[39] This is the only example there is of an original entrance covering. The west entrance to the Bent Pyramid predates the Great Pyramid north entrance by about 20 years and the closure method was probably similar for both pyramids and was not Petrie's hinged door.

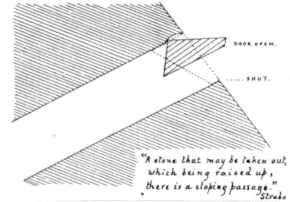

The entrance to the Great Pyramid as proposed by Petrie. His proposal would significantly reduce the available entrance height.

---

1. Sakovich, *Counting the Stones*, KMT Fall 2002. The article presents an update to the previous 2.4 million estimate. I recreated the calculation and got virtually the same number.
2. Petrie, *Pyramids and Temples of Gizeh*, First Edition, 1883, p 39.
3. Cole, *Determination of the Exact Size and Orientation of the Great Pyramid of Giza*, pp 7,11.

4. Based on the architects intent being a pyramid with sides of 440 cubits, a height of 280 cubits, and a side angle or seked of 5 palms, 2 digits.

5. Petrie, op cit, p 39.

6. Lepre, *Egyptian Pyramids*, p 68.

7. Maragioglio and Rinaldi, *L'Architettura Delle Piramidi Menfite, Parte IV,* p12.

8. Lepre, op. cit., p 65 and p 71. Of the 138 casing stones remaining 18 are on the north face, 15 on the east face, 20 on the south face, and 85 on the west face. Most are in bad condition. The average size is 5' long, 5' high, and 6' deep which would result in a weight of 10 to 12 tons.

9. Petrie, op. cit., p 44.

10. Herodotus, *The History of Herodotus.*

11. Tompkins, *Secrets of the Great Pyramid*, p17.

12. While we cannot be sure how high the rubble pile rose against the face, we do know that the pile against Khafre's Pyramid hid the entrance which is 38' above the pavement and the rubble pile against the north face of the Red Pyramid today is about 75' high. Therefore it is possible that the rubble pile against the face of Khufu's Pyramid rose higher than the entrance.

13. Maragioglio and Rinaldi, op. cit., p14.

14. ibid., p44.

15. Davidovits, *Pyramids, An Enigma Solved,* p38. They counted 203 steps and measured a height of 456.3'.

16. Smyth, *The Great Pyramid,* p172.

17. Petrie, op. cit., p 41 and Plate viii.

18. Davidovits, *Pyramids, An Enigma Solved,*p38.

19. Dieter Arnold in *Building in Egypt,* page 63 reports a study which showed that a 1 ton load on a sledge riding on a flat, wet surface could be pulled by 2 men for a pulling power ½ ton per man. The number increased to nine men when pulled up a 9° slope. He also cites the picture from Djehutihotep's tomb which shows 172 men pulling a 58 ton (estimated) statue and the Herodotus account that 2,000 men pulled the 580-ton "green naos". Both result in a pulling power of 1/3 ton per man.

20. A vertical height of 38" when applied against the pyramid sloping side of 51°50' creates a passage height of 48". While this is not suggesting the architects knew trigonometry, the math is:

Sine 51°51' = 38"/passage height

.7864 = 38"/passage height

passage height = 48.3".

21. Petrie, op. cit., Plate VIII.

22. Lepre, op. cit., p 69 and Maragioglio and Rinaldi, op. cit., p16.

23. The height of the remaining top 20 existing courses average 21" high. This would mean that the missing 27' would require about 15 courses and bring the total number of original courses to about 218.

24. Petrie, op. cit., p 43.

25. Lehner, *Archaeology of an Image,* p 7.

26. Lepre, op. cit., p 66.

27. Petrie, op. cit., pp 43-44.

28. Petrie op. cit., pp 37 – 38.

29. Petrie, *Pyramids and Temples of Gizeh,* 1985 version, pp 10 – 11.

30. Maragioglio and Rinaldi, op. cit., p 14.

31. Hancock and Bauval, *Message of the Sphinx,* p 102.

32. Vyse, *Operations Carried on at the Pyramids of Gizeh,* Vol 1, p 276.

33. Ibid., p 276.

34. Gayer and Jones, <u>Metallurgical investigation of an iron plate found in the Great Pyramid at Giza</u>, Journal of the Historical Metallurgy Society, Vol 23, no 2, (1989) pp 75-83. Craddock and Lang, <u>Gizeh Iron Revisited</u>, Journal of the Historical Metallurgy Society, Vol 27, no 2, (1993) pp 57-59. Both sets of investigators looked at the same piece and their metallurgical analysis produced similar results. The only difference was that Gayer and Jones found traces of gold while Craddock and Lang found none on either the specific piece nor the whole article

35. Prodigy Compton's Encyclopedia

36. Petrie, op. cit., 1883, p 55.

37. Petrie, op. cit., p 53. Sizes identified by Petrie are averaged. The size is multiplied by 155 pounds per cubic foot to get the weight estimate.

38. Petrie, op. cit., 1883, pp 167 - 169. Petrie believed Strabo was writing about a hinged door, but the translation is "a stone that can be taken out." Vyse in *Operations Carried on at the Pyramids of Gizeh* translates the same passage by Strabo as referring to a "…removable stone."

39. Fakhry, *Monuments of Sneferu at Dahshur, Vol 1, p 49.*

Chapter 3
Khufu's Pyramid Interior

The Pyramid has remained open since 820 AD when Caliph Al Mamun penetrated the core and gained access to the interior. With the exception of the relieving chambers above the King's Chamber and the "air passages" in the Queen's Chamber, all of the passages and chambers have been known since Al Mamun's time. During much of the intervening period, the Pyramid was a fearsome place to explore: dark, stench filled, and the home of thousands of bats. Today the Antiquities Department keeps the interior clean, well lit, and ventilated.

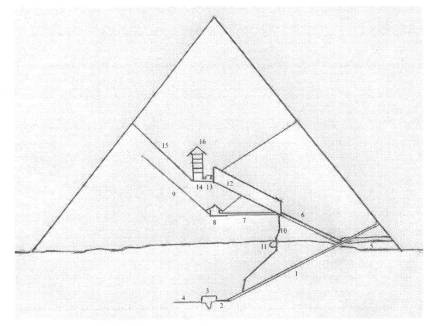

1 Descending Passage
2 Lower Horizontal Passage
3 Subterranean Chamber
4 Cul de Sac
5 Al Mamun's Hole
6 Ascending Passage
7 Upper Horizontal Passage
8 Queen's Chamber
9 Queen's Chamber Shafts
10 Well Shaft
11 Grotto
12 Grand Gallery
13 Ante Chamber
14 King's Chamber
15 King's Chamber Shafts
16 Relieving Chambers

Descending Passage

The Descending Passage runs straight from the entrance for a distance longer than a football field and maintains a constant incline, height, and width. For the first 110' the passage is within the pyramid core; the remainder is cut through the limestone bedrock. The Antiquities Department has made several additions for the convenience of the visitor: electric lights, cleated floorboards, and handrails were built into both the Descending and Ascending Passages. It is difficult to imagine negotiating these steep passages bent over without the rails to lean on and the cleats to provide a surface to push against.

Much has been made about the Descending Passage pointing at the north star or north pole position. With the Great Pyramid essentially at 30° north latitude[2], the pole position would be 30° above the horizon. Since this is 3 ½°

Looking down the Descending Passage with the cleated floorboards and the railing along each side. Because of the limited height, the passage has to be negotiated bent over. The best way to descend is to place your arms on the railing, and go backwards.

higher than the position at which the passage points, we look for a simpler explanation. The odd slope (see table) actually represents a lateral displacement of 2 units for a drop of 1 unit, or a 2 to 1 slope.[3]

Descending Passage	Dimension[1]
Descending Passage Length	345'7"
Vertical Depth below Pavement at Bottom	98'
Passage Slope	26°31'23" + or - 5"
Passage Size	48.5" High by 40.8" Wide

This simple ratio has to be more than a coincidence and leads us to conclude that there is no mystery in the determination of the Passage slope, they just used a simple to build ratio.

What at first glance appears to be a featureless low and very long passage has a number of interesting and sometimes mysterious features. In the portion within the pyramid core all of the wall blocks are aligned with the passage incline except a single horizontal block on either side of the passage 35' from the entrance.[4] The blocks preceding and following are inclined and cut to accept the horizontal blocks. No reason is apparent for these horizontal blocks. At the junction of the Descending and Ascending Passages, there is a vertical scored line 7" long and 1/2" wide on the east wall. The line is not inscribed, but appears as if it was gouged by the edge of something heavy falling. Further up the passage, at 40' from the entrance there are reported similar vertical lines on the passage walls. We have looked, but could not find these lines. If they exist, and are similar to the scored line, they might be an indication of a hidden passage.

At 92' 6" from the entrance is the junction of the Descending and Ascending Passages. The Descending Passage sidewalls rise vertically into a 7' long recess in the ceiling which provided access to the Ascending Passage. The Descending Passage ceiling is flared on the up-passage side to aid in making the transition between passages. But entrance to the Ascending Passage is blocked by a granite

Plug Block in Ascending Passage

Descending Passage

Looking down the Descending Passage (left,) the dark face granite block in a ceiling recess plugs the Ascending Passage. A line marking the level of the passage ceiling runs along each side. This space is the prism shaped area from which a covering block became dislodged and fell making a loud noise. From the floor of the Descending Passage (right) looking up at the plug face. Notches are visible in the side walls on both sides of the face.

plug block which was slid down from above to seal the passage. The flat black face of the plug stands in stark contrast to the surrounding white limestone walls. Notches 11" deep with an undeterminable purpose were cut in the limestone walls on the east and west sides of the plug block. We measured the plug bottom at 46" high by 37 ¾" wide. [5]

The granite block discovered by Petrie in the Descending Passage and later moved outside the entrance. Lying on top is a 1' black ruler. The partial third hole is in line above the two holes.

Tradition holds that the plug block was covered and hidden by the missing Prism Stone, named because of the wedge shaped space it would have filled. This single stone would have weighed a massive 7,000 pounds[6] and had to be raised 4' from the floor into position and secured. Since the confined space of the Descending Passage would have permitted no more than four workmen to be positioned to raise the stone, we are led to the conclusion that there was not one Prism Stone, but several stones raised and positioned to conceal the plug blocks. Exactly how the stones were held in place for several thousand years is difficult to imagine since there seems to be no provision for securing them. However, we can be reasonably certain that the granite plug blocks were covered and hidden from view. If the plugs were uncovered and visible, they would have been a clear indication to the first robbers of a blocked passage. The robbers would have certainly cut a passage through the softer surrounding limestone and penetrated to the upper chambers. Since this was not the case, we can conclude the plugs must have been hidden from view by a false ceiling.

But 8' further down the Passage, the ceiling opens to a rising, roughly cut 11' long shaft inclined to the west at a steep 60° angle. At the top, the shaft enters Al Mamun's Hole. This provided the means to bypass the plug blocks. More at the end of this chapter about this passage, the Prism Stone, and Al Mamun's Hole.

Just below this juncture, in 1881 Flinders Petrie found a large red granite block in the Descending Passage. This block was moved and now sits just outside the pyramid entrance. The block's upper, lower, and two side faces are finished and one corner is squared. The other surfaces are rough, broken from a larger block. There are three holes in a row cut completely through the thickness, two are complete holes, and the third is broken. This stone and three others like it which will be found as we describe the pyramid interior were a mystery for many years; the solution will be described later in this chapter.

At 110' from the entrance the Descending Passage enters the bedrock. This spot defines the plateau surface which is 6'7" above the level of the exterior pavement,[7] providing evidence a bedrock knoll was incorporated within the pyramid core. Later we will find that the plateau in the area of the Grotto is somewhat higher.

The Well Shaft opening with a wooden cover. The white tube provides ventilation to the Subterranean Chamber. See additional photos page 64

The Passage is tunneled through the bedrock for the next 264'; the natural rock forms the walls, floor, and ceiling. There are two natural fissures in the rock at 131' and 257'. The first contains a large stone which was inserted, apparently to fill and permit sealing of the space. During the many years the Descending Passage was open to explorers, the filling was mostly removed and the fissures probed.

The framed transition from the Descending Passage to the smaller Lower Horizontal Passage. A 1910 Edgar brothers picture (left) shows the top and right edges were relatively straight. The floor was still covered by debris. Charlie Rigano sits in the same position 91 years later (right). The frame top and right have suffered and are no longer straight.

On the west side of the Descending Passage near the bottom, 318' from the entrance, is the covered mouth of the Well Shaft. With a slight downward slope the shaft entrance cuts 8' west before a narrow rough shaft rises steeply towards the north. The Well Shaft was likely used as an escape route for the work crew that closed the upper chambers and released the plug blocks down the Ascending Passage. There is no evidence to indicate whether the entrance was sealed, but sealed or not it would have drawn the attention of the first robbers and provided the path to the upper chambers and the riches buried with Khufu. At the bottom of the Descending Passage a raised inclined lip perpendicular to the passage floor was likely intended as a stop for plug blocks. This marks the transition to the narrower Lower Horizontal Passage.

Lower Horizontal Passage

The low ceiling forces the visitor to crawl through the passage before emerging into the Subterranean Chamber. The Horizontal Passage is squared and straight; the sides are dressed and appear to be the intended final size. The sarcophagus in the King's Chamber (38.5" wide by 41.3" high) would not fit through this passage and it is difficult to imagine any stone sarcophagus being small enough to fit through the Passage and still be able to hold the king's remains.

Near the Passage end, just 3' from the Subterranean Chamber is a recess cut into the west wall, the ceiling is raised a few inches, and there is a slight cutting into the opposite east wall. Inside this recess is another

Lower Horizontal Passage	Dimension[8]
Size	27'2" Long, 36" High, 33" Wide
Recess	6' Long, 6' Wide, 4' High
Recess Granite Block	17" by 25 ½", 20"

The recess in the Lower Passage and the granite block. The ceiling is rough and unfinished indicating construction was not complete when the recess was abandoned. The Subterranean Chamber is at the end of the passage.

red granite block. This block has no holes and is rough on all sides. The recess appears unfinished so whatever its intended purpose cannot be directly determined.

Subterranean Chamber

After the confined space of the Descending Passage and Lower Horizontal Passage, entering the large Subterranean Chamber is like emerging into an auditorium. This chamber is cut deep within the bedrock; the outside is 375' away through narrow passages. Overhead is 100' of limestone bedrock and 450' of pyramid. Some comfort for the visitor may be provided by the realization that this Chamber has been here for 4500 years without mishap and there is no reason to anticipate it will collapse during a short visit.

The entrance from the Lower Horizontal Passage is in the Chamber northeast corner and requires a step 18" down to the Chamber floor. The Passage east wall is continuous with the Chamber east wall without a break providing evidence the architect did not plan a limestone or granite lining around the Chamber. From the entrance the Chamber floor slopes gently downward to the south (opposite the entrance) broken by a large hole in the Chamber floor. Another passage exits from the Chamber southeast corner. To the west (the right) the floor rises abruptly to a raised platform on which bedrock humps raise towards, but do not touch, the ceiling. The Chamber walls and ceiling are generally flat but unfinished, the ceiling defining the Chamber intended length and width. The Chamber was obviously not completed. [10]

In the center of the low area is a wide irregular shaped hole surrounded by a modern metal fence. About 4' down, the irregular shape forms a 5' square, 25' deep pit which is diamond shaped relative to the Chamber walls.

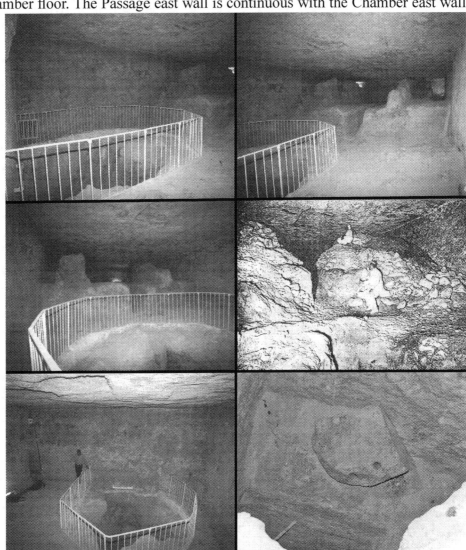

From the entrance to the Subterranean Chamber looking south (top left), across the fence surrounding the pit, to the barred Cul de Sac on the opposite side. The wall to the left is flat except for the projecting stone near the top. From the entrance the view to the right (top right) shows the "platform" area with vertical projections. The two pictures (middle row) taken from the same position but about 90 years apart. The Edgar Brothers photo (middle right) shows the chamber largely encumbered by debris, likely from Perring's excavation of the Pit. From atop the "platform" (bottom left) the entrance is to the left, the Cul de Sac to the right, and the pit in the center. The granite block (bottom right) sits on the ledge in the pit.

Subterranean Chamber	Dimension[9]
Chamber	46'1" E-W 27'1" N-S Height Various About 12' at East End

Captain G. B. Caviglia reported that when he first entered the Chamber in 1818 he found an excavation that appeared to be the beginning of a shaft, but he did not describe it further.[11] Caviglia may have further opened the excavation.[12] Vyse considered that Khufu's real burial chamber as described by Herodotus[13] might be below the Subterranean Chamber and accessed from the surface by a second lower descending passage. In a search for this chamber, Vyse had John Perring cut the hole deeper. After penetrating 38' through solid rock and finding nothing, Perring abandoned the excavation in September 1838.[14] The hole has partially filled in since that time.

On the pit south side, 5' down is a ledge on which rests the third red granite block. This block, again a large fragment of a more massive block, has two finished surfaces and two holes near one edge similar to the block outside the entrance. The block was first discovered in the early 1900's by L. Dow Covington in the Descending Passage and moved to its present location.

Exiting from the southeast corner of the Chamber, 7" above the floor, is a passage known as the Cul de Sac. Because the Chamber floor slants 3' downward from the north to the south, the ceiling of the Cul de Sac is below the level of the Horizontal Passage floor. The Cul de Sac is obviously unfinished as it has great variation in its height and width and is not straight. The passage itself provides no evidence of its use and since there is no precedence in other Dynasty IV pyramids; even a guess would be hazardous.

The western half of the Chamber appears to be an excavation in progress. On top of a platform, about half the Chamber height, stands a number of long, slim vertical limestone humps still connected to the bedrock. These appear to be an intermediate step in cutting the pieces at the bases and removing the large pieces whole, rather than chipping them away a piece at a time.

Cul de Sac	Dimension[15]
Length	53' 10"
Size (Very Irregular)	27" to 38 wide 27" to 31" high

Down the middle of the platform an east – west depression was started. While the depression has been described as a ramp or stairs, it was likely the start of a slot to isolate and remove stone. The entire raised area has been left very rough and the workmen's chisel marks are easily visible.

The state of the Chamber leads us to believe that it was abandoned. Since there are no cracks in the walls or ceiling, structural reasons do not seem to be the cause. One day, with work in progress cutting the raised platform, extending the Cul de Sac, defining the Recess, and removing debris from the Chamber to the surface; work was halted. A change in plan which resulted in the architects abandoning this chamber seems to be the only explanation.

Ascending Passage

The Ascending Passage slope is very close to the angle of the Descending Passage and was also likely intended as a 2 to 1 slope. The lower 15' of this Passage is completely filled with three granite plug blocks held in place by a narrowing of the Passage side walls at the lower end. The Passage height remains the same for its entire length. The west side of the Ascending Passage in Al Mamun's Hole is missing making visible the

Ascending Passage	Dimension[16]
Length	128' 10" (75 Cubits)
Height	47.3"
Width	41.6" Upper End, 38.2" Lower End
Passage Slope	26°2'30'

full length of the upper and middle granite plugs and the top of the lower granite plug. The higher (southern) end of the upper plug has a rough, irregular surface. Based on Petrie finding a piece of granite cemented to the floor, he estimated that the top plug was 24" longer than it appeared.

A portion of the middle and the upper plug blocks visible in the Ascending Passage where the wall is cut away in Al Mamun's Hole (left). The Ascending Passage (right) with floor cleats, handrails, and electric lights.

We wondered why part of the hard granite plug is missing when the lim Passage are softer and easier to cut away. Likely the end of the granite plug facing up the passage was hit many times by hard material being thrown down the Ascending Passage (pieces of limestone plug blocks, granite portcullis, granite sarcophagus lid, and other material that was removed from the upper chambers) and millions of human touches over more than a thousand years slowly wore away the granite surface.

The Ascending Passage is constructed of a combination of vertical blocks named girdle stones and blocks set at the same incline as the Passage. In 1872 Waynman Dixon identified the vertical stones. These were either single stones through which a hole for the passage was cut or two stones, an upper and lower, which completely surround

Top of the Ascending Passage as seen from the Grand Gallery. Ramps on the side go up the Grand Gallery. The path below enters the Horizontal Passage.

the passage on all sides. These became known as girdle stones. In 1909 the Edgar Brothers confirmed the girdle stone existence by measuring and plotting every stone in the Passage. They found that for 25' above the topmost granite plug the Passage is composed of seven partial or full girdle stones. About 10 cubits up the Passage is another vertical girdle stone followed by two more at 10 cubit intervals. Though there is space for an additional girdle stone before the Grand Gallery, another one is not present.[18] The other blocks forming the walls are inclined at the same angle as the passage. Likely additional girdle stones surrounded the plug

The junction of four passages. Some of the features will be explained later. This shows a bridge over the Horizontal Passage.

[Diagram labels: Grand Gallery; Niche & Hole; Slot; Horizontal Passage; Ascending Passage; Well Shaft]

blocks at the lower end of the passage, but since this area is either destroyed or hidden by the plugs a positive determination cannot be made.

Borchardt considered that the horizontal blocks in the lower passage and the inclined blocks in the upper passage provided evidence for a change in plan. His theory suggested that at a point after the Pyramid reached a height of several courses, the architects decided to abandon the lower chamber and place the burial chamber high in the pyramid core. To build a passage upward required tunneling through already existing limestone courses represented by the horizontally laid blocks (girdle stones) and from this point upwards, the builders laid blocks to match the Passage incline. There was general acceptance of the idea that the original plan identified the Subterranean Chamber as the burial chamber, which was abandoned when the upper chambers were planned. The only physical evidence supporting this theory is the possible tunneling of the Ascending Passage through already laid core blocks.

We tested the "tunnel through existing core blocks" theory. While the builders squared and laid casing blocks to high tolerances, they did not square core blocks and placed them with offset, wide joints.[19] If the Passage was tunneled through existing masonry, we should find the wide joints plastered to form a smooth surface, some ceiling blocks would not span the entire passage width but would have joints where blocks meet in the ceiling between the walls, and some ceiling blocks would be just a few inches wide while others would be several feet wide depending on where the tunnel was cut relative to the already laid blocks. On close examination of the Passage, we found very tight joints between well-squared blocks, all ceiling blocks span the full passage width, and all ceiling blocks were of approximately the same size. These findings are visible in the Edgar Brothers detail drawings.[20] The observations completely invalidates the "tunnel through existing blocks" theory and indicates the upper chambers were either included in the original plan or added to the plan shortly after construction commended.

So we look elsewhere for a purpose to the girdle stones and find two. First, when blocks are laid on an incline, they exert a force in the direction of the incline. If the Ascending Passage was composed of all inclined blocks butted against each other, the thrust build-up along the incline would be substantial and push against the ceiling of the Descending Passage. The first three or four vertical girdle stones from the passage top may have extended outward, deep into the pyramid core and used to interrupt this thrust build-up. Second, a possible purpose for the series of lower girdle stones may have been to contain the outward thrust of the plugs as they impacted the bottom of the Ascending Passage. If single blocks lined the lower end of the Ascending Passage, the impact of the sliding plugs might have pushed them outwards, widening the Passage, and not containing the plugs.

Upper Horizontal Passage	Dimension[21]
Width	41.3" (2 Cubits)
Height Before Drop	46.4"
Height After Drop	67"
Length (at ceiling)	110'4"

Upper Horizontal Passage

The Ascending Passage opens into the lower end of the cavernous Grand Gallery. From this point there are two possible paths: up to the Grand Gallery and the King's Chamber or straight ahead to the Upper Horizontal Passage which leads to the Queen's Chamber.

The entrance to the Upper Horizontal Passage forms a break in the floor of the Grand Gallery. The Passage width matches the Ascending Passage and the central ramp of the Grand Gallery. At the beginning of the passage the sidewalls are two courses high with each block two cubits long. Oddly, the vertical joints are one above the other making a continuous line from floor to ceiling. This is the only known exception in the Great Pyramid to the ancient Egyptian builder's rule of offsetting joints to make the masonry stronger. J. P. Lepre found 1/8" wide red ocher construction lines painted the length of the Passage 22" up from the floor. The lines are not visible today in this dim light, worn off, or obscured by the grime collected over the ages.[22]

At a distance of about 92'(measured along the ceiling) from the passage entrance, the floor steps down 21" (about 1 cubit) and continues at this level into the Queen's Chamber. After the step Caviglia cut a hole in the floor which was later enlarge by Vyse to a depth of 4' and 10' long, but they found nothing.[23] This lower floor is rough and that roughness extends into the Queen's Chamber.

Queen's Chamber	Dimension[24]
Height Above Exterior Pavement	69'5"[26]
Width (North - South)	17'2" (10 Cubits)
Length (East - West)	18'11"(11 Cubits)
Height at: North and South Side Walls Center of Gabled Roof	 15"5" (9 Cubits) 20'5"

Queen's Chamber

The misnamed Queen's Chamber (no queen was entombed here) is entered at the northeast corner directly from the Upper Horizontal Passage. There is no antechamber or portcullis or evidence that one was planned. A raised torus surrounds the entrance, a method used to protect surfaces during construction.

The floor level after the drop in the Horizontal Passage continues into the Queen's Chamber. The floor is very rough and was not intended to be the final product. Around the Chamber edges, the floor has a depression about 1" wide cut into the rough floor. The evidence leads us to several different theories:

- Finely finished paving blocks were laid on the floor and later removed by stone robbers
- Finely finished paving blocks were intended but never introduced
- The depression around the edge was a control surface and the floor was intended to be cut and finely finished to that level

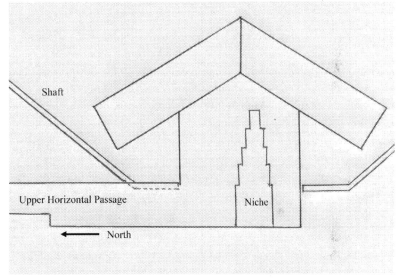

The Queen's Chamber looking towards the east with the Niche and entrance the far wall. "Air" shafts are shown stopping short of the Chamber as in their original state.

In the previous major pyramids - Maidum, Bent, and Red - corbelled ceilings were used to remove weight from chamber ceilings. In the Queen's Chamber a gabled ceiling was used for the first time as a weight-relieving device in a pyramid chamber. In future pyramids this advancement in roof design became the standard method and corbelled ceiling were no longer used. The gabled roof apex marks the Pyramid east-west center line, equidistant from the Pyramid north and south sides.

The ceiling is pitched at an angle of slightly more than 30° which transfers the weight bearing on the Chamber ceiling to the pyramid core. In the northwest chamber corner, Perring excavated beneath one of the ceiling blocks to determine the full size of these beams. Petrie measured the length of this ceiling

Niche	Dimension
Depth	41" (2 Cubits)
Base Width	62" (3 Cubits)
Height	184.6"
Width at Top	21" (1 Cubit)

block within the Chamber at 120.0" and behind the wall face at 121.6".[27] It is likely that the gable blocks were laid first on the core blocks and then the final chamber walls built under them so as to free the walls from any weight bearing pressures. Later settling has made the gables lie directly on the walls and the resulting downward pressure has caused a number of cracks.

The most distinctive feature in this Chamber is a deep Niche in the east wall. The Niche is framed by two courses at the bottom with the next four courses projecting ¼ cubit beyond the one below. It is interesting that in this Chamber the architects used both corbelling and gables as weight relieving devices. The Niche is not centered on the east wall as might be expected but the Niche midpoint is 25.2" to the south of the Chamber center.[28] To the rear of the niche robbers cut a rough tunnel horizontally for 50', curving slightly north near the far end. This tunnel provides a view into the Pyramid core. The first 22' penetrates four large

The gabled ceiling at the chamber west end (upper left). The white mark at the right is where Perring cut into the wall to determine the length of the gable. The entrance from the Horizontal Passage to the Queen's Chamber in the center(bottom left), Niche to the right, and the shaft opening marked by the arrow. Charlie Rigano stands in the Niche (right). To his back is the barred hole cut by robbers. The robber's chisel marks are visible above his head.

well-squared blocks which apparently surround the chamber on all sides. After this point the core blocks are roughly dressed only on the upper and lower faces, with wide joints, and show no evidence of mortar fill.[29][30] Apparently chamber walls were not built directly against core blocks, but to provide stability, the chamber was surrounded by several layers of finely squared and laid blocks.

The Niche's purpose is a mystery. We are tempted to envision a large freestanding statue of Khufu here. Petrie suggested a diorite statue since he found a number of diorite fragments, some with polished faces, in line with the Pyramid entrance.[31] Of course there could be any number of explanations for the fragments and there is really no evidence to support the statue theory. In looking for purpose, we should consider that the shape of the Niche was likely caused by weight relieving requirements and not by the shape of the object enclosed.

The other interesting Chamber features are the "air" shafts opening from the north and south walls. In 1872 Waynman Dixon noticed a crack in the south wall. When he was able to push a wire to a great depth, he had Bill Grundy cut a hole at the spot with a hammer and chisel. After just a few strokes, the chisel broke through revealing the shaft. They measured for the same spot on the north wall and quickly broke through to the northern shaft.[33] Both shafts travel horizontally through the wall before rising towards the Pyramid surface. The covers were not a block inserted in the shaft but a 6.7" thick part of the wall block which had not been cut through.[34] In one of the shafts, probably the north though he did not say, Dixon found three objects: a copper "grappling hook", a small gray-green stone ball, and a wooden rod 5" long and broken at one end.

In 1928 Morton Edgar probed the shafts with flexible metal rod sections he had manufactured with threaded ends for connectors. The leading end had a wooden ball so the rod would not get stuck against minor projections. Edgar inserted the rods 175' up the north shaft when they broke. A week later with new rods he tried again with the same result. Twice he used the rods to probe the south shaft. Both times at 208' he encountered an obstruction that he could not get beyond.[35]

In 1993 Rudolf Gantenbrink sent his camera equipped robot Upuaut II up both shafts. The robot was able to penetrate only 59' up the north shaft before encountering a 45° turn to the west (left) constructed so that the shaft would miss the Grand Gallery. At the turn the robot found Edgar's round metal probing rod and a square rod which was possibly Edgar's second try. Both rods continued up the shaft. The robot was not able to negotiate the turn leaving further exploration for a later time.[36]

Upuaut II was able to travel the full length of the southern shaft and found the obstruction Morton Edgar

"Air" Shafts	Dimension[32]
North Shaft	
Face Size	8" High, 8" Wide
Horizontal Depth	76"
Inclined Angle	Fluctuates between 33°18' to 40°6' before the 45° bend, after the bend the angle is unknown.
Height Above Floor	59" above current floor 38" above possible missing floor
South Shaft	
Face Size	8" High, 8" Wide
Horizontal Depth	77"
Inclined Angle	39°36' Average of 24 measurements
Height Above Floor	59" above current floor 38" above possible missing floor

encountered; the shaft was closed with a finely finished block of Tura limestone. The block has two copper pieces attached to its surface, one broken with a piece lying in the shaft; possibly this piece was broken by Edgar's probing. This block was unfortunately called a "door" and expectations ensued about what might lie beyond.

Exploration of the shafts continued in 2002 with a robot, Pyramid Rover, drilling a small .78" hole in the block at the end of the south shaft. On live TV the robot inserted a camera on a rigid boom into the hole finding a small space 7" deep and another blocking of roughly finished local limestone. Pyramid Rover also traveled 207' up the Queen's Chamber north shaft and found a similar blocking slab with two copper pins, but did not drill through the block.

In 2011 the Djedi robot inserted an articulating camera through the south shaft hole made by the Pyramid Rover. It found three red hieratic glyphs, which might be read 121 or 221, and a red line on the floor. We note that this spot is 121 cubits up the shaft from the Queen's Chamber. On the reverse side of the block Djedi found the copper pins each formed a very small loop, .1" in diameter. It appears two holes were drilled through the block, copper pins inserted and held in-place by some black material and mortar, the very small loops were created on one side, and the pin hammered flat against the opposite side. The loops are not in the block center, but are approximately a third of the distance from the top. Plans for Djedi to further explore both shafts were interrupted by political unrest in Egypt.[38]

Based on the south shaft slope and length we can calculate that the shaft was abandoned at a height of 204' above the outside pavement.[39] The peak of the top relieving chamber above the King's Chamber is 210'[40] above the pavement. This might indicate that the builders did not stop work on the Queen's Chamber south shaft until they were completing the uppermost parts of the relieving chambers. This supports a contention that construction of the Queen's Chamber continued until the King's Chamber was nearing completion. An alternative explanation could be that there is an internal step pyramid as an early phase of construction, and these shafts terminated at the step pyramid face.

The Queen's Chamber was constructed relatively early; started about year 7 and there was plenty of time to finely finish the Chamber.[41] However, there are indications the Chamber was never completed:

- Red leveling lines not removed from the Horizontal Passage,
- Rough unfinished condition of the chamber floor and horizontal passage floor,
- Covered shafts
- Shafts not extended to the outside surface

- Rough raised lip (torus) around the entrance not removed

None of these conditions should have existed in a finished chamber. From being an unfinished chamber we can easily jump to it being an unused chamber. As we have already hinted, the Queen's Chamber may have not even been accessible since the entrance to the Horizontal Passage leading to the Chamber may have been blocked by a bridge over the entrance on which plug blocks were slid into the Ascending Passage. Like the Subterranean Chamber, the Queen's Chamber seems to have been abandoned and unused.

Grand Gallery

This space is the most impressive in any Old Kingdom structure. But the architect's intent was not to build a grand place, but to design and build a space which served two functions: to continue the ascent to the burial chamber and to store plug blocks.[42] Simply stated, the design of the Gallery efficiently serves these functions, if it had any other primary function, it would have been designed differently. To achieve this result the architects planned a long, wide inclined passage with a central ramp bounded by low platforms running the gallery length. Above the side platforms, the walls rise vertically for the first seven feet,[43] then seven corbelled courses shift the walls inward

Grand Gallery	Dimension[37]
Incline at Floor	26°16'40"
Incline at Ceiling	28°11'
Height - Vertical	28'2" Average
Length - Ascending Passage to Great Step	153'6"
Width - Bottom Including Side Platforms	6'10" (4 Cubits)
Width – Between Side Platforms	3'5" (2 Cubits)
Side Platforms	20.5" Wide, 20.5" High (1 Cubit Square)
Width Ceiling	3'5" (2 Cubits)

3" per course to reduce the width and remove weight from the ceiling. We can imagine that by the dim light of the ancient torches or oil lamps, the walls disappeared into blackness above.

The Gallery continues upward at the same slope as the Ascending Passage but the floor is broken by the entrance to the Upper Horizontal Passage. Since the plug blocks at the bottom of the Ascending Passage had to be initially stored in the Grand Gallery (more on this later) and slid down into the Ascending Passage, the break must have been bridged. An 8" drop in the upper central ramp provides an area on

which a bridge could rest and a raised edge at the entrance to the Ascending Passage provides a stop for the bridge at the bottom. The distance from the upper drop to the lower raised edge is almost 20'. Along each sidewall of the break at the entrance to the Upper Horizontal Passage, there are five holes matching position and size to holes on the opposite wall except that one of each pair is deeper. The bridge must have been supported by five beams inserted in the hole sets, one side being deeper to facilitate their insertion.

The side niche (left) with the filling removed and one of the platform holes with the side niche filled In (right). Both have a black 1' ruler in them.

The beams were likely wood and not stone since some remnant of a stone beam would have likely remained in the holes when the bridge was removed or destroyed by robbers. The use of a wood would also have permitted easier construction and removal to allow access to the Queen's Chamber at any time during construction or burial if necessary. All remnants of the beams and bridge are now gone.

Niches and Holes	Dimension
Side Niches (In Walls)[44]	
Height	~26"
Width	~11"
Depth	~8"
Holes (In Platform)[79]	
Length (Along Gallery Wall)	19.7" - 25.0"
Width (From Gallery Wall)	5.5" - 6.5"
Depth (Into Platform)	7.0" - 11.5"
Adjacent Hole Edges	41.5" - 50.4" Apart

Along the east and west Gallery sidewalls there are raised platforms running from the lower north wall to the Great Step at the top of the Gallery. Between these platforms the central ramp flows into the Ascending Passage; the platform sides and the Ascending Passage walls form a continuous surface and, with the bridge in place, continuous floors.

At the top of each platform 25 niches are cut into each wall (total 50) most of which have an angled trapezoidal feature chiseled across its face. There are also 27 rectangular holes[78] cut downward into each side platform (total 54). The rectangular holes are next to the walls and generally centered on the niches cut into the side walls; the two rectangular holes against the north (lower) face of the Gallery do not have companion side niches.

All of the 50 side niches and trapezoidal features are completely filled with blocks and mortar of the type used elsewhere in the pyramid with the exception of the 7th and 11th side niches from the bottom on the west side, the first of which is empty and the second has a hole cut into the mortar. Because the depth of only two side niches is known, we cannot determine if opposing side niches were of different depths to facilitate insertion of a beam as is the case with the holes at the entrance to the Upper Horizontal Passage.

What purpose did these side niches, trapezoidal features, and rectangular holes serve? First the rectangular holes. We look to the Bent Pyramid subsidiary pyramid, built just a few years before the Great Pyramid, with much the same design as the Great Pyramid: descending passage leading to an ascending passage leading to a gallery in which four plug blocks were stored prior to being slid down into the ascending passage. As evidenced by holes in the subsidiary pyramid gallery wall, these four plugs were originally held in place by a beam anchored in the holes and passing in front of the lowest plug. When this subsidiary pyramid was ready to be closed, the cross beam was replaced by a retaining pole which was angled from a hole in the floor upward to the lowest block face to temporarily hold the

plugs in place. The plan was then to pull the retaining pole away with a rope from below and release the plugs to side down and block the ascending passage. This was only partially successful since two plugs slid into the ascending passage and two plugs became stuck and are still in place in the gallery.

We look for this same arrangement in the Grand Gallery. The three granite plug blocks were originally stored at the bottom of the Grand Gallery. The rectangular holes in the Grand Gallery platforms were clearly part of the mechanism designed to hold the plug blocks in place until ready for release. A tool in the rectangular holes could hold a cross beam which

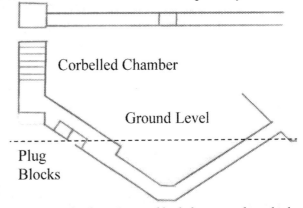

The Bent Subsidiary Pyramid had plugs stored in a high-ceiling passage before being lowered into the ascending passage.

passed in front of each plug holding it back. When the pyramid was to be closed, this beam could be lifted straight up freeing the block evenly in one motion and letting it slide into the Ascending Passage.

Since niches and trapezoidal features are filled in, either they were replaced or their purpose was completed and they were no longer necessary. Since they are located with the rectangular holes, they could have been used in a discarded method to hold back the plugs. Or they could have been used in the construction of the Grand Gallery and once that purpose was fulfilled, the niches and trapezoidal features were filled in.

From the Ascending Passage entrance into the Grand Gallery looking straight ahead to the Upper Horizontal Passage and the two side ramps going up the Grand Gallery. This center area was covered by the bridge which started at the lip in the center ramp (just below the light) and supported on beams placed between the holes on either side of the center space.

While the three granite plug blocks were obviously stored in this central ramp, the slotted shape of the Grand Gallery floor leads us to conclude that plug blocks were stored for its entire length. Based on the number of rectangular holes there were as many as 23 plugs; not considering the space over the break for the Upper Horizontal Passage. These 23 plugs could have filled almost the entire Ascending Passage.[45] Likely the architects would not have planned to store blocks on the bridge over the break for the Lower Horizontal Passage. The lower rectangular holes here could have been intended to stop the plugs and provide control before sending them careening down the Ascending Passage. Looking at this from a slightly different perspective, if there were only three plugs stored in the Grand Gallery instead of plugs stored for its entire length, the slotted shape of the Gallery central ramp would have been designed differently. It is apparent that the slotted shape was necessary to hold the plugs and move them directly and smoothly into the Ascending Passage entrance. If plugs were not stored the entire length of the Grand Gallery, there would have been no need for the central slot to run the full length of the Gallery. The plugs had to be held back by some mechanism. The only mechanism present are the holes in the side platforms; there just is not any other choice.

The sidewalls contain one of the most mysterious features in the Pyramid. Halfway up each wall, 14' above the center ramp, 5" above the bottom of the third corbelled course a groove on each wall 7" high and about 1" deep runs the full length of the gallery. Along virtually the full length of each groove, hundreds of chisel marks were cut downward. It is difficult to imagine either the purpose of the shallow grooves or why such an enormous effort was applied in trying to destroy them.

Borchardt and others have proposed variations on the idea that a wood or stone floor spanned the passage resting in these grooves and supported by posts placed in the ramp holes.[46]

A small section of the slot with many chisel marks cutting through it. On the left side is the lower edge of the third corbel.

The Great Step (left) circa 1909 (Edgar Brothers) shows the center front was cut or worn away. In a recent photo(right), in addition to the rungs, rails, wires, and lights, the surface has been restored. When the damage was done to the Great Step and what caused it is unknown.

All variations fail. No reasonable architect would rest either a 65" wide stone or wooden floor in a 1" deep groove. Additionally, the third corbelled course projects 9" out from the sidewall. With the ramp holes 6 ½" wide, the groove is 2 ½" further from the side wall then the outer edge of the hole. If the holes were intended to hold supports, the holes would have been positioned differently. We are moved to propose other alternatives: golden objects, construction supports to hold the walls apart, a canopy. But there is no evidence supporting these alternatives. However, the grooves and chisel marks are there without a compelling explanation, a condition which will probably remain unchanged forever.

The ceiling is not easy to examine up close because of the incline floor and the difficulty of placing a ladder on the incline. Petrie examined the ceiling at the ends of the Gallery where the bottom of a ladder could be placed flat. The individual roof blocks are inclined at an angle which is steeper than the floor. The walls on which the ceiling blocks rest were cut in a saw-tooth fashion so that the roof blocks lay against the lower end of the saw-tooth and not against the next lower ceiling block. This prevents a cumulative force buildup of the roofing stones from bearing on the north Gallery wall.[48]

At the upper (south) end of the Grand Gallery the Great Step rises from the ramp and forms a platform. The single block forming the Step does not stop at the Gallery wall but extends an additional 66" into the Ante Chamber. At a minimum this single stone weighs 15 tons.[49] Petrie determined the northern face of the Great Step to be equal distance from the north and south sides of the pyramid and directly above the Queen's Chamber gabled roof. In each corner of the Great Step platform at the junction of the side walls and back (south) wall are two shallow holes similar in size to the holes in the Gallery side ramp. Their purpose is not known.

As we stated at the outset of this section, to the architect and the builder, the Grand Gallery was likely meant to be only functional: to continue the ascent to the burial chamber and to store plug blocks. We might ask why did they have to build such a large space. We believe the reasoning is simple and straightforward. The width of the Gallery was determined first by the two cubit width of the Ascending Passage which was carried into the central ramp of the Grand Gallery. To each side of the central ramp, a space was necessary for the workers to stand when they removed the beam from in front of each plug block. The workmen were not

Great Step	Dimension[47]
Height Above Central Ramp	33 ¼"
Size	82" Wide by 60 ¾" Deep
Corner Holes	6 ¾" Wide by 21 ¼" Long

allowed a lot of space, only a minimal one cubit on each side for a total width of four cubits - about 82". The 47" height of the plugs and the need for moving over the blocks and working around them resulted in the need for a minimum height of about 100". From here the height of the Gallery was not left to the whims of the stonemasons but determined by a multiple of the space spanned.

The size and shape of the Grand Gallery were a natural outgrowth of the functional requirements, and the architectural approaches and technology available to fill the requirements. But the result should not only be appreciated for the efficiency with which the architects and builders filled requirements but for the magnificence of their product. The visual impact can best be captured from the top of the Great Step. We have stood there and looked at certainly one of the world's grandest views captured in stone. The torches and oil lamps which turned the once glistening white walls to a smudged brown have been replaced by subdued lights. In person, the space can be seen in detail but due to its length, photos are not adequate and words too frail to convey the majesty of the space and the awesomeness of the moment.

Antechamber

Lying between the upper end of the Grand Gallery and the King's Chamber, the Antechamber housed three portcullis blocks as the final protection for Khufu's body. This space was poorly designed, badly executed, and easily penetrated. Petrie found what he considered poor workmanship in that the length of the central chamber varied from 114" to 117" and the width from 64.5" to 65.5".[50] The floor is inexplicably uneven: the first granite floor block is raised ½" above the preceding limestone block and at the entrance to the King's Chamber there is another rise of ¾". Since the floor is finely finished, the uneven surface cannot be attributed to an unprepared surface or the possible intention to overlay the area with another floor. The only apparent reason for these differences is sloppy workmanship.

From the top of the Great Step the Grand Gallery extends into the distance below. The center slot initially contained plug blocks which were held back by beams secured in the side ramp holes before the plugs were released into the Ascending Passage The mysterious slot is visible on the third corbel.

The exactness found in laying out the exterior and in the Descending and Ascending Passages and the excellence of the initial architecture had seriously degraded over the years to permit wide differences in the dimensions of this small Chamber and poor quality construction. While we might be tempted to attribute some of these differences to settling or earthquakes, we note that the discrepancies do not pervade the entire structure but become evident with height above the pyramid base and removal in time from the start of construction.

The Chamber is entered through the First Low Passage from the Great Step. The architrave over the entrance and the jamb on the west side are partially broken away, likely when robbers removed a block closing the entrance. On the west side of this low passage in 1817 Caviglia cut a rough tunnel to gain access to the north "air" channel. This tunnel provides another view of the internal core construction. It is cut through finely finished limestone blocks separated by very thin joints, providing support to the hypothesis that the formal chambers were surrounded by a thick lining of finely cut and precisely laid blocks.[52]

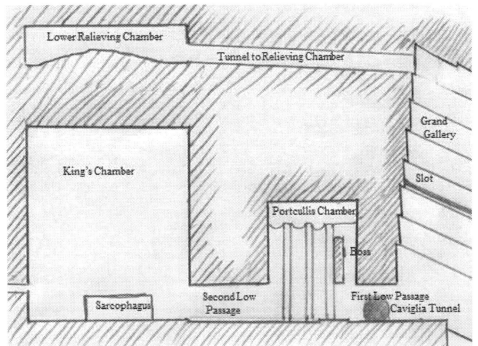

The first section of the Portcullis Chamber is a small space as wide as the passage but only 21" long north to south. The north limestone wall rises to the Chamber ceiling. To the south, two granite blocks (known as leafs), one on top of the other, start 44" above the floor. The top of the upper leaf was broken away at a height of 8'. At eye level on the top leaf is a protractor shaped, half round construction boss protruding from the block surface about 1" and measuring 5" wide by 3.5" high. Because of the small size of this space, most visitors do not even look up as they pass through this area, much less stand to look at the boss. In 1864, Piazzi Smyth found in the shape and measurements of this boss a unit which he named the "pyramid inch."[53] Using one pyramid inch to represent one year, followers of Smyth correlated historical events to passage measurements and theorized that the ancient builders predicted events by the length and changes in the pyramid passages. Based on this methodology, believers tried to predict the future, but the future was never successfully predicted and several dates for the end of the world have come and gone without the world apparently ending. In recent years these theories have, with reason, fallen by the wayside.

Antechamber	Dimension[51]
First Low Passage	52" Long, 43.7" High, 40.5" Wide
Portcullis Chamber	116" Long, 148.4" High, 65" Wide
Portcullis Grooves	21.5" Wide
West Wall	112.6" High
East Wall	103.9" High
Second Low Passage	100.7" Long, 43.7" High, 41.3" Wide

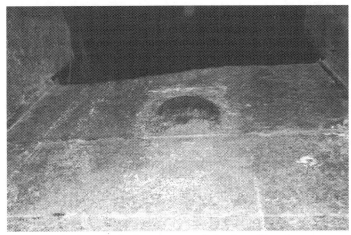

The boss in the first section of the Ante Chamber.

To the south of the granite leafs is the area which housed three portcullises. Along the east and west side walls, three grooves each

Both photos were taken from the floor with a wide angle lens looking up at the space that housed the three portcullises. The King's Chamber is through the passage under the slotted wall. The ceiling is surprisingly flat for an area this wide; indicating there is likely a relieving space above.

originally held a portcullis, all now missing. Supporting the contention that the portcullis were granite, the limestone projections which formed the grooves were partially cut away in an irregular fashion to a height of 6' to 8' so the portcullis could be removed whole instead of being broken up in place indicating they were hard granite. The top of the east and west walls were finished differently. The west wall top has a semicircular cutout 9" deep filling the width of each vertical groove below. At the top of the east wall we would expect to find matching semicircular cutouts, but strangely the east wall is topped by a flat ledge at the level of the opposite semicircular cutout's bottom. Above the east and west ledges, there is a space 3' high. Unless it was necessary for a person to have access to this area above the raised portcullis, the ceiling would undoubtedly be lower.

Likely a wooden beam spanned the chamber with one end in the semicircular cutout and the other on the flat opposite wall. Why this arrangement was used and whether there was a structure to hold the beams in place on the flat ledge cannot be determined. Ropes from the portcullis were likely run up and over the wooden beams, over the granite leafs, down through the First Low Passage, and out to the Great Step. The portcullis furthest south laid directly against the south wall. In the south wall, above the entrance to the Second Low Passage are four vertical grooves 3 ¼" to 4" wide, set 6 ½" apart. The ropes used to lower this portcullis rode in these grooves providing evidence that each portcullis also had four rope holes which matched this spacing. In the initial raised position the portcullis were probably held in place by supports from below rather than place a strain on the ropes for many years while the Pyramid was under construction.

Granite Fragments

Recall the four granite fragments we found around the pyramid. Following is some background on each of these fragments and their locations can be followed on the pyramid drawing.[54] The sizes of these blocks are identified in the table for comparison to the maximum possible portcullis dimensions listed at the bottom of the table.

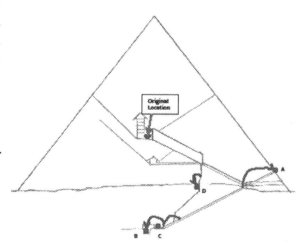

A - Fragment Outside the Entrance	First noted by Petrie in 1881 in the Descending Passage just below the intersection with the Ascending Passage. In the early 1900s L. Dow Covington placed an iron gate on top, blocking access below this point. In 1926, Morton Edgar moved it further up the passage.[55] Maragioglio and Rinaldi in the early 1960's found the block still in the passage. Sometime later it was moved to its current position outside the entrance.
B - Fragment on the Ledge in the Subterranean Chamber Pit	First noted by Covington in the Descending Passage just above the Well Shaft entrance. In 1910 men working for the Edgar brothers were clearing debris just below the granite block discovered by Petrie (see above), when they dislodged a small granite block. The block slid 200' down the passage and ran into Covington's block sending both to the bottom of the Descending Passage. Since these barred entrance to the Lower Horizontal Passage, Morton Edgar moved both blocks slightly up the passage, then in 1926 he moved them into the Subterranean Chamber.[56] The small granite block has since disappeared, but an Edgar photograph shows the shape of Covington's block matches the block now located on the ledge in the Subterranean Chamber pit. Apparently someone unknown tried to dispose of the block in the pit and it came to rest on the ledge instead of falling to the pit bottom.
C - Fragment in the Lower Horizontal Passage Recess	First mentioned and photographed by the Edgar brothers in 1910 in its current location. Previously, Petrie only mentioned that the Recess was filled with large stone blocks.[57]
D - Fragment in the Grotto	Caviglia identified a measurement in the Well Shaft as, *"Depth of the Well to a block of granite that had fallen into it – 38'."* The Edgar brothers found the block in the Grotto, 58' down the Well Shaft. Likely when Caviglia was clearing the Well Shaft, rather than raise this heavy block he lowered it and placed it in the grotto.

The comparison shows that the fragment dimensions do not exceed the maximum possible portcullis dimensions.

The diameter of the holes and the distance between holes in the granite block outside the entrance show them to be close to the spaces and grooves in the chamber south wall.[59] This data draws us to a conclusion that each of these granite fragments was once part of a portcullis. Robbers likely broke-up the portcullis blocks to ease removal of objects from the King's Chamber. They threw the fragments to the bottom of the Grand Gallery than disposed of them either down the Well Shaft or down the Ascending Passage and into the Descending Passage.

Granite Blocks				
Location[58]	Height	Width	Thick	Holes
Outside Entrance	31 1/2"	44"	21"	3
Recess	17"	25 ½"	20"	0
Subterranean Pit	---	---	---	2
Grotto	17"	18"	21"	2
Portcullis Max Dimensions	~58"	48 ½"	21"	4

King's Chamber

The Antechamber's Second Low Passage provides access to the northeast corner of the King's Chamber. There is a simple beauty to this flat-ceiling, rectangular shaped, granite room. Eyes immediately find the only object, the battered sarcophagus at the west end and notice the mouths of the two "air channels." In designing the Chamber the architects employed whole cubits in multiples of 5 to the maximum extent possible.

King's Chamber	Dimension[60]
Height Above Exterior Pavement	50th course, 141'
Length - East to West	413" 20 Cubits
Width - North to South	206" 10 Cubits
Height	230" 11.17 Cubits
Center Diagonal (Top Corner to Opposite Bottom Corner)	515" 25 Cubits
Diagonal Across North and South Walls	472" 22.9 Cubits
Diagonal Across East and West Walls	309" 15 Cubits

The Antechamber's granite floor continues into the King's Chamber. The Chamber 21 granite floor blocks are laid between the walls instead of having the walls placed on top of the floor. As in the Antechamber, here we find additional evidence that the quality of workmanship evident at the start of Pyramid construction had declined. Petrie found the King's Chamber floor to be uneven, with a variation of 2.29". Taking the joint at the top of the lowest granite wall course as a level line, Petrie measured the level of the floor below this joint and found a range from 40.65" to 42.94", a significant difference over a relatively small area.[61] While this difference could be attributed to settling or earthquakes, with no weight on the floor and a great weight on the walls, we would expect the walls to be impacted more severely. This is not the case and the poor workmanship displayed in laying the Antechamber floor has been carried into the King's Chamber.

In the northwest corner robbers pried up the granite floor blocks and cut a hole in the underlying limestone in an apparent search for treasure in a hidden space under the King's Chamber. The hole descended about 30' into an area 6' to 10' wide.[62] While the hole was unfortunate, it did provide an opportunity to directly observe that the bottom of the granite walls sit on the underlying limestone 5" below floor level. This hole was closed during the 1999 restoration and the floor returned to its original condition.

The walls are composed of 101 finely dressed granite blocks rising in five even courses of nearly equal height to a roughly finished flat ceiling. The largest block, two courses high, sits across the top of the Chamber entrance and is partially hidden behind the Chamber east wall. Across the center of this block a depression starts at the upper west side and runs diagonally across the face but disappears behind the east wall 18" above the block bottom. Assuming the diagonal continues to the lower corner, we can calculate the length of the block at 140". With a measured height of 94" and depth of 59", this single block weighs 35 tons.

The King's Chamber is empty except for the sarcophagus (left). The entrance is in the corner (right). The North Shaft is at the arrow. The depression across the face of the large block above the entrance indicates the block extends into the wall.

The ceiling is formed of nine flat granite beams laid across the short north – south dimension. These are the largest known blocks in the pyramid, weighing an average of 50 tons. Compared to the walls, the ceiling beams are roughly dressed and each has cracks along the south side. Petrie identified cement daubed in by fingers filling the cracks at the Chamber's eastern end and plaster covering a foot square area at the southwest corner.[63] The filled cracks provide evidence that at least some of the cracks occurred before the pyramid was closed.

The uninscribed and undecorated sarcophagus was cut from a single block of red granite; the missing lid would have been cut from the bottom of the block. The outside surface is relatively smooth but not finely finished with saw marks visible on each side. These marks can be easily identified by shining a flashlight across the surface of the north (short) end which will plainly reveal two places where the saw cut too deeply and was backed out. The saw lines show that the long east and west sides and the short north side were cut horizontally while the short south side was cut vertically. Considering the length of the sarcophagus, the saw would have been at least 9' long. Petrie raised the sarcophagus and found it sat on the chamber floor with nothing below but a large flint pebble.[65] This pebble may have been introduced when ancient robbers also checked underneath, but while there should have been pieces of granite and limestone readily available resulting from the break-in, flint had to be brought from the outside.

The top surface of the sarcophagus sides are badly damaged, but through similarities with the intact Khafre sarcophagus, enough information is available to

The large granite blocks of the King's Chamber flat ceiling. Cracks are barely visible in the rear left corner.

Sarcophagus	Dimension[64]
Outside Dimensions	89.6" Long, 38.5" Wide, 41.3" High
Inside Dimensions	78.1" Long, 26.8" Wide, 34.4" Deep
Wall Average Thickness	5.8"
Base Average Thickness	6.9"

The line at the sarcophagus top edge (left) separates the flat lower surface and the now destroyed overhanging lip. Inside of the sarcophagus with a black 1' ruler (right). Interior surfaces are flat and corners are squared.

determine the construction and locking method of Khufu's sarcophagus. Along the short north and south sides, and the long east side, the top was divided into a flat 1 ½" wide lower inside surface above which was an overhanging lip. The back west side top is flat with three holes cut into the surface and at the level of the lower inside surface. The lid probably first rested on blocks between the sarcophagus and the back west Chamber wall. After Khufu was placed in the sarcophagus, the lid was slid into place so that it rested on the lower inside surface and projected under the overhanging lip which prevented the lid from being raised. Three holes cut in the lid, probably completely through, matched the holes in the sarcophagus west side top. Pinions placed in the holes and "glued" with resin locked the top in place. These precautions would not have posed much of a problem for a robber with time to work.

The sarcophagus was too large to pass through the Pyramid passages. The outside measurements of the sarcophagus are slightly larger than the 38.2" wide bottom of the Ascending Passage, the smallest part of the passage system, providing evidence that the sarcophagus was placed into the King's Chamber before the Chamber ceiling was closed.

King's Chamber Shafts	Dimension[66]
North Shaft	
Height Above Floor	39"
Face Size	5" High, 8" Wide
Distance to Surface	235' (Original Surface)
Exit Course	101
Inclined Angle	
Initial 8.5'	Horizontal
Next 7.2'	17°
Next 9'	25°
Next 6.7'	29°30'
Next 8'	34°
Next 186'	32°36' Average
South Shaft	
Height Above Floor	39"
Face Size	6" High, 7" Wide
Distance to Surface	175' (Original Surface)
Exit Course	101
Inclined Angle	
Initial 5.6'	Horizontal
Next 7.2'	39°12'
Next 14.1'	50°32'
Next 137'	45°

As in the Queen's Chamber, both the King's Chamber long north and south walls have openings for "air shafts" at the top of the lowest wall course. While the position of the Queen's Chamber shafts are at mid-chamber and the shafts in the larger King's Chamber are closer to the east end, they are within 15" of being placed one above the other. If the architect intended a vertical alignment, he could have easily come closer since the east walls of both chambers are aligned. Both King's Chamber shafts penetrate horizontally through the Chamber granite lining, then rise at varying angles towards the pyramid surface. Rudolf Gantenbrink cleared the King's Chamber shafts in 1992 and explored both for their full length with a video camera equipped robot called Upuaut I. He also installed a ventilation system in the southern shaft to improved temperature and humidity inside the Pyramid.[67]

The north shaft does not rise at one angle or at one azimuth but makes five incline changes and at least four and likely five changes in azimuth. At the lower end the shaft initially both rises and angles towards the west to miss the Grand Gallery by more than 17' before turning back to the north. The rough tunnel Caviglia cut into the west wall of the Antechamber first low passage intersects with the north "air channel" and follows its path for 16'. From this passage an observer can see the turns. At the upper end where the shaft opens on the pyramid surface, robbers excavated downward along the shaft for a distance of 37' without apparently finding anything.

The wall around the south shaft opening was seriously mutilated and is closed and hidden today by a ventilating fan blowing air up the shaft. The initial rising section changes angle twice, then after 27' rises at a steady 45° angle to the surface.

Relieving Chambers

In 1765, Nathaniel Davison, hearing odd echoes high in the Grand Gallery, discovered an opening in the top course of the east wall, in the corner and directly above the Great Step. Davison entered the hole and found a 32" high by 27" wide passage filled to a depth of 16" with bat dung.[68] He was apparently undaunted by the dung and crawled south through the passage 24' to the space over the King's Chamber. While the passage is not finely finished, it is squared and straight, and though it may not have been part of the original plan, it was part of the original construction and not a robber's hole.

Apparently as a result of the cracks which opened in the King's Chamber ceiling, the builders wanted to determine the condition of the relieving chambers and they cut an access passage from the Grand Gallery to the lowest relieving chamber. Satisfied with the condition of the lowest chamber, they did not tunnel into the higher relieving chambers.

The lowest relieving chamber matches the length and width of the King's Chamber. The uneven floor, composed of the tops of the nine granite beams roofing the King's Chamber below, and the flat ceiling formed by eight finished granite beams running north – south forms a chamber averaging about 3' high.[69] Davison found nothing of interest in this chamber, inscribed his name, and left. With his name on the wall, this space became known

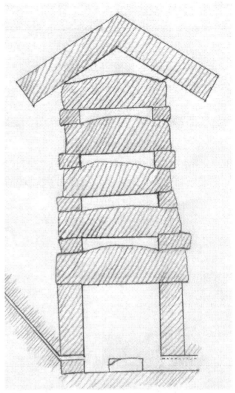

The King's Chamber and five relieving chambers above with the sarcophagus, entrance passage, and south shaft.

as Davison's Chamber. Caviglia cleared out the bat dung and explored the spaces. The cracks on the south side of the King's Chamber ceiling led him to believe there was an open space to the south of the chamber causing the cracks. In a search for a secret room, he hired a gang of workman to cut a tunnel through the soft limestone east side of the relieving chamber and behind the granite south wall. They found nothing but core blocks.[70]

In 1837, Colonel Howard Vyse explored the Pyramid with the tool of the day, gunpowder. Believing that the flat ceiling of Davison's Chamber would not bear the weight of the pyramid, he assumed there were additional spaces above. Blasting a vertical passage, Vyse found four more relieving chambers which had been sealed for 4500 years. The first three resembled Davison's Chamber in construction, size, and height while the 7' high top chamber had a limestone gabled roof similar to the ceiling in the Queen's Chamber. Vyse named the chambers from the bottom up Wellington's, Nelson's, Lady Arbuthnot's, and Campbell's. A floor stone in Lady Arbuthnot's chamber may be the largest single stone in the Great Pyramid measuring 27' by 5' by 7' and weighing 70 tons. Since the chambers were never intended to be visible to anyone, they were left in a rough condition with construction bosses, carved basins, and level lines.

Vyse found workman graffiti and construction marks written in red ocher in the top four chambers. The red ocher marks proved to be the confirming evidence that the pyramid was built by Khufu. Three forms of his name were found here: Khufu, Khnun-Khuf, and Mdjedu, his Horus name. Some have alleged that these marks were forged by Vyse, but the evidence supporting this contention is inaccurate.

The work gangs who built the Pyramid wrote their names on the Relieving Chambers stones. Gangs named "The crew, the White Crown of Khnum-Khuf is powerful" and "The crew, Khufu excites loves" left their marks. While these names must lose something in the translation, they indicate that the workers were willing participants in the construction.

Well Shaft

Almost 200' feet long, the Well Shaft connects the lower end of the Grand Gallery to near the lower end of the Descending Passage. The Shaft starts at the very bottom of the Grand Gallery where on the west side there is an opening in the raised platform from which a block was roughly removed. Chisel marks indicate the block was cut away from within the Grand Gallery. We believe the plug blocks stored in the Grand Gallery could only be lowered into the Ascending Passage by a crew in the Grand Gallery. As a result, the crew needed an exit route so they would not be trapped and the Well Shaft provided that route. An intact Grand Gallery side ramp was needed to guide the plug blocks into the Ascending Passage and the block covering the Well Shaft entrance could not be cut away until that job was complete.

The Well Shaft is composed of five sections 28" square or smaller, two sections are vertical and finished; the other three are steeply inclined. A hollow space, the Grotto, was dug into the side of the lower vertical section. The lower end of the shaft exits to the Descending Passage.

About 1638, John Greaves was the first person in the modern era to enter the Well Shaft, penetrating from the Grand Gallery to about the area of the Grotto. Though the Shaft was open below him; he was not able to continue due to the foul air and the large number of bats. Since Graves found the Descending Passage completely clogged below the level of its junction with Al Mamun's Hole, he did not find the Well Shaft lower end.

Caviglia also tried to penetrate the Well Shaft from the top and reached a point below the Grotto where he found the shaft filled with sand and loose rocks. He hired a gang of workmen to clear the Shaft but bad air prevented completion of the job. Having failed here, Caviglia turned to clearing the Descending Passage of rubble. Near the bottom of the Descending Passage on the west side, he found an entry to a rising shaft clogged with debris. He set his workmen to clear the debris which soon fell down on them. In the debris they found a basket and rope they had earlier left in the Well Shaft.[72] The full length of the Well Shaft was now open.

Entrance to the Well Shaft at the lower end of the Grand Gallery with side ramp blocks cut away. At bottom right is the inclined floor of the Ascending Passage. (Edgar Brothers)

The Well Shaft starts at the lower end of the Grand Gallery, where below the missing block a 2' deep hole enters a short horizontal passage to the west. The entrance and floor of the horizontal passage seem to have been roughly cut to larger dimensions. From the end of this entrance passage the first Well Shaft section made of finely finished limestone blocks descends vertically. This connects to the rough walled second section which extends at a steep angle

Well Shaft Sections[71]				
Section	**Construction**	**Direction**	**Angle**	**Length**
Entrance	Finely Finished	E-W	Horizontal	4'
1	Finely Finished	---	Vertical	26"
2	Rough Surface on Core Blocks	N-S	~70°	26'
3	Block Line Shaft, Grotto to the Side	---	Vertical	17'
4	Cut Through Bedrock	N-S	48°	87'
5	Cut Through Bedrock	N-S	75°	31'
Exit	Cut Through Bedrock	W-E	Slight Up Slope	7'

through the pyramid core blocks until it meets the top of the finished vertical third section. While the temptation is to describe this inclined section as being cut through already laid block, the finished sections above and below do not support this conclusion. Caviglia found the inclined section nearly filled with large stones which he had great difficulty removing. Likely he had to cut into the sidewalls to gain an advantage in removing the stones giving the walls their rough appearance. The third section starts in the pyramid core and enters the bedrock. The top surface of the bedrock here is 18' 8" higher than the exterior pavement. At the place the builders wanted to construct a vertical shaft, they either encountered an area of loose material or filled a depression with loose material.[73] In either case the material was not suitable for a shaft. The builders laid 10 courses of small, well-worked limestone blocks to hold back and form a vertical shaft through the loose material. Apparently the small limestone blocks attracted the attention of robbers. The robbers removed a section of blocks and dug out some of the loose material behind it forming a small hollow which became known as the Grotto. This material likely formed part of the fill which Caviglia found blocking the Shaft's lower end.

The Grotto is a roughly outlined space that is 12' by 16' at its broadest dimensions and generally 4' high except for a hole which extends the depth to about 10'.[74] Sitting in the Grotto is the fourth granite block which was likely thrown down the Well Shaft as a convenient method of disposal. Below, the loose material the shaft enters the bedrock. The fourth Shaft section slopes to the south, cutting through the bedrock and connects to the fifth section which continues south but at a steeper slope. At the bottom a short, slightly rising passage turns to the east and exits just 25' from the lower end of the Descending Passage.[75] Possibly the original intent was for the Well Shaft fourth section to continue and provide the lower exit within the Lower Horizontal Passage; maybe the purpose of the Recess. The Well Shaft lower opening would then be protected by plug blocks placed in and closing the Descending Passage.

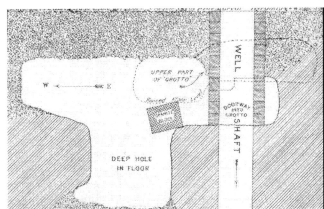

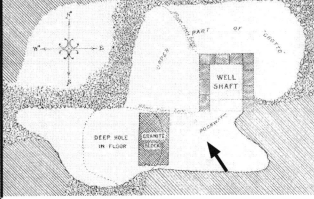

Drawings of the Grotto by the Edgar Brothers looking horizontally from the south (top left) and looking down (top right). The arrow identifies the location of the photographer for the photo (bottom left). The photo shows the bottom four courses of limestone blocks sitting on top of the bedrock. A small piece of the granite block is visible at the bottom left, and the loose ceiling material at the top foreground. It would have been extremely difficult to lay the 10 rows of blocks through the loose material as part of a later construction.

But for some reason, possibly to speed completion, the builders increased the Well Shaft angle and instead made it exit in the Descending Passage, still with an intent to hide it behind plug blocks in the Descending Passage.

1910 photos of the Well Shaft opening in the Descending Passage (left), and looking into the Shaft (right) from the Descending Passage. Opening is horizontal across the top (instead of incline with the passage), square, and with flared sides. Inside the square opening changes to a round tunnel. (Edgar Brothers)

The area in the Descending Passage surrounding the opening is roughly square with rounded flared edges left in a rough condition. Inside, the squared opening transitions abruptly to a rounded profile, appearing as though this final section was cut from both sides. Since the exit is cut in the bedrock and not a finished part of the Passage, any covering over the hole would have quickly drawn the attention of robbers and led to further exploration.

Al Mamun's Hole

Al Mamun's Hole today is used as the tourist entrance into the Pyramid and provides a window into internal pyramid construction. In this tunnel we can see that the tight fitting blocks on the exterior gave way in the pyramid core to roundish stones set with wide joints. Near the far end the tunnel makes a turn to the east (left) and opens into a larger space in which the side of the Ascending Passage is cut away revealing three granite plug blocks. The top and middle plug blocks are clearly visible. Chisel marks cover the sides of a pocket cut down along the middle plug revealing a small portion of the lower plug. A 12-step stairway of recent construction leads up to the Ascending Passage above the top plug block. At the foot of the stairs a rough inclined hole leads downward to the Descending Passage.

In 820 AD the Caliph Al Mamun at-

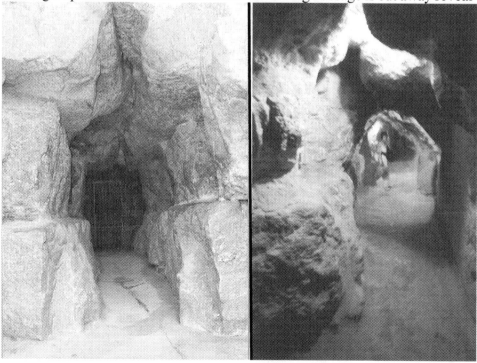

The entrance to Al Mamun's Hole (left) was more than two courses high. Deep inside the pyramid Al Mamun's Hole (right) remains high and roughly cut.

tempted to enter the Pyramid in search of treasure. His story, reported by the Arab historian Abu Abd Allah Mohammed ben Abdurakin Alkaisi, is probably a mix of real facts and embellishments.

Though the pyramid was likely entered and robbed during the First Intermediate Period, at some later time the pyramid entrance was resealed. Reports from Herodotus in 450 BCE through the 13th century indicate the casing was intact. So Al Mamun likely found the exterior Pyramid casing undamaged and the entrance hidden.

The story goes that hoping to run into an interior passage or chamber, Al Mamun had a tunnel forced in the center of the north face, six courses up from the pavement. To create the tunnel it is reported the Arabs set fires next to the blocks, poured vinegar on the hot stones, and pounded the stones. Al Mamun did not settle for the small cramped passages of the Dynasty IV builders, but instead cut his tunnel irregularly but comfortably large, about 5' wide by 8' tall. After tunneling 100', Al Mamun was about to give-up when the workmen heard the muffled noise of something heavy falling to the east, inside the pyramid. They changed direction of the tunnel and broke into the Descending Passage. In the Passage they found the Prism Stone had fallen on the floor revealing the face of the granite plug filling a passage (Ascending Passage) which sloped up into the Pyramid. Unable to move or chip the granite plug, Al Mamun had his men cut around the plug (no evidence for this, see later). They tunneled for 16' along three granite plugs before finding the passage filled with softer limestone plugs, the number of limestone

Two photos taken from the same spot about 90 years apart of the end of Al Mamun's Hole where it runs into the granite plugs and the Ascending and Descending Passage. Size of the topmost granite plug is estimated based on Petrie's measurements. The Descending Passage was accessed by a steep downward hole. The original limestone plugs which filled the Ascending Passage were likely cut away and thrown down the Ascending Passage, hit against the face of the granite plug, and tossed downward into the Descending Passage. Note the degradation of the granite plug face just in the short time between the two photos.

plugs not recorded, which they were able to cut away gaining access to the upper chambers: Grand Gallery, Queen's Chamber and King's Chamber. There is no record of what was discovered in the chambers, so likely nothing of value was found, but even any tattered remains would have been of significance to us today.[76]

In considering this story, refer earlier in this chapter to the photos of the granite plug face where the Ascending and Descending Passages intersect. The limestone around the plug is pristine and obvious that no one cut around the plug invalidating some of the story.

The available evidence points to a somewhat different story than told by Alkaisi. Possibly the workmen's pounding did dislodge the ceiling blocks hiding the plug blocks in the Ascending Passage. The sound inside the Hole lasting for just a moment must have startled, possibly frightened, the workmen. We can see that the Hole turns to the east which resulted from the workmen following the sound. Since the connection to the Descending Passage is almost vertical, likely they did not break into the Descending Passage. Instead, the direction and level of the Hole indicates the workman first encountered the granite plug blocks. Finding granite in the midst of all this limestone pyramid was likely a surprise. They cut away the limestone, going left and right along the blocks to reveal two full granite plugs and the start of a third (the lowest plug). At this point they realized this was a blocked inclined passage connecting to another passage immediately below and the most direct line to that undiscovered passage would be to tunnel down instead of continuing along the plugs. They tunneled down, under the plugs and quickly broke into the Descending Passage.

Al Mamun would have immediately investigated the Descending Passage down to the Subterranean Chamber, but finding nothing in the lower levels he would have returned to the granite plugs in his Hole and focused on cutting upwards along the granite plugs. Likely above the third granite plug he found limestone plugs and instead continued cutting away the plugs from within the Ascending Passage. The full length of the Ascending Passage was probably filled with plug blocks which were lowered from the Grand Gallery after Khufu's burial. Al Mamun's workman cut upwards through the plug blocks and threw the resulting debris down into the Descending Passage; this passage being of no matter to them since there was nothing of interest in the lower areas.

Caviglia, Petrie, and the Edgar brothers cleared the Descending Passage, but they did not describe in detail the make-up or the quantity of debris they removed. The debris were likely the remains of the now missing plug blocks which once filled the Ascending Passage. While Petrie described one piece of granite in the Descending Passage[77] and the Edgar brothers wrote about several granite blocks, neither they nor Caviglia mention removing large amounts of granite debris and they surely would have due to the rarity of granite in this pyramid. Additionally, if the Ascending Passage was filled with granite plugs, Al Mamun would have cut through the softer limestone along the blocks rather than try to break-up the hard granite inside the passage. As a result, we can be sure that while the bottom three plug blocks were granite, the rest were limestone.

Having emptied the Ascending Passage of blockage, Al Mamun's men gained access to the upper passages and chambers. They may have been responsible for digging the hole into the Queen's Chamber niche and the hole under the King's Chamber. Since both holes appear rough, there is no indication that they broke into any chamber or found anything of value.

The Great Pyramid remained open for the next 800 years until John Graves arrived in 1638 though it was probably not a popular place to visit since a large number of bats had taken up residence and the resulting bat dung and stench made the interior a very uncomfortable place to visit.

---

1. First two from Maragioglio and Rinaldi, L'Architettura Delle Piramidi Menfite, Parte IV La Grande Piramide di Cheope, Tav 3, last two from Petrie, "Pyramids and Temples of Gizeh," PP 18-19.
2. Actually the Great Pyramid is 2 miles south at 29 degrees 58 minutes.

3. The incline is measured by taking the tangent of the Descending Passage angle. The tangent required to represent a 2:1 slope would be .5 which is the tangent for 26°33'54 This is only 2'31" different from the angle as measured by Petrie and provides evidence that the 2:1 slope was intended.

4. Lepre, "Egyptian Pyramids", p73.

5. Lepre in his book "The Egyptian Pyramids", page 73 identified the bottom of the Ascending Passage as 47 ¼" by 38 ½", a difference we cannot explain. In our research on the Great Pyramid we discovered that different investigators found significantly different measurements for the same feature.

6. We can determine the weight of a single stone filling this space by its likely dimensions. The formula for the estimated weight is 7' long x 3.4' wide x 2' (est) high x 155 pounds per cubic foot = 7,378 pounds.

7. In "Pyramids and Temples of Gizeh" pages 17 and 18 Petrie identified the original entrance as 668.2" above the pavement and the distance from the entrance to the transition of the Descending Passage from pyramid core to bedrock as 1318.5" Using trigonometry we can determine the height of the entrance above the transition point by: Sine 26.523 = A/1318.5. This provides a height of 588.8". Finding the difference between the entrance height above the pavement (668.2") minus the height above the transition (588.8") determines the height the transition is above the exterior pavement of 79.4" or 6'7".1

8. Maragioglio and Rinaldi, op. cit., TAV 4, granite block per author's measurements.

9. Ibid, TAV 4.

10. Vyse, "Operations Carried on at the Pyramids of Gizeh in 1837", Vol II-A, p290.

11. Ibid, p290.

12. In a sketch John Perring drew of the Subterranean Chamber in 1837, he shows a hole about 8' deep. This was likely the result of Caviglia's work. Perring, "Pyramids of Giza from Actual Survey and Measurements", TAV IX.

13. In his Histories, Herodotus described "…underground chambers, which Cheops intended as vaults for his own use: these last were built on a sort of island, surrounded by water introduced from the Nile by a canal." There is no indication that Herodotus actually saw this, but was likely recording the description provided by the priests.

14. Vyse, op. cit., Vol I, p223.

15. Maragioglio and Rinaldi, op. cit., TAV 4.

16. Petrie, op. cit., pp61-63.

18. Maragioglio and Rinaldi, op. cit., TAV 5 and p34.

19. Core blocks can be observed in Al Mamun's Hole and in the excavation cut from the Queen's Chamber niche.

20. Edgar, "Great Pyramid Passages and Chambers" 1910 edition, plate CX

21. Maragioglio and Rinald, op. cit., TAV 6.

22. Lepre. op. cit., p110. Lepre uses the term "lines" so the assumption is that there is a line on each side of the passage, but he is not clear on the point.

23. Maragioglio and Rinaldi, op. cit., TAV 6 and p42.

24. Ibid, TAV 6 unless otherwise noted.

26. Petrie, op. cit., p66.

27. Ibid, p69.

28. Petrie, op. cit., p70.

29. Maragioglio and Rinaldi, op. cit., p44, TAV 6.

30. The excavation behind the niche today is protected by a heavy grating. Maragioglio and Rinaldi propose that robbers observed a 2'9" by 3'1" block in the back niche wall which was set symmetrical with the niche sides. Possibly the robbers saw this as a blocked passage and removed the block by breaking it and the niche above and to the south side. Since both these sides are damaged for 3 cubits indicating the block size, the robbers might have seen this block as a plug filling a passage. Excavating further they found only the pyramid core and gave up. Maragioglio and Rinaldi, op. cit., page 124.

31. Maragioglio and Rinaldi, op. cit., p124.

32. Gantenbrink, The Upuaut Project, www.cheops.org, except Height Above Floor from Maragioglio and Rinaldi, op. cit., TAV 6. Gantenbrink did not provide the details of the angle measurements, Petrie, op. cit., p71 identifies the angle of the north shaft at 37°27' and the south shaft at 38°37'28".

33. Smyth, "Great Pyramid", p428.

34. Maragioglio and Rinaldi, op. cit., p 42.

35. Edgar, "Great Pyramid Passages and Chambers" 1929 edition, page xxi.

36. Gantenbrink, op. cit..

37. Ibid.

38. http://emhotep.net/2012/03/07/locations/lower-egypt/giza-plateau-lower-egypt/the-djedi-project-the-next-generation-in-robotic-archaeology/

39. If the shaft terminated 195' from the entrance and the first 6.5 ' is horizontal, then the shaft rising length is 188.5'. The vertical height above the shaft start where the shaft ends is determined by the formula Sine 39°36'=Shaft End Height /188.5' = 120'. The height of the shaft end above the pavement is determined by adding this result to the height of the shaft start

above the Queen's Chamber floor and the height of the Queen's Chamber floor above the pavement or 120'+5.5'+69.5' = 195'.

40. Maragioglio and Rinaldi, op. cit., TAV 3 identifies the height of the apex in the top relieving chamber as 64.09 meters or 210' above the pavement.

41. We can calculate that the pyramid volume below the Queen's Chamber is 30,485,990 cubic feet (91,013,990 total - 60,528,000 above the chamber) represents 34% of the pyramid volume. Using an approximation of 20 years for pyramid construction (Khufu reigned about 23 years), we can take 34% of 20 years to determine that the Queen's Chamber was started about year 7.

42. There are only three possible storage places for the plug blocks: the Horizontal Passage to the Queens Chamber, the area between the entrance to the Horizontal Passage and the Ascending Passage, and the floor of the Grand Gallery central ramp. The 47.3" height of the bottom plug is greater than the 46" height of the Horizontal Passage and therefore the plug would not fit. Petrie determined the length of the three plugs as 178.5". The distance between the entrance to the Horizontal Passage and the edge near the Ascending Passage upper end is 178.3". Even if we discount the .2 difference between the two measurements, storing the plugs here would block the entrance from the Ascending Passage to the Grand Gallery. This leaves only the floor of the Grand Gallery central ramp, which is shaped perfectly to store the plugs.

43. Maragioglio and Rinaldi, op. cit., TAV 6.

44. Ibid.

45. Piazzi Smyth provided data on the size and distances between the rectangular holes in his *Life and Work at the Great Pyramid*, vol 2, pp 80 - 81. Based on this data we can determine the average distance between rectangular holes to be 68.04". Leaving an estimated 4" for a cross beam we can approximate the average plug to be 64.04" long. For 23 plugs released into the Ascending Passage this would fill 122.7' (23 times 64.04"). The Ascending Passage is 127' long. We tried to confirm that the three plugs now located at the bottom of the Ascending Passage would fit in the spaces between the lowest Grand Gallery rectangular holes above the bridge over the Upper Horizontal Passage but we were unable to determine accurate measured lengths for the three plugs.

46. Maragioglio and Rinaldi, op. cit., p116.

47. Author's measurements.

48. Petrie, op. cit., p72.

49. Calculation: weight = volume in ft3 x 155lbs, ((33.5 x 82 x 126.75)/1728) x 155 = 31,232 lbs or 15.6 tons.

50. Petrie, op. cit., pp76-77.

51. Maragioglio and Rinaldi op. cit., TAV 7.

52. Maragioglio and Rinaldi, op. cit., p 46, 126.

53. Smyth, op. cit., p205-210, 1 pyramid inch equals 1.001 inches, based on the depth and 1/5 the width of the boss being equal.

54. The descriptions which follow are taken from several sources: Maragioglio and Rinaldi, op. cit., p 28; Petrie, op. cit., p60; Edgar Brothers, op. cit., pp 281-283.

55. Edgar, op. cit., 1923 edition, p xxiii.

56. Edgar, op. cit., p xxiv.

57. Petrie, op. cit., p60.

58. Measurements are author's except measurements for the block in the Grotto from Lepre, op. cit., p118.

59. We measured the spaces between slots on the south wall as 6 ½" and the width of the slots starting from the east side as 3 ½", 4", 3 ½", 3 ¼". We measured the granite fragment outside the entrance as space (S) 6 7/8", hole (H) 2 7/8", S 7 ¼", H 3", S 7 ¼", H 3". While these measurements do not match and do not indicate this granite block was against the south wall, the measurements are similar and provide evidence the granite block was part of a portcullis.

60. Length, width, height from Maragioglio and Rinaldi, op. cit., TAV 7, center diagonal from Lepre, op. cit., p 101, other diagonals from authors calculations based on Maragioglio and Rinaldi measurements.

61. Petrie, op. cit., p82.

62. Lepre, op. cit., p101.

63. Petrie, op. cit., p82.

64. Ibid, p86.

65. Ibid, pp 84-85. Petrie writes that the sarcophagus was "…tilted up at the S. end by a large pebble under it…" Piazzi Smyth, op. cit., p 154 writes 3 years before Petrie that the south end was tilted up by a 1 ½" high black jasper pebble which is very common at Giza. He also says that the pebble was recently pushed under the sarcophagus. What additional information he had is unknown.

66. Gantenbrink, op. cit., except Height Above Floor from Maragioglio and Rinaldi, op. cit., TAV 7. Petrie, op. cit., p73 identifies the angle of the north shaft averages 31°33' and the south shaft averages 45°13' both near the top end.67. Gantenbrink, op. cit..

68. Lepre, op. cit., p106, and Tompkins, Secrets of the Great Pyramid", p36.

69. Maragioglio and Rinaldi, op. cit., TAV 8.

70. Maragioglio and Rinaldi, op. cit., TAV 8 and Tompkins, op. cit., p 56.

71. Maragioglio and Rinaldi, op. cit., TAV 5.

72. Tompkins, "Secrets of the Great Pyramid", p58.

73. The Edgar brothers described the material as "…gravel embedded in caked sand which crumbles in the hand with comparative ease." Great Pyramid Passages and Chambers, p277.

74. Dimensions are based on the sizes shown in the Edgar Brothers drawing assuming the shaft is 28" wide. op. cit., plate CL.

75. Edgar Brothers, op. cit., pp 271-285. Morton Edgar provides a detail description with photographs, drawing, and plans of his descent through the Well Shaft with his brother John and his Arab helper Judah.

76. Tompkins, op. cit., pp7-15.

77. Petrie, op. cit., p28.

78. Maragioglio and Rinaldi report the lower (north) side of the holes to be perpendicular to the incline of the Gallery. A knowledgeable friend who specifically looked at the orientation of the lower side reported it to be vertical. In either case the holes will act to accept a hold back mechanism.

79. Smyth, Life and Work at the Great Pyramid, Vol 2, p 80-81, provides detail measurements of all rectangular holes.

Chapter 4
Khufu's Mortuary Complex

By Dynasty IV the king's funeral complex had evolved into a standard set of structures. The formal entrance to the complex was the valley temple located on a canal or harbor. From the valley temple a causeway ran uphill to the mortuary temple located adjacent to the pyramid east face. The pyramid was surrounded by an enclosure wall which could be entered only from the mortuary temple. Boat pits were placed outside the enclosure wall, often in the vicinity of the mortuary temple. Subsidiary pyramids for the burial of close relatives lay to the east, southeast or south of the main pyramid.

The Causeway and Valley Temple

Herodotus described Khufu's Causeway as *"...five stades (3,051') in length, ten orgyae (60') wide, and in height, at the highest part, eight orgyae (48'). It is built of polished stone, and is covered with carvings of animals."*[1] Today, only the barest remnants of the base remain stretching 800' northeast from the Mortuary Temple to a modern stone wall at the Plateau edge. Over the wall the steep side of the escarpment gives way to the town below. Only a few large limestone blocks mark the missing Causeway path as it continued towards the Valley Temple. Maps from the 19th and early 20th century provide evidence that much of the Causeway base, after it left the Plateau, survived until relatively recently and that the Causeway made a slight turn to the north. However, they do not indicate the end or the location of the Valley Temple.

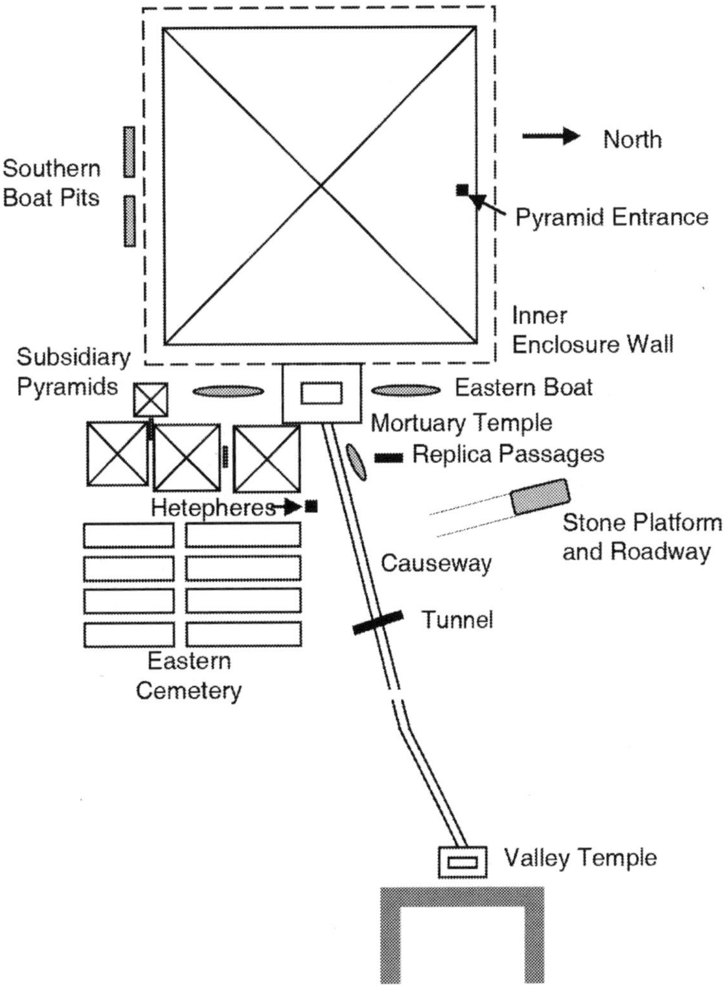

Major elements of Khufu's Mortuary Complex. The context of the Valley Temple and its relationship to water is unknown, but likely it was fronted by either a canal (as shown here) or a harbor.

From the Mortuary Temple the Causeway is angled north of east by 15° so as to avoid the eastern cemetery. It appears to have been about 30' wide (conflicts with Herodotus above, see Endnote 2) with thick walls surrounding an inner corridor about 10' wide.[2] From the Mortuary Temple to the Plateau edge the Causeway was built directly on the bedrock. At the edge of the Plateau, a ramp constructed of large blocks was necessary to carry the Causeway down to the ground below.

There is no direct evidence for the existence of the Valley Temple but there is no doubt that it existed, the remains now hidden under the city of Nazlet-el-Samman. Hishmat Messiha made soundings (opened trenches) in the possible location of the temple and found limestone and basalt blocks.[3]

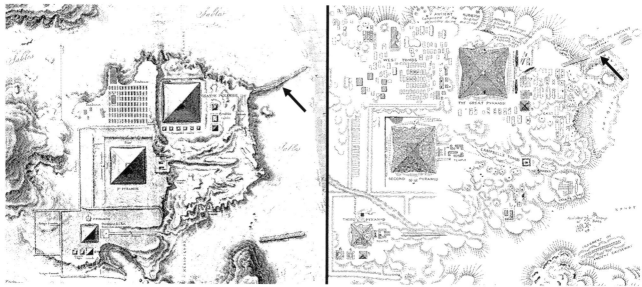

A map by Napoleon's Savants from about 1798 (left) and a map from the Edgar Brothers 1909 Giza expedition (right) were both drawn when more remained of Khufu's Causeway. Additionally, Perring's 1837 map (not pictured here) includes much of the Causeway. All three show the Causeway made a turn to the north (arrows) after leaving the Plateau. The Valley Temple location was likely already lost below the cultivation.

However, older villagers suggest it is under a house which has a garden covering a paved area and rooms built of huge stones under the house.[4] But Zahi Hawass proposes that the site was found in March 1990 during construction of a sewage system when a basalt pavement and mud brick wall were uncovered.[5] But then possibly it is someplace else. While we anticipate the existence of the ruined Valley Temple, there may be other ruined stone buildings hidden under the ground which are being uncovered and presumed to be the Valley Temple.[6] We should be extremely careful in drawing conclusions based on what is found in a few small holes dug over a very large area.

With the Valley Temple located at the water's edge; the water, Valley Temple, Mortuary Temple, Causeway, and pyramid would have created a barrier approaching a mile long, limiting access to the Eastern cemetery for mourners arriving from the north. To avoid the long walk around the pyramid, the builders cut a short tunnel under the Causeway about halfway between the Mortuary Temple and the edge of the Plateau.

The blocks at the left mark the end of the Causeway at the Plateau northeast corner. Below the large blocks are all that remains of the Causeway. In the distance someplace below the houses of Nazlet-el-Samman once stood the Valley Temple.

The tunnel under the Causeway looking south at the mastabas in the Eastern Cemetery. Not much but a rough surface remains of the Causeway.

To the north of the Causeway at the edge of the escarpment, approximately in line with the second row of mastabas, is a platform built of large roughly cut limestone blocks. Leading from the platform towards the Causeway is a cutting 21' wide which indicates some form of short roadway. While the cutting would make a right angle with the Causeway, there is no indication that they were actually connected. There is what appears to be a column base on each side of the cutting, about halfway between the platform and the Causeway. There is an additional 36" square column base at the northeast corner of the platform. The size of the platform

Charlie Rigano stands on the stone platform. Parts show roughly laid courses (below author), others just a jumble of stones indicating it may have been constructed in two phases. The "roadway" extends to the left.

blocks indicate a construction contemporary with the rest of the site and the use of large stone blocks instead of a more temporary material suggests a permanent structure. However, while great effort went into its construction, the platform's purpose is not apparent, even a guess would be hazardous.

Mortuary Temple

The Causeway connects directly to the east side of the Mortuary Temple. Sockets for a door cut 3 ½' apart into a basalt block mark the entrance. Today, little remains of the Temple but a partial limestone foundation upon which was laid a floor of black basalt blocks. While flat on the top, the basalt blocks are otherwise irregularly shaped. Long straight saw marks on the sides provide evidence they were individually cut to fit together in a puzzle-like fashion; the softer limestone foundation cut to accept individual basalt blocks. The much ruined floor and surrounding area provide clues to the Temple layout. Some of the layout is clear, some confused, some missing.

The Temple at 171' by 145',[7] while larger than the temples built by Khufu's predecessors, was not of the monumental proportions of the temples which followed his reign. Its design was straightforward and symmetrical. With white limestone walls, black basalt floor, and red granite pillars, it likely presented a simple elegance in design and color against the pyramid backdrop. The Temple was entered from the Causeway directly into a large open

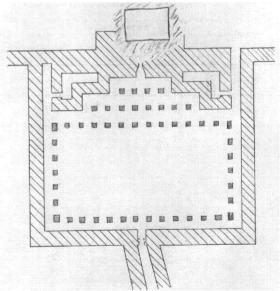

The Causeway at bottom enters the temple courtyard. The pyramid is out of view at the top. The Enclosure Wall extended left and right from the Temple. Access through the wall and into the pyramid court is at top right. The Dynasty XXVI pit at top destroyed the sanctuary layout.

courtyard. While this was the only obvious entrance, based on other contemporary mortuary temples, additional access points probably existed but evidence of them is lacking due to this temple's ruined condition.[8]

The courtyard was surrounded by 34 square granite pillars along the sides and 4 larger rectangular granite pillars at the corners. Regular squared holes in the pavement identify the location of each pillar; some still contain a broken granite base. These pillars likely supported a roof forming a cloister around the outside of

The Mortuary Temple looking from the Great Pyramid. The Dynasty XXVI pit is surrounded by a fence. The entrance block (pictures below) is at the arrow. About 25% of the basalt floor remains which originally extended to where the person is standing at the right.

the courtyard. Larger pillars at the corners were necessary to carry the additional weight of multiple roofing blocks. A recess on the courtyard's west side contained 12 square granite pillars in two north-south rows which likely supported a roof. From the recessed center there is a cutting that indicates a doorway to the sanctuary. Many Egyptologists have tried to analyze the shape and contents of the sanctuary - false doors,

Door sockets cut into a basalt block (top left) marks the entrance to the Mortuary Temple from the Causeway. The open tape measure is 12" long. The same block (bottom left) from the corner reveals a second set of slightly wider, larger door sockets (there is a corresponding socket on the other side of the block). From atop the "socketed" block (top right) looking into the courtyard. Saw marks (bottom right) which look like long straight lines are visible on a number of the basalt floor blocks.

74

steles, statue niches, long halls - but all is conjecture since a Dynasty XXVI Saite burial pit 13' by 21' and 53'9 deep has obscured the original sanctuary plan.

Two corridors exit from the courtyard corners. At the end of the northern corridor a granite threshold identifies the access point from the Temple interior through the Enclosure Wall to the court surrounding the pyramid. Since no threshold is present at the end of the southwest corridor, Jean-Philippe Lauer believes it led to a stairway to the roof.[10] There are indications that off each corridor may have been a room, possibly used for storage, since no other storage space is obvious within the Temple.

Besides Herodotus' description of a decorated causeway, there is other evidence that Khufu's Temples were inscribed. In clearing the Mortuary Temple, Reisner found two blocks which he believed came from the courtyard wall. The blocks show portions of a king wearing the Red Crown, a partial Khufu cartouche, mention of Khufu's pyramid, and the torso of a seated king holding a flail,[11] reminiscent of the Snefru picture inscribed on a stele now located outside the Cairo Museum.

When the Metropolitan Museum of New York excavated the Middle Kingdom Dynasty XII Amenemhat I (1991 – 1962 BCE) complex at Lisht during the period 1906 to 1934, they found 92 inscribed blocks taken from other funerary monuments used as fill within the pyramid core and temple foundations. Six of these blocks contained Khufu's cartouche, which along with four blocks with nautical scenes, were attributed to Khufu's Valley Temple. Another 16 blocks with scenes depicting animals, officials, attendants, ships being rowed and under sail, and scenes from the Sed-festival were assigned to Khufu's Valley and Mortuary Temple. Hans Goedicke, who published the investigation results, suggested that these Old Kingdom blocks were incorporated into Amenemhet's Middle Kingdom complex in an attempt to symbolize that he was building on past traditions.[12] However, more likely the blocks were readily available and could be transported to Lisht easier than new blocks could be cut in the quarry and moved to Lisht. We might think of this not so much as destroying important monuments, but as ancient re-cycling.

Enclosure Wall and Pavement

There were two walls surrounding the pyramid. The Inner Enclosure Wall, which was obviously part of the architect's plan, is a continuation of the Mortuary Temple west (back) side and surrounds the pyramid only 33' from the pyramid base.[13] There are wall remnants on all four pyramid sides. This wall is estimated to have been about five cubits (8 ½') wide at the base, with narrowing sides, and a rounded top. The height is unknown but was likely in the order of 20' to 40'.[14][15] Excavators found pieces of the wall and created a reconstruction near the Mortuary Temple. This wall bounded a 20 cubit wide apron around the pyramid which was paved with white limestone blocks some of which are still in-place. As in the Mortuary Temple, the pavement blocks were flat and finished on the top, but otherwise irregularly shaped and cut to fit together. Seats for each block were cut in the bedrock to match the contours of the individual block bottoms rather than leveling the whole area and laying squared blocks of a standard thickness.

The Outer Enclosure Wall was erected 77' from the pyramid base on the north and west sides, 61' from the base on the south side, no remains have been identified to the east.[16] On the west side the wall is well preserved along the edge of the Western Cemetery. To the south, this wall went over the top

Fragment of the rounded wall top restored near the Mortuary Temple. This example is 4' high, the original was much higher.

of the completed boat pits (more later in this chapter) which therefore dates the wall to sometime after Khufu's burial.

Subsidiary Pyramids

To the east of Khufu's pyramid stand three subsidiary pyramids in a north - south row. A fourth minor pyramid was uncovered in 1993. Subsidiary pyramids from this period were typically found to the south of the main pyramid. However in the case of the Great Pyramid, the quarry and pyramid construction covered the ground to the south and an alternate location for the subsidiary pyramids was necessary.

When we refer to one of the three major Giza pyramids by using the king's name there is no confusion. However, there are eight subsidiary pyramids at Giza; none of which can be firmly attributed to specific people or purposes. George Reisner solved the identification

From five courses high on the Great Pyramid looking southeast across the remains of the Mortuary Temple, at the three subsidiary pyramids (from left) GI-a, GI-b, GI-c

problem by assigning a simple, logical identifier to each pyramid. Reisner used the letter "G" to identify Giza; the Roman numerical I, II, and III to identify the three primary pyramids in chronological order; and letters to identify the minor pyramids.

Originally, GI-a, b, and c were quite similar in appearance and size, each with a volume slightly less than 1% the volume of Khufu's main pyramid. Today the three pyramids look quite different. GI-a in old photos appears to be not much more than a pile of sand. With the sand removed, the pyramid is revealed to have been heavily quarried and at 20' high today stands only 1/5 of its original height. GI-b has a stepped appearance and though also in a ruined condition is somewhat taller at about 30'. GI-c is in the best condition, maintaining a pyramid form and rising to almost its original height.

The surface on which these subsidiary pyramids stand slopes from the northwest to the southeast. While the builders cleared the area to bedrock, they did not level the surface. Instead of adapting the surface to the pyramids, they adapted the pyramids to the sloping surface. This caused problems for the architects in laying out the site resulting in pyramids that are not square, opposite sides which are not parallel, and corners which are not right angles. The fineness which characterized the early portions of the main pyramid was not evident in the layout of the subsidiary pyramids.

Since the main quarry was to the south of the site, the large pyramid was being built to the west, the mastabas were being built to the east, and the Causeway and edge of the Plateau nearby to the north, material used in constructing these three pyramids must have arrived from the south. It is likely that due to the surrounding construction, the confined space created around these pyramids resulted in them being built one at a time starting with GI-a and working south. Judging from their current state, they were also likely dismantled starting with GI-a and moving to the south.

By comparing the volume of burial chambers in the three pyramids to similar spaces in mastabas within Khufu's complex, Reisner found comparisons of GI-a to early mastabas in the Western Cemetery and

Reisner's Pyramid Identifiers	
Pyramid	**Reisner Designation**
Khufu (Great Pyramid)	GI
Subsidiary – North	GI-a
Subsidiary – Middle	GI-b
Subsidiary – South	GI-c
Subsidiary – New	GI-d
Khafre	GII
Subsidiary	GII-a
Menkaure	GIII
Subsidiary – East	GIII-a
Subsidiary - Middle	GIII-b
Subsidiary - West	GIII-c

comparisons of GI-b and GI-c to slightly later mastabas in the Eastern Cemetery. Based on this analysis he determined they were built in order from north to south and placed the construction of GI-a at about years 15 to 17 of Khufu's reign.[19] Additionally we can see that neither the entrances nor the burial chambers for the three pyramids were cut on the same north – south line providing evidence that they were excavated one at a time based on conditions surrounding the construction of the specific pyramid. However, the measured dimensions and similar floor plans reveal an architect's initial intent to build three identical pyramids with a base of 90 cubits (155') to a side and a face angle identical to the main pyramid. Site constraints and other changes made during construction led to variations among the three.

GI-a, b, and c are thought of as forming a straight line, however GI-c is offset almost 12' to the west of the line formed by GI-a and GI-b. Each was built with three steps which were filled in to form a true pyramid.

The same basic internal plan was used for all three subsidiary pyramids with only slight modification. The entrance on the north face provides access to a descending passage built for a short distance first through the core,

GI-a (top), GI-b (middle), GI-c (bottom). The large blocks forming the flat surfaces of the GI-c stepped face and the smaller fill blocks can be identified.

	GI-a	GI-b	GI-c	GI-d
Est Height	99'	100'	95'	45'
Face Angle[17]	51°50'	51°50'	51°40'	51°45'
Base[18]	156'	157'	151'	71'
Volume (ft³)	803,000	822,000	722,000	76,000
Probable Burial	Merytyetes	Djedefre's Mother	Henutsen	Unknown

then the bedrock. The passage opens to a turning space which permitted the handling of long objects such as the sarcophagus and ceiling beams around the 90° turn to the west and down another short descending passage to enter the limestone lined burial chamber above floor level. Each of the burial chambers were cut entirely into the bedrock, and then lined with finely finished limestone, much of which is still in-situ. Each of the three burial chambers at one time likely contained a stone sarcophagus and a royal burial. However, they were all robbed, probably during the First Intermediate Period, and the sarcophagus broken up and removed when the pyramids were reused as communal burial places in the Ptolemaic-Roman period.[20]

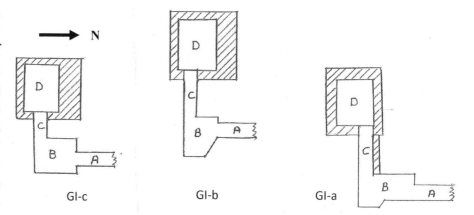

The three subsidiary pyramid substructures with actual east-west offsets (though the distance between pyramids is much greater) showing they are not aligned. However the internal layouts are very similar. A descending passage (A) leads to a turning space (B) designed so that long objects could make the 90° turn into the short descending passage (C) which leads to the burial chamber (D). Cross-hatching indicates laid limestone blocks. The short descending passage (C) in GI-a was cut wider, and then reduced to normal passage size through the insertion of limestone blocks.

As much as GI-a, b, and c are alike, the recently discovered GI-d is clearly different. How can a new pyramid be discovered at Giza, a site visited by millions each year and excavated by Egyptologists for 200 years? After 4500 years of despoiling and stone robbery, all pyramids do not look like pyramids, today some are no more than holes in the ground.

The entrance to GI-a (top left). The large architrave was originally well under the casing. Looking up (top center) at the Descending Passage as it widens and continues the decline. Looking down to the bottom of the Descending Passage (top right) with the turning space behind the banister to the left and the short passage to the burial chamber behind the banister to the right. Looking down the short passage (bottom left) to the burial chamber entrance. At the entrance to the Burial Chamber (bottom center) and from inside the Burial Chamber (bottom right) looking back at the entrance at the top of the ladder near the ceiling.

That is much the case here. What remained of the pyramid was hidden under debris when an asphalt road was built from the northeast corner of Khufu's Pyramid, over top of the Mortuary Temple

Looking down (left) at the GI-d descending passage and chamber. The blocks along the passage are reconstructions. The chamber interior (right) with the inward slanting walls cut in the bedrock.

and the debris covering GI-d, and down to the Sphinx. In the winter of 1992/1993 this road was removed and the surface cleared to bedrock revealing the small pyramid. It was totally ruined with only a few core and casing blocks remaining in-situ along the east and south sides. The substructure was cut into the bedrock and open to the sky. Parts of the pyramidion were found, rebuilt, and placed on display at the site.[21]

The substructure was simple; composed of a descending passage which enters a 9' deep rectangular chamber with inward sloping walls. There is no evidence that the chamber was lined with blocks, but there remain significant amounts of pink plaster on the walls. The descending passage enters the chamber 18" above the floor. In the chamber floor, just below the passage there is a shallow hole in the floor that may have held a stone to continue the ramp down to the chamber floor.

While the general belief among Egyptologists is that GI-d was a planned part of Khufu's Mortuary Complex and possibly served as his ritual pyramid, the facts argue against this belief. Its size at only 10% the volume of the other subsidiary pyramids and its "T" shaped substructure clearly sets GI-d apart from the other three subsidiaries but bears a strong resemblance in size and internal layout to GII-a, the minor pyramid to the south of Khafre's Pyramid.

From ground level there seems to be nothing special about the location of GI-d. However when seen from the air, a different picture emerges. South of the Great Pyramid the Outer Enclosure Wall was built over top of the two boat pits sometime after Khufu's reign. Ten mastabas, dated by Reisner to the end of Khafre's reign or the beginning of Menkaure,[22] about 30 years after completion of the Khufu's Mortuary Complex, are aligned with this wall and apparently built after the wall. If they were built before the wall, likely the mastabas would have been sited closer to the Great Pyramid, on top of the hidden southern boat pits and aligned with the Inner Enclosure Wall. While there are no remains of the Outer Enclosure Wall to the east of the Great Pyramid's, likely it was also present on this side. This wall, the mastabas, the three subsidiary pyramids, and boat pit set the boundaries of a small, relatively flat area in which GI-d was constructed.

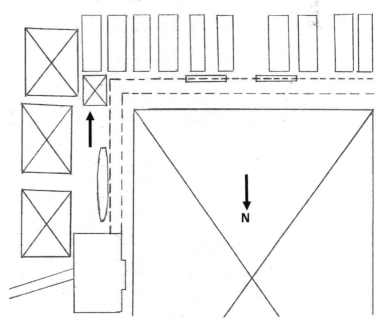

South and east of the Great Pyramid. The enclosure walls are dashed lines. The position of the Outer Enclosure Wall to the east is estimated. It appears GI-d (arrow) was built last in the small space defined by the already existing structures.

It is very unlikely that GI-d was built first and defined the locations for the outer enclosure wall and mastabas. It is much more likely that the boundaries created by these constructions were there first and defined the space and size of a pyramid built after all were in place. This sets the earliest possible construction date for GI-d to after completion of the southern mastabas. The timing makes GI-d and Khafre's

Similarities of GI – d and GII - a		
Feature	GI – d (Khufu)	GII – a (Khafre)
Base	71" Square	69' Square
Height	Estimated 45'	Estimated 46'
Exterior Angle	51°45', essentially the same as the main pyramid	53°, essentially the same as the main pyramid
Descending Passage	39" wide, height unknown, enters chamber above floor level	41" square, enters chamber above floor level
Passage Incline	32°	31°
Chamber	27' by 10', 9' high, lined with pink plaster	25'9" by 8'8", 6'11" high, lined with pink plaster
Pyramid Volume	76,000 cubic feet	73,000 cubic feet

subsidiary pyramid (GII-a) contemporary and explains the similarities between the two pyramids. For whom GI-d was built and why a site was chosen next to Khufu's Pyramid instead of the reigning king is unknown.

All four of the Khufu's subsidiary pyramids are outside of the enclosure wall making them actually part of the Eastern Cemetery instead of the main complex. There is no evidence that they were accessible directly through the main pyramid enclosure wall, or were enclosed by a wall of their own, or separated from the mastaba field in any manner. There is also no evidence that there was an exit from the Causeway which served these pyramids.

There is a boat pit at the center of the GI-a south face which is likely associated with that pyramid. GI-b and c are separated by only 17' (about half the distance between GI-a and b) which was not enough for a boat pit and still have room to get to the GI-c entrance. Instead the boat pit was placed to the southwest of GI-b. The ground south of GI-c was cleared to bedrock without finding a third boat pit.

As a mortuary temple served the main pyramid, small mortuary temples served each of the three subsidiary pyramids. There is no evidence for a temple next to GI-d. There is an outline on the bedrock for a temple on

The boat pit south of GI-a (left) and southwest of GI-b (right). Ledges are visible on each side of the pit on which covering blocks may have been placed. Stone walls at the bottom of the GI-a pit were likely not original but later additions to separate intrusive burials.

the east side of GI-a. Some blocks remain in- place identifying the GI-b temple. The GI-c temple was enlarged and altered during Dynasty XXI to honor Isis, Mistress of the Pyramids. The Saites in Dynasty XXVI further enlarged the Isis Temple.[23] In 1880 Mariette found a stele in this temple which has caused much controversy. Known as the Inventory Stele it reads in part:

> *"Live Horus Medjdu, king of Upper and Lower Egypt, Khufu given life. It was besides the house of the Sphinx on the northwest of the house of Osiris, Lord of Rostaw, that he established the house of Isis. It was beside the temple of this goddess that he built his pyramid. It was beside this temple that he built a pyramid for the king's daughter, Henutsen."*

These words imply that the Sphinx came first, near which the Temple of Isis was built, next to which Khufu built his pyramid and a pyramid for his daughter Henutsen. This timing would have the Sphinx predate Khufu. Since the Isis Temple blocks were laid against the finely dressed subsidiary pyramid cas-

ing and the temple is not bound to the pyramid,[24] clearly GI-c was not built next to the Isis Temple, but the Isis Temple was built at a later time next to the subsidiary pyramid. According to Petrie *"this insignificant looking tablet is cut in scratchy intaglio, worse than any of the poorest tomb decorations of the early times, and looking like nothing but a degradation of the work of the decadence of the twentieth dynasty."*[25] In agreement with Petrie, just about every Egyptologist rejects the notion that the stele was a product of the Old Kingdom and considers it at best a copy of an-

Remains of the Isis Temple on the east side of GI-c. The inclined pyramid face is on the right; the Temple entrance was through the center of the four columns to the left center.

other older stele or a complete fabrication to honor Isis. Petrie also noted that Isis was never connected with the pyramids in the Old Kingdom and her name is one of a later period. It is unlikely that she would be viewed as the Old Kingdom Mistress of the Pyramid. There is really no evidence to support this stele as being anything but a fabrication of a later period.

There is no textual evidence to identify who was buried in each of the minor pyramids. Since ownership cannot be determined directly, some detective work is necessary. An inscription from the chapel of Kawab identifies Merytyetes as his mother who bore him by Khufu. Kawab was heir to the throne, but he seems to have died before he could claim it. Kawab had the place of honor at the north end of the first row of mastabas. It is likely that his mother would be the chief queen and be buried next to Kawab in GI-a. The owner of GI-b rests on less evidence. Reisner proposes it belongs to the unidentified mother of another group of Khufu's children; the most important was the next king, Djedefre.[26] GI-c is assigned to Henutsen solely based on the Inventory Stella found in the GI-c temple. These attributions are based on very little evidence and there are other possibilities proposed by Egyptologists which are also slimly supported.

Trial Passages or Replica Passages

East of Khufu's Pyramid, north of the Causeway, and generally in line with the subsidiary pyramids is found a system of connected passages excavated into the bedrock. The passages do not lead to chambers but end in a blank wall below, and above break the surface in three places. This feature is often called the "Trial Passages", but we find Mark Lehner's term "Replica Passages" preferable since it better suits the evidence. While the surface is generally flat, there is neither a superstructure nor any indication that there ever was a super-

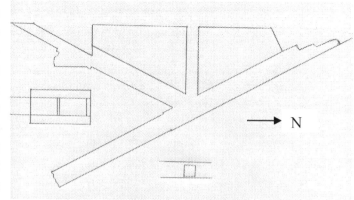

The Replica Passage layout. Entrance is on the right.

structure. Inside the passages are squared and unlined; there is little remarkable to see. When were the Replica Passages built and what was their intended purpose?

The passages have the typical north-south pyramid passage orientation. From the north a passage descends for 72' to a dead end. At a point 40' down the passage[27] there is an intersection with an ascending passage. Where the ascending passage opens to the sky, the passage widens, and with raised platforms against each wall, continues to the surface. Here also is a short horizontal cutting. At the intersection of the descending and ascending passages a shaft rises vertically to the surface.

The area around the passages appears to be leveled as if a building was intended. However we searched for some sign of a superstructure or any sign that blocks were ever laid on the limestone bedrock, and we found nothing. While this passage system is clearly of a different design then the

The Replica Passages (top) north entrance is the railed area to the left, the covered vertical shaft in the center, and the railed gallery area to the right. The north entrance (bottom left). In the background and to the south is GI-a. The ascending passage exits through the partially open door into the gallery area (bottom right). The area is highly eroded but the platforms are visible on either side.

subsidiary pyramids, we find striking similarities when we compare the Replica Passages with the passage system of Khufu's Pyramid. Both have a descending passage and an ascending passage exiting the ceiling of the descending passage. The Replica Passages ascending passage has a slight funneling aspect; the height at the lower end being slightly restricted, a construction technique matched in the Great Pyramid as a means to hold plug blocks in place. At the upper end of the ascending passage in both, the ceiling rises vertically and the passage widens into a gallery space with raised platforms against the east and west walls. At the spot where Khufu's Pyramid has a passage leading to the Queen's Chamber, the Replica Passages has a cutting for what might have been the start of a similar horizontal passage. Above and below this cutting there are small cut-outs which have corresponding features in Khufu's Pyramid to hold a bridge in place on which plug blocks slid over the opening to the Queen's Chamber Passage and into the mouth of the Ascending Passage.

Two constructions in the Replica Passages have similar but not exact matches in Khufu's Pyramid. First, in the Replica Passages below the point in the descending passage where the ascending passage branches upward, the descending passage height and width narrows forming what would appear to be a frame around the passage and creating a "stop" for plug blocks. This same narrowing and framing occurs in the Great Pyramid at the bottom of the Descending Passage where it meets the Horizontal Passage forming a "stop" for plug blocks. Second, in the Replica Passages at the intersection of the descending and ascending passages is a vertical shaft 28" square. In Khufu's Pyramid, the Well Shaft which runs from the Grand Gallery to near the bottom of the Descending Passage is also 28" square.

The similarities between the two structures are not only in the layout of the passages but in the dimensions and angles. Petrie compared measurements in the two structures,[28] we have added the Ascending Passage measurements[29] to the table.

The comparisons are so many and so close that we can be assured the relationship did not occur by chance. This evidence ties the Replica Passages to Khufu's Pyramid and to the time that the Pyramid was being built. Petrie and others have suggested that these passages cut into the bedrock were a "trial run" before building the real thing. However, with the trail passages cut totally in the bedrock and the main pyramid passages built almost entirely in the pyramid core, we can immediately eliminate this idea. Instead we should look for other purposes.

The evidence points us to the conclusion that the Replica Passages were intended to be the substructure of Khufu's first subsidiary pyramid which was planned to match the internal layout of his main structure, the Great Pyramid. We can estimate the intended size of the pyramid over the Replica Passages through comparison with the Great Pyramid. In the Great Pyramid the length of the Grand Gallery approximates the length of the Ascending Passage. The Great Step at the top of the Grand Gallery is on the Great Pyramid center line. We can use this same relationship in the Replica Passages. By extending the gallery to match the length of the ascending passage we can estimate the position planned for the pyramid center line. To determine the planned position of the pyramid's north side we can assume an entrance slightly above the bedrock as was typical of the other subsidiary pyramids. These two positions define a pyramid 100 cubits on a side,[30] only slightly larger than GI-a, b, and c.

Similarities: Replica Passages and Khufu's Pyramid		
Feature	Replica Passages	Khufu's Pyramid
Descending Passage Angle	26°32'	26°27'
Descending Passage Width	41.5"	41.5"
Descending Passage Height	47.4"	47.2"
Ascending Passage Angle	26°10'	26°2'
Ascending Passage Width	41.3"	41.6"
Ascending Passage Height	47.2"	47.3"
Ramp Height	23.6"	23.9"
Gallery Width	81.2"	82.4"
Well Width	28.6"	28.2"

Based on the elements included in earlier pyramid complexes, Khufu's original plan for the east side of his pyramid would have included a mortuary temple in the center of the pyramid's east face and a causeway leading from the mortuary temple to the valley temple. We

Possible Pyramid Over Replica Passages	
Face Angle to Match Main Pyramid	51°52' Assumed
Estimated Base	172' (100 cubits)
Calculated Height	110'
Calculated Volume (cubic feet)	1,085,000

can easily imagine an extended time when the main pyramid was many courses high with the internal spaces essentially completed and the area to the east of the pyramid largely bare of the structures we see there today. During this time the plan could have included a subsidiary pyramid built over the Replica Passages. For unknown reasons the plan for the Eastern Cemetery was changed. The three minor pyramids, the initial eight mastabas, the causeway, and the boat pits were sited. The 100 cubit pyramid planned over the Replica Passages would cover both a large section of the Causeway, the boat pit to the north of the Causeway, and the north east corner of the Mortuary Temple. Since the structure over the Replica Passages interfered with the new site plan, the passages and planned pyramid over the passages were abandoned.

Boat Pits

Though boats are identified with earlier royal burials, Khufu is the first king known to have boat pits associated with his pyramid,[31] but they would become standard pyramid complex features after Khufu. There are five boat pits to the east and south of Khufu's Pyramid, all outside the Inner Enclosure Wall. Three uncovered boat pits lie east of the Pyramid, two of them are parallel to the pyramid eastern face, one north and one south of the Mortuary Temple. The third is parallel with and north of the Causeway. Two covered boat pits just south of the pyramid were covered and hidden when the Outer Enclosure Wall was constructed.

We see the boat pits to the east of Khufu's pyramid today and imagine them always free of debris; however, this was not the case. Petrie excavated the three eastern pits, but referred to them as "trenches."[32] What he did not see was they are shaped in the form of boats with bows and sterns being evident and in some cases with a hull shaped, ribbed bottom.

The Boat Pits are not standard in size or shape. The three pits to the east of the pyramid were likely never covered since they lack obvious side ledges completely around the edges on which covering blocks could have rested. Additionally, the great width of these pits would have required covering blocks 30' long weighing in the order of 35 tons each. While this may not have been beyond the ability of the ancient builders, sliding the large covering blocks along the open pit sides would have been extremely difficult.[33] Internally these three pits are all boat shaped and may have represented a boat carved into the stone. When Reisner excavated the pit parallel to the Causeway, he found rope and pieces of gilded wood providing some indication that boat parts may have been built within the pit.[34]

In 1954, while clearing the 65' high debris piled against the south side of Khufu's Pyramid, Kamal el-Mallakh discovered the southern Outer Enclosure Wall beneath which was a series of closely fitted limestone slabs that roofed two boat pits.[36]

Boat Pit Dimensions[35]				
Boat Pit Location	North of Mortuary Temple	South of Mortuary Temple	Along Causeway	Opened Pit South of Pyramid
Length	174'	169'	141'	102'
Width	23'	23'	16'	8.5' plus 2 ledges each 3.5' wide
Depth	23'	23'	23'	17.5' including ledges 6' deep

The boat pits to the east of the Great Pyramid. The pits north (top left) and south (bottom left) of the Mortuary Temple have no apparent ledges to support covering blocks. The building in the background of both photos once belonged to King Farouk. The pit paralleling the Causeway (right) had a ribbed bottom. While there are side ledges, it does not appear they were to hold covering blocks.

The eastern boat pit was opened and found to contain a dismantled boat while the western pit was left for later investigation. The opened pit is not boat shaped, but instead has an unusual rectangular shape with straight vertical sides. Ledges on each side supported 41 covering blocks joined by a thick mortar which sealed the pit. A large number of quarry marks, including 18 cartouches of Djedefre, Khufu's son and successor, were found on the pit walls and roofing blocks.[37] One of the informal marks on a roofing block reads "Djedefre is ruler"[38] providing some evidence that placing of the boat and covering of the pit occurred after Khufu's death and that King Djedefre was responsible for finishing his father's monument and properly burying him.

Lying in the pit bottom was a dismantled boat, constructed of Lebanon cedar and local acacia wood. The 1,224 pieces ranging from a few inches to 75' long were carefully placed in 13 layers to approximate the location of the parts in the original boat. The bow and stern posts were placed at either end.

Hag Ahmed Yusuf had the task of restoring and rebuilding the boat. He had no written plans to follow, but boats are often shown in tomb scenes. Still much delicate trial and error was involved. After 14 years the completed job produced a near perfect 142' long - longer than the pit - 45 ton boat[39] which today sits on pedestals in a museum built over the pit. By comparison, this boat is longer than the 117' Santa Maria, Christopher Columbus's flagship, and the 100' long Mayflower. The boat has no sails but was powered by 10 oars near the front and steered by two tillers in the rear. A large windowless cabin with doors fore and aft occupies the center of the craft. At the foredeck stands a small construction of poles which may have originally been roofed. Ropes and wooden pegs held the whole boat together.

The boat pit to the west, with 40 limestone covering slabs still in-place, is protected by a metal shed. In 1985 a group sponsored by the Egyptian Antiquities Organization and National Geographic magazine drilled through a slab and photographed the interior. Special equipment was designed to permit penetrating the interior without changing its environment. The photos showed a rectangular, vertical sided pit and ancient timber pieces from a disassembled ship laid down in an orderly fashion. Four oar blades, two pieces for a deck house, a beam to support the deck house roof, hull

The Boat Museum (top left) is just south of the Great Pyramid. The pit (top right) in which the boat was found is under the Museum. Some of the covering blocks rest on the ledges; the remainder sit outside, next to the Museum. Inside the Museum the boat sits on pedestals; the stern (bottom left) and the bow (bottom right).

planking, and green cooper loops were seen among the pieces. There was no evidence of a mast, sails, or rigging but these parts could be hidden in lower layers. Informal hieroglyphics painted on the interior limestone walls again included a Djedefre cartouche. The investigators hoped the pit was sealed and they would be able to sample 4500 year old air. However, pictures showed marks where water had leaked between the covering blocks and a beetle was photographed on the wood. When the air was tested, it was found to be indistinguishable from the outside air except that it contained double the amount of carbon dioxide from the decaying wood in the pit.[40]

The plan is to remove the boat from the second pit, preserve and rebuild it, and put the boat on display. This will be a many year process that started in 2011 with removal of the 40 blocks covering the pit. Samples of the wood were taken in 2012 to create a restorations plan and the first boat parts were removed in 2013. The plan is to remove all the pieces over two years and photograph them with a 3-D Digitizer camera so that trial reconstruction runs can first be done on a computer before the real wood is handled.

These last two pits are clearly different from the boat pits to the east of the pyramid and apparently had a different purpose. We theorize that the pits to the east side in the shape of boats were for symbolic purposes and for use by the dead king in the afterlife. If the intent was for Khufu to use the two boats found in the southern pits in the afterlife, the pits could have been made larger and the boats placed in them whole. Instead, the boats were disassembled. The rectangular pits appear to be burial places for the two boats used in transporting Khufu and his funerary equipment to Giza.

Hetepheres I

On February 2, 1925, the leg of a photographer's tripod scratched a patch of plaster which covered what turned out to be the entrance to the tomb shaft of Khufu's mother. The word "tomb" might be misapplied since while Hetepheres' sarcophagus, furniture, and canopic packages were present, her body was missing.

Just south of Khufu's Causeway and in line with the "street" between the row of subsidiary pyramids and the first row of double mastabas, there is a large square shaft cut into the bedrock and surrounded by a protective fence. Here Alan Rowe and George Reisner of the Harvard - Boston Museum of Fine Arts Expedition worked for 27 months clearing Hetepheres' unplundered tomb with meticulous care. The tomb was unplundered because mysteriously, there was nothing to beckon looters and explorers: no pyramid, no mastaba, no temple, no building or marker of any kind.

Reisner found a flight of 12 steps open to the sky which cuts to the south and 10' down through the shaft wall. The 90' deep shaft cut into the bedrock was completely filled with layers of small limestone blocks, sometimes neatly arranged, sometimes laid haphazardly, and interspersed with layers of clean sand and chips. As Reisner worked downward, removing the shaft blockage, he found a walled up niche cut into the west shaft wall 24' below the surface. This niche contained a crushed horned skull, three bull leg bones wrapped in a reed mat, two wine jars, a limestone boulder, two chips of basalt, and some charcoal.

In the shaft blockage at different levels Reisner found smashed pottery, parts of eight vessels which appeared to be from Hetepheres' original tomb, some copper fittings, limestone pieces which appeared to be bases for canopy poles, and small pieces of wood, one of which had traces of gilding. At the bottom Reisner found several mud sealing pieces inscribed with the name of Khufu's mortuary workshop. All these items should have been in the burial chamber.[41]

At the shaft bottom on the south side Reisner found the entrance to an irregularly cut chamber 17' long, 9' wide, and slightly over 6' tall. The chamber entrance was not sealed and chisel marks could be plainly seen on the unlined chamber walls. Inside the chamber, was a closed alabaster sarcophagus against the east wall with poles from a disassembled canopy laying on top. The rest of the chamber was filled with the decayed remains of Hetepheres' furniture. On first entering the chamber Reisner noticed the sarcophagus upper edge was chipped which indicated a metal tool had been used to pry off the lid. When clearing the chamber, Reisner found a chip from the sarcophagus edge wrapped in linen in one of the cases. Oddly, 13 copper tools were found among the chamber contents[42] apparently left behind by the workmen. Reisner carefully removed the decayed remains and through the genius of the restorer, today in the Cairo Museum we can see the sedan chair, two arm chairs, a bed and bed canopy, and wooden chests with gold and ebony accents.

The tomb today, the fenced stairway leading to the pit (top). GI-a is to the right. The bedrock vertical faces and channels indicate quarrying, probably related to the nearby Causeway. Looking from the opposite side (bottom) with the Great Pyramid in the background.

Replicas are displayed in Reisner's Boston Museum of Fine Arts. Inscriptions on the furniture describe Hetepheres as the wife of Snefru while other inscriptions identify her as the

When Reisner entered the tomb, all of the Queen's burial goods had turned into rubbish. The sarcophagus (left) and canopic box (right) now in the Cairo Museum remained intact.

"Mother of the King of Upper and Lower Egypt", obviously this was Khufu.

Professional patience required Reisner to clear the tomb before turning his attention to the sarcophagus. Two years after the burial chamber was first entered, he lifted the sarcophagus lid. As anticipated, the interior was empty. Reisner found the sarcophagus lip was damaged on the side against the wall, likely from when robbers pried off the lid. Since this could not have occurred with the sarcophagus against the wall, he concluded that this chamber was not the original burial but that the contents were moved here from Hetepheres' tomb and reversed in the process.

The tomb was not completely devoid of Hetepheres' remains. In the chamber west wall Reisner opened a sealed, roughly cut recess in which he found Hetepheres' alabaster canopic chest sitting on a badly decayed small wooden sledge. The chest was divided into four compartments which contained what was presumed to be Hetepheres' internal organs; three chambers amazingly still contained a 3% natron solution in water.[43] The chest and its contents, which appear to be an unformed mass at the bottom, are also on display in the Cairo Museum.

Reisner looked at the evidence and developed a scenario. He believed that Hetepheres died early in Khufu's reign and was buried near Snefru's Red Pyramid. Shortly after her burial, thieves broke into the tomb, forced open the sarcophagus lid, and destroyed or removed her body. The Vizier ordered the lid replaced and convinced Khufu to move his mother and burial equipment to a place near his pyramid where Hetepheres could be properly guarded. For further protection, no marker was placed over the tomb to draw attention. Khufu apparently never checked to see if his mother was still in the sarcophagus and no one told him the truth.

Mark Lehner questions Reisner's theory. Why would the thieves have gone through the trouble to remove the lid, when in fear of being discovered, they could have quickly smashed it and gained access to the interior? Why would the burial be moved from Dahshur where an offering chapel and priests would have continued to make offerings to her spirit? Why was a secret tomb required for Khufu's mother at Giza but not for the other members of his family? How could the tomb be cut and the burial made in secret in a place where thousands of people worked?

As an alternative explanation, Lehner offered that early in Khufu's reign Hetepheres was initially buried in this tomb shaft. A superstructure was planned to be constructed above the shaft, but as the plan of the eastern cemetery developed, the monument over her shaft was no longer viable. Instead either pyramid GI-a or GI-b was built for her. Hetepheres' body was removed from the shaft tomb and with a new set of funerary equipment was buried in a subsidiary pyramid. After the transfer the shaft was refilled.[44]

Zahi Hawass in turn questions Lehner's theory. As Lehner himself suggests, the canopic box remaining in the shaft tomb argues against an official transfer of the burial to one of the subsidiary pyramids. Instead Hawass had another alternative. His theory proposes that Hetepheres was initially buried in GI-a or GI-b. Late in the Old Kingdom or during the First Intermediate Period, Khufu's complex was being vandalized. The priests, responsible for Khufu's cult moved Hetepheres burial to the Dynasty II or III shaft tomb to hide it from the vandals; the body had already been removed by robbers in a search for jewels.[45]

These theories do not fit the facts or a test of reasonableness.

For Reisner:

- There is no known Dahshur burial for Hetepheres. However, if there was one, it is difficult to imagine that thieves could have violated the tomb during Khufu's reign, so shortly after Snefru's death, while the area was still being attended to by likely a large number of mortuary officials.
- Burying a person as important as the Queen Mother, with Khufu believing she was in the sarcophagus, without a superstructure and any means to make offerings is inconsistent with burial practices of the day. Khufu's other close relatives were placed in very obvious tombs.

For Lehner:

- The chamber was roughly and unevenly finished, unlined and not plastered. Chisel marks are readily apparent. If this was initially the planned final burial place for a queen, it would have been finely finished.
- The presence of the canopic box argues against the official removal of the body. We cannot imagine that the body was moved and the canopic box forgotten.
- Snefru would have made provision for his wife's burial near one of his pyramids.
- The tomb was neatly arranged, the lid to the sarcophagus was in-place, poles were laid on the top of the sarcophagus, and some trouble was taken in neatly closing the shaft. This "neatness" argues against a removal of her body.

For Hawass, though he is closer, there are still inconsistencies:

- Hetepheres would more likely have been buried near her husband at Dahshur, not her son at Giza.
- Outside of the gold foil covered furniture, the only objects of value left in the burial were one set of silver bracelets. Likely there were many pieces of gold and silver jewelry buried in the tomb. The robbers had already done their work, taking everything of value, missing the one set of bracelets and considering the foil covered furniture too bulky to carry and to time consuming to strip. There was little left to protect from future robbery – the body and valuables were already gone.
- Preparing the shaft for a burial, extracting the sarcophagus from GI-a, and then lowering it 90' down a shaft would have been a visible, major undertaking. Resealing GI-a would have been easier and just as effective.
- The shaft was not of the type cut during Dynasty II or III.
- If there was a Dynasty II or III shaft, it would have had to stand open and unused for the intervening 200 or so years.

The data points lead us to other conclusions. The lack of a superstructure or temple, the unfinished and very rough nature of the tomb, the tools left in the chamber, the funerary pieces found mixed with the shaft filling all argue against a formal ritual-filled reburial during Khufu's life and for a less ritualistic reburial distant in time from Khufu. Snefru would have made provisions for Hetepheres burial near one of his pyramids at Maidum or Dahshur. These would have been locations with multiple royal and high official burials, an active priesthood, and supporting communities. It is extremely unlikely that a queen's burial could be robbed within the 20 plus years that Khufu reigned. However, all indications are that the original burial was robbed: the chips along the edge of the sarcophagus lip, the complete lack of jewelry with the exception a set of silver bracelets, and the missing queen's body.

We see a scenario as follows. Hetepheres died during Khufu's reign and was buried in the tomb prepared for her by Snefru at Dahshur. Sometime during the Old Kingdom, possibly as early as Khafre's or Menkaure's reigns, Hetepheres' Dahshur tomb was robbed. The robbers made off with almost everything of value missing only one set of silver bracelets and leaving the less valuable and more difficult to carry gold foil covered boxes and furniture behind. They took the body for a more thorough search of the wrappings when they were not concerned about being discovered. When the robbery was discovered, there was no body to rebury, but the objects used as part of the royal burial were sacred and had to be properly disposed. A shaft was cut at the still active and protected Giza necropolis in Khufu's precinct near his queen's pyramids. Since this was more a religious disposal of grave goods than a burial, a roughly finished chamber was sufficient, and no superstructure was needed. As soon as the chamber was of adequate size, the Queen's equipment was lowered down the shaft. Since this was not a burial, the chamber did not have to be sealed, the shaft just had to be filled. The area around Snefru's Red Pyramid is still largely unexcavated. Maybe someday more digging will provide new clues to this mystery.

---

1. Herodotus, "*History of Herodotus*", Book II, pp124-126.
2. Hassan, "*Excavations at Giza Vol X, The Great Pyramid of Khufu and its Mortuary Chapel*", p19. On page 18 Hassen repeats Herodotus' value of 60' for the width, then on page 19 says the width is about 9 m, or about 30' wide. Our observation of the width makes it closer to 30' wide.
3. Messiha, Hishmat, "The Valley Temple of Khufu (Cheops)," *ASAE 65 9-18* (1983).
4. Hawass, "*Funerary Establishments of Khufu, Khafra, and Menkaura During the Old Kingdom*", p134.
5. Hawass, "The Programs of the Funerary Complexes of the Fourth Dynasty," in "*Ancient Egyptian Kingship*", pp224 – 225.
6. For instance, Khafre's Valley Temple and the area around it were covered by a deep layer of debris. If we cut a small hole into the debris, we might mistake parts of Campbell's Tomb, the Sphinx, Sphinx Temple, or tombs in the area for Khafre's Valley Temple.
7. Maragioglio and Rinaldi, "*L'Architettura Delle Piramidi Menfite, Parte IV La Grande Piramide di Cheope*", TAV 9
8. For instance at Abusir, Sahure's Mortuary Temple has a columned entrance separate from the causeway. At Dahshur, there is an entrance to the Bent Pyramid's Causeway near the point where it connects to the enclosure wall. Khafre's temple has an entrance at the southwest corner.
9. Abou-Seif, "Degagement de la Face Est de la Pyramide de Cheope", *ASAE Vol 46*, Plate LXV.
10. Maragioglio and Rinaldi, op. cit., p62.
11. Reisner, *History of the Giza Necropolis*, Volume II, pp4, Fig 5, 6a, 6b.
12. Goedicke, *Re-used Blocks from the Pyramid of Amenemhet I at Lisht*, pp6, 8-118. Blocks without cartouches were identified to specific kings through style of execution and the form and details of the scenes. Based on an analysis of the scene content, some blocks were assigned to specific buildings.
13. Hawass, *Funerary Establishments of Khufu, Khafra, and Menkaura During the Old Kingdom*, p31.
14. Assuming an 8.6' (5 cubit) base, an 80° sloping side, and a 2' wide rounded top, the wall would be 18.7' high. If the wall had an 85° slope instead it would be 37.7' high.
15. Maragioglio and Rinaldi, op. cit., p66.
16. Ibid.
17. GI-a, b, and c from Maragioglio and Rinaldi, op. cit., pp 80, 86, 92.
18. GI-a, b, and c were not built on a flat surface but on a slope. Therefore the length of each pyramid face is different as the builders accommodated each side to the incline. For purposes here we measured the east-west distance through the pyramid center from Maragioglio and Rinaldi, op. cit., TAV 11.
19. Reisner, *History of the Giza Necropolis*, Vol I, p135.
20. Reisner, op. cit., Vol I, p135.
21. Hawass, "Discovery of the Satellite Pyramid of Khufu," *Studies in Honor of William Kelly Simpson*, pp379-398.
22. Reisner, op. cit., Vol I, p83.
23. Reisner, op. cit., Vol I, p17.
24. Maragioglio and Rinaldi, op. cit., p94.
25. Petrie, *Pyramids and Temples of Gizeh*, p156.
26. Reisner, op. cit., Vol II, pp6-7.

27. Measured from Maragioglio and Rinaldi, op. cit., TAV 9.

28. Petrie, op. cit., p50.

29. Replica Passage measurements per Maragioglio and Rinaldi, op. cit., TAV 9, Great Pyramid measurements per Petrie, op.cit. pp61-63.

30. Based on measurements taken from Maragioglio and Rinaldi, op. cit., TAV 9. 40' down the descending passage is the intersection with the ascending passage, the ascending passage floor 18.7', the cut for the horizontal passage 7.4'. By assuming a gallery the same length as the ascending passage the centerline would be at 82' from the north side. If the ascending passage is extended 6' (inclined distance) to emerge above ground level, typical of the other subsidiary pyramids, the centerline is 86' from the north side producing a pyramid 172' or 100 cubits on a side.

31. No boat pits have been found around earlier pyramids though the area to the south of Zoser's Pyramid within the Enclosure has been cleared, excavations at Maidum uncovered north and south burials but no boat pits, Fakhry found several structures when he cleared the area around the Bent Pyramid but did not find a boat pit. The surfaces around Sekhemkhet's and the Red Pyramid are still largely covered by rubble and whether boat pits lie beneath awaits future excavations.

32. Petrie, op. cit., p47.

33. There are granite blocks spanning the Great Pyramid King's Chamber that weighed up to 70 tons. However, the chamber may have been filled with sand forming a solid base when the blocks were placed.

34. Hawass, *Funerary Establishments of Khufu, Khafra, and Menkaura During the Old Kingdom*, pp59-62.

35. First three Hassan, *Excavations at Giza Vol X, The Great Pyramid of Khufu and its Mortuary Chapel*, p38. I have seen several different measurements for these boat pits, therefore these measurements should be considered only approximate. Last from El-Baz, "Finding a Pharaoh's Funeral Bark," *National Geographic* April 1988, p514.

36. Abubaker and Mustafa, *Aufzaetze Zum to Geburtstag von Herbert Ricke*, "The Funerary Boat of Khufu", p1.

37. Hawass, op. cit., p56.

38. Edwards, op. cit., p114.

39. Jenkins, *Boat Beneath the Pyramid*, pp78, 83, 108.

40. El-Baz, op. cit., pp518 – 542.

41. Reisner, op. cit, Vol II, p14.

42. Reisner, op. cit, Vol II P34.

43. Reisner, op. cit, Vol II, pp21-22.

44. Lehner, *Pyramid Tomb of Hetep-heres and the Satellite Pyramid of Khufu*, pp4-5, 35-40.

45. Hawass, op. cit., p108.

Chapter 5
Khufu's Pyramid – Designing, Closing, and Opening

In the last three chapters we described Khufu's mortuary complex in detail. Now we will use the physical evidence embodied in the descriptions to build scenarios describing:

- How the design of Khufu's Pyramid evolved from the designs his father, Snefru, used at Maidum and Dahshur.
- The likely sequence of the build.
- The process in which Khufu was entombed and the pyramid sealed.
- How the pyramid was later entered and robbed of its contents.

We place high confidence in the following and provide descriptions in non-wavering terms. But of course we do not claim to be absolutely correct.

The Pyramid Design

Khufu's architects and master builders also served his father, Snefru. In designing Khufu's Pyramid they did not start with a "blank page" but with the lessons and techniques they personally learned at Dahshur and Maidum and the experiences and advances passed down to them from 100 years of pyramid building.

While earlier Dynasty III pyramids – Djoser, Sekhemkhet, and the Layer Pyramid - had deep underground burial chambers, those immediately preceding the Great Pyramid had main chambers that were not only within the core, but were built progressively higher within the pyramid core:

- Maidum burial chamber floor is at ground level with the chamber within the core,
- Bent's Upper Chamber (presumably the burial chamber) is wholly within the core,
- Bent's Subsidiary Pyramid has a layout similar to the Great Pyramid with the main chamber in the core,
- Red Pyramid passages and chambers are all within the pyramid core.

Based on the progression of the four preceding pyramids, we would be surprised if Khufu reverted to a deep underground burial. Placing Khufu's burial chamber higher in the pyramid core was a logical next step in pyramid evolution. But Khufu's architects changed the method for hiding and gaining access to the main chamber. The entrance to the main chambers in the three previous large pyramids at Maidum and the Bent and Red were all hidden high above the previous chamber and required a vertical climb to reach the burial chamber.[1] Khufu's architects abandoned that plan and instead expanded on the design used just a few years previously in the Bent's South Pyramid (see the description of this subsidiary pyramid in Chapter 4). In this

Pyramid Main Chambers	Chamber Height Above Pavement	Chamber Height to Pyramid Height
Maidum[2] Chamber	0 – 16.6'	0% - 5.4%
Bent Pyramid[3] Upper Chamber	10.5' – 64.5'	3.1% - 18.8%
Red Pyramid[4] Burial Chamber	28.2' – 76.3'	8.2% - 22.3%
Great Pyramid Queen's Chamber[5]	69.5' – 89.9'	14.4% - 18.7%
Great Pyramid King's Chamber[6]	141.1' – 160.3'	29.3% - 33.3%

Note: The Bent's Subsidiary Pyramid was excluded from the list since it is significantly smaller than the other pyramids and may not offer a valid comparison. Its measurements show the burial chamber to be 9.2' to 22.6' above the pavement which equates to 10.7% to 26.3%[7].

small pyramid, from the entrance a descending passage connected to an ascending passage which opened into a high ceiling gallery in which four plug blocks were stored. The blocks were initially held in place by a beam anchored in the side walls and running in front of the lowest block. When the pyramid was ready to be closed, the beam was replaced by a retaining pole which had one end in a hole in the floor and the other end against the lowest block. A rope tied to the retaining pole allowed the pole to be pulled away from below and have the plug blocks slide into the ascending passage, sealing it. When the pole was actually pulled away, the two lower blocks slid into the passage and the two upper blocks stayed in the gallery where they remain today. We do not know if the architects were aware of the partial failure.

As we addressed in Chapter 4, the design of the Grand Gallery was optimized to hold the plug blocks and facilitate lowering them into the Ascending Passage. If the Grand Gallery had another purpose, it would have been designed differently. The architects wanted to completely close the Ascending Passage which required 23 plug blocks. Plugs in this quantity had to be released individually from the Grand Gallery which required men to be present in the upper gallery and that required a method for the men to escape the Pyramid after they sealed the Ascending Passage. So an escape shaft, which we know as the Well Shaft, was included in the plan. Since there was no good way to block and/or hide the escape shaft, it's exit would have to be in the Lower Horizontal Passage (during construction, the shaft exit was moved to near the bottom of the Descending Passage) and the Descending Passage filled with plug blocks to protect the shaft exit and access to the upper chambers.

Design Changes?

The incomplete Subterranean Chamber and the unfinished Queens Chamber tempt us with the idea that there were two major changes in pyramid design that moved the burial chamber from the Subterranean Chamber to the Queen's Chamber to the King's Charmer. This would lead us to consider that the original plan had the burial chamber deep underground in the Subterranean Chamber with a solid pyramid built over top. We see it unlikely that the Subterranean Chamber was ever planned as the burial chamber:

- When we look at the group of pyramids following Khufu, we see Djedefre apparently planned a deep underground burial, Khafre's burial was at ground level, Baufre's was deep underground, and Menkaure was underground but not deep. But the pyramids preceding Khufu's placed the burial chamber higher in the pyramid core, not deep underground – see table.
- The bottom of the Descending Passage was designed as a "stop" for plugs blocks slid down the passage. This "stop" defined the dimensions of the Lower Horizontal Passage as 36" high and 33" wide; too small for a stone sarcophagus to pass.
- At the bottom of the Descending Passage there is no horizontal section or raised ceiling which would permit a sarcophagus or other long burial goods to be maneuvered into the Lower Horizontal Passage.
- As we will discuss later in this chapter, the building of the Well Shaft needed for a burial chamber high in the pyramid core, had to be initiated before pyramid construction covered the top of the internal knoll. We would have to consider whether the Descending Passage, most of the Subterranean Chamber, and the Cul de Sac could all be created prior to this point.
- Generally the pyramids of the time had a portcullis system protecting the burial chamber even if the passages were filled with plug blocks – Bent, Khafre, Menkaure.

The Queen's Chamber does not appear to have been ever planned as the burial chamber:

- In Chapter 3 we discussed our finding that the Ascending Passage was not cut through already laid blocks. Therefore a change from the Subterranean Chamber to the Queen's Chamber would have had to occur at the start of building the Ascending Passage which occurred during the time the lowest few pyramids courses were being laid.

- There was time to complete the Queen's Chamber but it was left unfinished.
- If the burial chamber was to be placed high in the pyramid core, then the Grand Gallery was required to seal the Ascending Passage. We can safely conclude that with the choice of placing Khufu's burial chamber at the bottom or top of the Grand Gallery, the architects would naturally pick the top.
- There is no provision in the Upper Horizontal Passage leading to the Queen's Chamber to block the passage – no portcullis or plug blocks.
- The entrance to the Upper Horizontal Passage would be covered by the bridge which allowed the plug blocks to slide from the Grand Gallery into the Ascending Passage.

Additionally, of significance, the Replica (Trial) Passages cut into the Plateau and abandoned early during construction appear to have provisions for all of the final pyramid passages and chambers. So instead of seeing two changes in plan, we believe that Khufu's architects planned the Great Pyramid in much the same form as we see it today with three main chambers and connecting passages.

Starting with a three-chamber plan with the top chamber intended for the burial, we look for the purpose of the other two chambers. The Dynasty III and IV Old Kingdom king's pyramids were all built with multiple chambers. But there was no standard design. We might find the Subterranean Chamber as being similar to the Bent Pyramid Lower Chamber and we find the Queen's Chamber as being similar to Khafre's Lower Chamber but we do not know the purpose of either of those chambers. All we can say is that all of those chambers were designed close in time to each other and showed some architectural consistency.

Building the Pyramid

Before the first block could be laid, the site had to be readied: the location accurately surveyed, the base outline determined, the surface prepared, and the center knoll shaped to accept core blocks. The infrastructure required for the construction at this new site had to be developed: canals and harbors laid out and dug, ramps and roadways prepared, and facilities to house and feed ten thousand or more workers built. The time required to accomplish these preemptory tasks likely consumed a year or more. During this time, the Descending Passage and the Well Shaft were started.

Because of the confined space in the Descending Passage, one stonecutter crouched and cut by the light of an oil lamp, lengthening the passage while others followed behind finishing the sides. Cutting a downward slope for 235', then an additional 29' horizontally, this small passage was completed in 3 to 5 months at a modest rate of 2' to 3' per day. Since the work was far from the sun, shifts could go continuously. On reaching a point just south of the planned pyramid apex, the excavation broadened to start cutting the large Subterranean Chamber. With increased space, more men were employed and the pace of the excavation increased. The intended size of the final subterranean chamber was approximately 15,000 cubic feet[8], about 70% of which was cut. We could assign a time in the order of a year to excavate the Subterranean Chamber as we see it today.[9] During this time, on the exterior the work crews laid the first core blocks. Somewhere between the first and second years of construction with the Descending Passage complete and the Well Shaft and Subterranean Chamber in progress, for some unknown reason - religious, architectural, whim - the Subterranean Chamber was abandoned, unfinished.

The Well Shaft was cut downward from the top of the central knoll. Where the Well Shaft was to penetrate the knoll top there was a large deposit of loose stone through which a tunnel could not be cut. To penetrate the layer a vertical shaft was constructed of blocks to hold back the deposit. We can recognize that the shaft was not cut from below since the loose stones would have cascaded down the shaft and the laid blocks which form the vertical shaft at the top of the internal knoll would have been impossible to construct from below. So the shaft had to be built before pyramid construction covered the area. At a point 17' below the surface, after the loose stones were penetrated, an inclined shafted was started, aimed at the Lower Horizontal Passage. The inclined shaft is generally straight and there is no evidence to indicate the shaft was cut from both ends and met someplace in the middle. The Well Shaft was steeper than the Descending Passage and had a smaller cross section. Working conditions inside must have been terrible.

At some point, possibly after the decision to abandon the Subterranean Chamber and Lower Horizontal Passage, the inclination of the Well Shaft was increased which reduced the shaft length and the time and effort necessary to complete it. With this change the Well Shaft would not exit in the Lower Horizontal Passage but into the Descending Passage. Measuring angles and distances the architects knew when the escape shaft reached a point near the Descending Passage. The pounding of stone inside the escape shaft could be heard from the Descending Passage and progress followed. Workers pounding on the wall of the Descending Passage gave a sense of location to the men in the shaft. At a point where the bottom of the escape shaft intersected with the level of the Descending Passage, a connecting passage was started. Based on the different shapes of the walls in the connecting passage, more round at the west end and more square on the east end, the men in the escape shaft must have tunneled to the east while men in the Descending Passage tunneled to the west. As they broke through a cheer must have gone up and congratulations passed around.

From the top of the knoll the escape shaft grew upwards as the Pyramid was raised. First as an inclined section through the Pyramid core, then on reaching a point directly below where the northwest corner of the Grand Gallery was to be built, the escape shaft became vertical. The entrance to the shaft from the Grand Gallery was covered with a block which formed part of the Gallery side ramp. This block had to be in-place so that during pyramid closure, the ramp sides were continuous with the sides of the Ascending Passage to guide the plug blocks from the Grand Gallery into the Ascending Passage.

The King is Entombed

The King died around his 27th year on the throne.[10] His body was brought to the Valley Temple, purified, and mummified over a period which lasted several months. His body was carried up the Causeway to the Mortuary Temple where additional rites were performed. To facilitate carrying the mummy, it was likely placed in a wooden coffin or laid on a wooden platform. Using anything heavier would have made movement through the pyramid passage system very difficult. The burial procession led by the new King Djedefre, Khufu's son, exited the Mortuary Temple and carried the body around the pyramid northeast corner. Since the Pyramid entrance was 19 courses up the steeply sloped pyramid side, a ramp was constructed from the pyramid northeast corner to the entrance.[11] The procession ducked low and entered the Descending Passage.

The interior passages were too low and narrow to permit several people to carry the mummy. Instead a coffin or wooden platform was laid on the incline and lowered down the passage by rope. On reaching the intersection with the Ascending Passage, the handlers raised one end and connected a rope from the Grand Gallery to start the movement upward, deep into the pyramid core.

On reaching the Grand Gallery the mummy continued up the wooden bridge covering the entrance to the Upper Horizontal Passage. The handlers moved to the Grand Gallery side ramps and lifting the mummy, they carried it across the top of the plug blocks stored in the Grand Gallery. The handlers and funeral procession moved carefully, being sure not to trip on the cross beams holding the plug blocks in place. The mummy continued over the Great Step, through the Antechamber, into the King's Chamber, and was placed into the granite sarcophagus. The King's Chamber was filled with Khufu's personal articles which would serve him in the afterlife. With some ceremony the sarcophagus lid was slid into place and locking pins seated.

With Khufu safely placed, the royal party left and a crew watched over by priests and probably Djedefre, started the job of closing the Pyramid. The first step was to lower the three portcullises in the Antechamber.

A workman climbed high into the Ante-chamber in the space above the portcullises[12] and one portcullis at a time he threaded ropes through the four holes at the top of each portcullis. From the four holes the four ropes went up and over the beams, horizontally to the top of the granite leaf, then down and out into the Grand Gallery. The ropes were pulled tight, the supporting beams between the floor and the portcullis bottom were removed, and the portcullis lowered, sealing the King's Chamber

The entrance to the Ante Chamber from the Great Step shows damage to the top and right sides. The damage was likely caused when the first robbers tried to cut behind a block that plugged this short passage.

entrance.[13] With each portcullis weighting about 3 tons,[14] there were 20 to 30 men on each of the four ropes[15] and a few more removing the blocking below the portcullis. Counting overseers, priests, and royal members, there numbered 100 to 140 people engaged in this part of the closing. Each of the three portcullises was lowered in turn and the ropes removed. The workmen then turned to a large block stored on the Great Step. Placing a plaster coating on the floor to reduce friction, the block was pushed into and closed the Ante Chamber entrance.

Blocking the Ascending Passage with the plug blocks stored in the Grand Gallery was the next step. Most of the crew left the pyramid leaving only a small group, possibly 10 men, to slide the 23 plugs into the Ascending Passage. The wooden bridge over the Upper Horizontal Passage provided a continuous floor from the Grand Gallery into the Ascending Passage. The crew lubricated the floors of the Grand Gallery, bridge, and Ascending Passage to reduce friction and make the blocks slide easier. One by one, the cross beams were removed and the plugs moved slowly down the Grand Gallery central ramp. To control the flow, each block was stopped several times by cross beams until each plug in turn was held in place at the opening to the Ascending Passage.[16] The beam was raised and the plug pushed into the Ascending Passage. The process continued until the Grand Gallery was empty and the Ascending Passage was full.[17]

The crew now turned to the Well Shaft to make their escape. The Well Shaft entrance was covered by a side ramp block which had to be in place during the Pyramid closing since it was part of the continuous surface from the Grand Gallery into the Ascending Passage mouth. The wooden ramp over the Queen's Chamber Passage partially covered and prevented access to this block. The covering side ramp block was laid about 18 years earlier, and while the plan was to remove the block and escape, the crew members probably were not completely satisfied they would find the Well Shaft with the removal of one block, or that they knew exactly which the covering block was, or that the plan would work. The crew had been sealed in the Pyramid for many hours at this point, the air was bad, they were under stress, and were not very gentle in removing the wooden ramp and the covering block. The mutilated surfaces in the area lend evidence to the lack of care.

But they removed the side ramp block and as planned found the upper entrance to the Well Shaft. The crew made its way through this long, very tight, steep passage and emerged at the bottom of the Descending Passage, very relieved, and climbed up the Descending Passage to the fresh air. This crew was not composed of normal workman, but of priests since they would carry with them the secret of the route to Khufu's burial chamber.

Another small group of priests descended to the junction of the Descending Passage and the Well Shaft. The priests covered and sealed the Well Shaft exit, trying unsuccessfully to make it look like the surrounding stone walls. Another crew of priests brought the prism stones to the junction of the Descending and Ascending Passage. They could see the bottom of the lowest

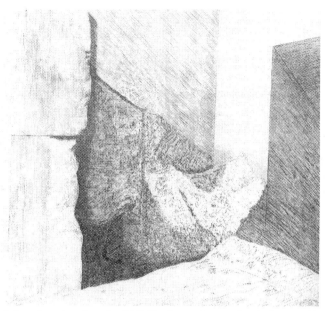

A drawing showing the Well Shaft opening as the dark area. To the right is the Ascending Passage and the lower lip against which the wooden bridge rested. The damage around the opening might indicate stress or indecision on exactly which block covered the entrance.(Edgar Brothers)

granite plug block recessed in the hole above their heads. They raised the prism stones and secured them in place, hiding the secret of the Ascending Passage for the next 3500 years. The original intent of the architect was to fill the Descending Passage with plug blocks to prevent access to the Well Shaft.[18] However, in the end they settled for sealing the Well Shaft entrance and possibly sliding a few limestone plug blocks down the Descending Passage to cover the Well Shaft opening. There is no evidence that the entire Descending Passage was filled with plug blocks. Interest was already being focused on Djedefre's pyramid at Abu Rawash and it was beyond their comprehension that anyone would attempt a violation of the mighty Khufu's tomb.[19] The last action was to cover the entrance to the Pyramid. A casing block was slid into place [20] and access to the pyramid interior completely hidden; forever they thought.

The Pyramid design from a security standpoint was not very good. However, the mass robberies of the royal tombs had not yet occurred, the central government was strong, the King was a god, and the architects of the time had no reason to think anyone would dare violate the tomb. While measures were taken to secure the pyramid, the architects should have seen the measures could be easily circumvented. This thinking might seem silly to us today, but we should put ourselves in their position. Today, the tombs of our important personages are well marked and unprotected but still their wholesale robbery seems extremely unlikely.

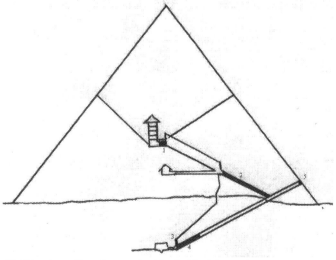

(1) The Ante Chamber and a block filled the entrance to the Ante Chamber, (2) the Ascending Passage was completely filled with plug blocks, (3) the opening from the Well Shaft to the Descending Passage was likely covered, (4) the plan was to fill some part of the Descending Passage with plug blocks but we cannot be sure if this occurred, (5) the entrance was closed by a block which appear as every other casing block.

Tourists visit the location of John and Robert Kennedy's graves daily. George Washington's coffin lies in plain sight behind a metal gate at Mount Vernon. The tombs of virtually every famous person are marked and could be easily violated by anyone with a little time and the simplest of tools. As with every previous nation, someday, the authority of our central government will likely fail and anarchy will take its place. With this anarchy we can expect that our graves will be opened and our tombs robbed. But this likelihood is as foreign to us today as the robbery of Khufu's pyramid was to the people of his time.

The Great Pyramid is Opened

About 400 years after Khufu's death, the last Old Kingdom king, Pepi II of Dynasty VI, died after a 96 year reign. Late in the Old Kingdom the nobles achieved increasing influence and wealth, control became decentralized, and the central government became continually weaker until, with Pepi II's death, it completely collapsed and the Old Kingdom died. The country fell into a 150 year long time of political disorder known today as the First Intermediate Period.[21] The Middle Kingdom followed and pyramids built during this Kingdom had significantly improved security measures providing evidence that the once sacrosanct Old Kingdom pyramids had been entered and robbed during the First Intermediate Period. We can guess that the robbers were not men who came in the dark of night to make off with whatever they could carry. Instead the robbers either had the approval of the local authorities or they were the local authorities. The plundering of the Giza monuments must have required an extended amount of time and effort. The Great Pyramid, being the largest and likely contained the richest treasure, must have been the first target.

The robber's first job was to find the Pyramid entrance. This should not have been that difficult. As we mentioned earlier, casing course 19 must have beckoned to them because of its extra height. Possibly the knowledge of the entrance location was still known to the priests and the robbers were able to obtain the information and go right to the entrance.

Once inside, the robbers proceeded down the Descending Passage to the Subterranean Chamber. Here they found much of what we see there today, an empty, unfinished room. They explored Chamber nooks and crannies without result. If there was any form of a pit in the floor, they investigated but only found the bottom. They crawled the length of the cul de sac and discovered the unfinished end. They moved back up the Descending Passage and found several places where the walls had been plastered over. The robbers set to work removing the plaster in search of hidden passages. At first they found only cracks in the bedrock which had been filled. When removing the plaster from an area on the west passage side near the bottom of the Descending Passage, they found more than cracks, they found the Well Shaft and its long rising passage. Climbing up this confined passage, they exited at the bottom of the Grand Gallery. They now found themselves high in the Pyramid superstructure.

They climbed the Grand Gallery, passing the wooden beams used to hold the plugs in place. On reaching the Great Step they found and cut away the block sealing the entrance to the Antechamber and revealed the portcullis stones. These stones were not much of a hindrance in other pyramids and the design of the Great Pyramid made them even easier to by-pass. Climbing over the Granite Leaf the robbers were atop the portcullis. They attacked the south Ante Chamber wall just above the portcullis, cutting a hole just barely large enough for a small man to squirm through and into the King's Chamber. Later to facilitate removal of the burial equipment, they broke-up and removed the three portcullises.

In the King's Chamber, Khufu's personal positions were arranged in neat piles. The robbers knew the wrapping around Khufu's body contained gold jewelry and precious stones and they went to work on the sarcophagus. Initially, they were unable to move the lid and instead hammered on the southeast corner wall.[22] After forcing their way through the corner, they again attacked the lid, completely destroying it in the process. With Khufu's mummy fully exposed, the robbers went about unwrapping it removing the valuables wrapped with the body. So as not to be menaced by Khufu from the afterlife, they destroyed the body.

Both pictures are from the Ante Chamber looking south through the short passage and beyond to the King's Chamber. When robbers entered the Ante Chamber they found the space filled with the lowered portcullises to the height of the entrance to the short passage. From atop the portcullis they cut a hole in the south wall. The 1909 Edgar Brothers picture (left) shows the hole. Since that time the hole has been repaired (right).

The robbers had a decision to make. They found the plugged top end of the Ascending Passage at the bottom of the Grand Gallery. They must have realized where it led and were able to estimate that the Passage contained a large number of blocks which would have to be removed to create a more direct route out of the Pyramid. The easier choice was to use the Well Shaft. Any object that could fit through the Well Shaft would come out whole. Any object that could not fit would be broken until it could fit through the 28" by 28" rough shaft. Since they were not troubled by time, the process of removing all of Khufu's belongings was accomplished in an orderly fashion. By the time the robbers finished, the Pyramid was emptied of any object of value. Even if the initial group of robbers did not complete the job, the pyramid remained open and the upper chambers accessible for possibly thousands of years. While the path to the upper chambers might not have been easy, it was probably well traveled.

After the Robbery

Evidence available from the descriptions of early visitors leads us to believe that the Great Pyramid was resealed.

- Herodotus visited Giza about 440 BCE and in his Histories correctly describes the Causeway and pyramid exterior, but incorrectly described interior underground chambers as an island surrounded by water from the Nile, a description he likely got from the local shamans.[23]
- Diodorus Siculus visited about 59 BCE and while he described the exterior he did not describe the interior.
- In 24 BCE Strabo described a removable stone which provided access to a passage leading to a pit dug 150' below the pyramid – a reasonably accurate description.
- Pliny the Elder in the first century AD describes a well 86 cubits (147') deep but it is difficult to tell if he visited the interior or was repeating what others had written.[24]

- In 820 AD Al Mamun likely found windblown debris had accumulated against the pyramid sides, but it is unlikely that they reached as high as the original entrance at course 19.

That neither Herodotus nor Diodorus Siculus described the entrance or the interior correctly provides evidence that the pyramid was re-closed at some point before 440 BCE. Strabo may have been describing a re-closure and we cannot tell if Pliny the Elder accessed the interior.

We look for candidates who might have resealed the Great Pyramid. The Saite Kings during their rule from 664 to 525 BC returned prosperity to a troubled Egypt and created art forms that copied the earlier Kingdoms. Djoser's Step Pyramid and Khufu's Great Pyramid were considered hallowed sites and burial near these structures was desired.[25] The Saites were responsible for the south entrance and passage under the Step Pyramid, while at Giza they built a number of deep pit burials including Campbell's Tomb and the pit immediately to the east of the Great Pyramid. Assuming that the Saites were also responsible for re-closing Khufu's Pyramid is not unreasonable, though there is no direct evidence for it.

Al Mamun's Hole at right center was below and slightly west of the original entrance under the gabled stones.

The Final Entry

The original entrance was not obvious when in 820 AD Al Mamun forced his entry at course 6 in the center of the pyramid north face which we described in Chapter 3. While reportedly Al Mamun found nothing of value inside the Pyramid, it is unlikely that stories told about him breaking into the pyramid would have recorded the presence of stone rubble or wood: the broken coffer lid, the pieces of the portcullis, the beams which held the plug blocks back, the ramp over the Queen's Chamber passage, the pieces of the block covering the Well Shaft, and the valueless remains of Khufu's burial gear. The granite portcullis blocks we earlier described outside the original entrance and in the lower substructure provide evidence that large, heavy granite stone pieces were thrown down the Grand Gallery and Ascending Passage. After Al Mamun, the Great Pyramid lay open with the upper chambers exposed for 800 years before being examined by John Graves in 1638 and then for another 130 years before the arrival and examination by Nathaniel Davison. During this period of almost 1,000 years there was ample opportunity for everything of interest to be removed.

The pyramid we see today is the result of careful planning, executed with precision, followed by 4,000 years of assaults by robbers, plunderers, explorers, and scientists. It has only been in the last century that Egyptologists have scientifically studied the monument and the current caretakers have carefully executed plans for its preservation. But in the layout and architecture of the passages, the centuries of debris which accumulated within and without, the marks left on its stones, and the reports of early conditions we can piece together the important events in the Great Pyramid's history.

---

1. At Maidum the main chamber was reached through a 21' 4" high vertical shaft. In the Bent Pyramid, access to the upper chamber was through a passage placed 41' high in the ceiling of the lower chamber. In the Red Pyramid, the main chamber is 25' 3" high near the ceiling of the second lower chamber. In all three cases, a stairway to the main chamber has been built for the modern visitor. But there is no evidence for any accommodation for the ancients.

2. Maragioglio and Rinaldi. L'Architettura delle Piramidi Menfite, Parte III: Il Complesso di Maydum, la Piramide a Doppia Pendenza e las Piramide Settentriola in Pietra di Dahsciur, TAV 4.

3. Maragioglio and Rinaldi, op. cit., TAV 9.

4. Maragioglio and Rinaldi, op. cit., TAV 18.

5. Maragioglio and Rinaldi, L'Architettura Delle Piramidi Menfite. Parte IV La Grande Piramide di Cheope, TAV 3.

6. Ibid.

7. Maragioglio and Rinaldi. *L'Architettura delle Piramidi Menfite, Parte III: Il Complesso di Maydum, la Piramide a Doppia Pendenza e las Piramide Settentriola in Pietra di Dahsciur,* TAV 4.

8. 46' long x 27' wide x 12' high = 14,904 cubic feet

9. To excavate a space of 11,250 cubic feet (75% of the intended final size) over 365 days results in an excavation of 31 cubic feet a day which is roughly the volume contained in a cube 3' 2" on a side. This leads us to believe the estimate of 1 year is conservative.

10. Our source for dating reigns is Clayton's *Chronicle of the Pharaohs* which identifies a 23 year reign to Khufu. A papyrus recently discovered at Wadi el-Jarf identifies a time during Khufu's reign as the year after the 13th cattle count. With cattle counts typically every two years this would date to Khufu's 27th year.

11. We can reject a ramp from the north since at a 2 to 1 angle of 26 degrees it would have consumed a length of 112', placing the start outside the enclosure wall.

12. The builders left a space 3' high between the beams spanning the Antechamber and the ceiling. If access to the area above the portcullis was not necessary, the ceiling would have been lower.

13. A vertical supporting beam was likely placed under each side of each portcullis to hold it in the raised position. Ropes alone would not have been trusted during construction to hold the portcullis in the raised position for a number of years, possibly 10 years or more, from the day the portcullises were placed in the channels to the day they were lowered. Ropes were likely not placed in the holes during construction since they would have deteriorated during the intervening time. We can arrive at several scenarios for the placing of the ropes: ropes placed through the holes in the period just prior to the burial or placed after the burial and during the closing; one set of four ropes used and moved from one portcullis to the next or one set for each portcullis; after the lowering the ropes were left connected or removed; or while provision was made for ropes, none were used and the supporting beams were just pulled out allowing each portcullis to fall down. We choose a scenario to use in the text, but there is no evidence supporting any set of choices.

14. Weight of the portcullis is estimated by determining the volume of the 21" thick, 42" wide, and 61" high stone and multiplying by 200 pounds per cubic foot.

15. If each man was allocated 75 pounds of the 6000 pound portcullis, there would be 80 man holding the ropes or 20 per rope. If each man was allocated a more conservative 50 pounds, there would be 120 rope handlers or 30 per rope.

16. There are holes in the side ramps to the sides of the wooden bridge. Likely plugs were not stored on the wooden bridge since this would have placed unnecessary weight on the wooden bridge for many years and blocked entry to the Queen's Chamber. The only purpose for these holes then would be to control the plugs prior to them being slid into the Ascending Passage.

17. There is a hole in each side ramp, of the same construction as the other holes, at the bottom of the Grand Gallery at the entrance to the Ascending Passage. This could only be the last stop before the plug was slid into the Ascending Passage.

18. The bottom of the Descending Passage is not vertical, but perpendicular to the angle of the Descending Passage. The narrowing of the passage as it transitions into the Lower Horizontal Passage, provided a frame at the bottom of the Descending Passage. The perpendicular angle and the frame provide a well-designed stop for a plug block.

19. If the Passage was filled with plug blocks, we would expect the walls to be mutilated during removal or tunneling obvious around the plugs. There are no indications of either providing evidence that the original intent to fill the Descending Passage was not executed.

20. Fakhry found the Bent Pyramid's west entrance closed with a casing block. While a swinging flap door has been proposed for Great Pyramid entrances, none have been found in other pyramids.

21. Clayton, *Chronicle of the Pharaohs*, pp. 65-70.

22. There is no reliable modern report that the sarcophagus was ever seen intact.

23. Herodotus, "The History of Herodotus".

24. Vyse, *Operations Carried on at the Pyramids of Gizeh in 1837*, pp 184-190; David, *Biographical Dictionary of Ancient Egypt*", pp 40, 107, 146; Tompkins, *Secrets of the Great Pyramid*, p3. In Vyse, which contains a translation of Strabo, the entrance is reported blocked by a "...removable stone. On taking this away there is a winding gallery to the vault." This also describes the removable casing stone Fakhry found closing the western entrance to the Bent Pyramid. In Tompkins the entrance is reported blocked by a hinged stone.

25. Alfred, *The Egyptians*, p176.

Khafre Pyramid Complex

Khafre's Pyramid Site

Khafre's Pyramid Interior

Khafre's Mortuary Complex

Sphinx

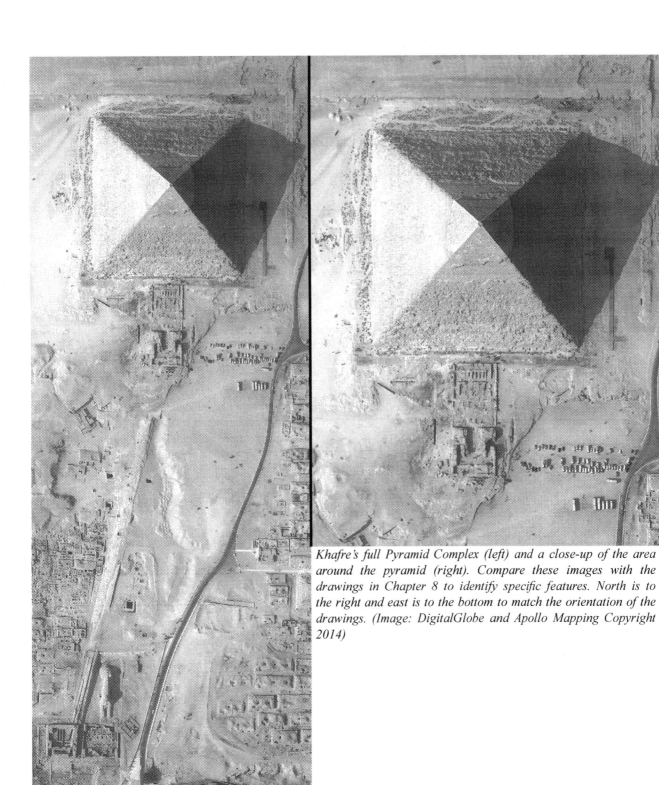

Khafre's full Pyramid Complex (left) and a close-up of the area around the pyramid (right). Compare these images with the drawings in Chapter 8 to identify specific features. North is to the right and east is to the bottom to match the orientation of the drawings. (Image: DigitalGlobe and Apollo Mapping Copyright 2014)

Chapter 6
Khafre's Pyramid Site

Khafre's Pyramid from the northwest. The north face with the entrances is on the left. The Tura limestone cap remains at the top. Except for some granite blocks at the base, the rest of the casing has been quarried away.

Khufu's son, Djedefre, abandoned Giza to build his pyramid at Abu Rawash. Then Khafre, another of Khufu's sons, chose to return to Giza for his pyramid. Tradition and allegiance to his father may have had some influence on Khafre's choice but more practical reasons probably prevailed. Possible reasons for Khafre's return to Giza are not hard to identify.

- The Plateau was large and good sites where still available.
- The infrastructure required to build and support a pyramid was still in-place and would not have to be duplicated: canals, harbors, ramps, quarries, and facilities to house, feed, and administer the work force.
- The limestone quarry for core blocks was literally at the foot of the pyramid and would provide an ample supply of material and permit the efficient employment of the workforce.

When we look at Khafre's Pyramid, the immediate impression is that he built a larger monument than his father's Great Pyramid. But this impression is not based on measurements but on the site Khafre choose 33' higher[1] on the Plateau and the illusion created by the large cap of casing stones remaining at the top of his pyramid. Though the pyramid was set on higher ground, it was well removed from the Plateau's edge and did not provide the prominence inherent in Khufu's site. Additionally, the site Khafre choose required significant modification and preparation to create a base for the pyramid.

Khafre Pyramid (left) is 86% (by volume) as large as Khufu's Great Pyramid (right) though both appear to be of about equal size

The Site

Preparing the site surface was not a trivial matter. The builder's first task was to shape the sloping surface to form a base on which to build the pyramid. The final shape was not a completely flat surface but a flat apron surrounding the square pyramid base within which the raised bedrock was left and incorporated into the pyramid core. Since rock had to be removed from the high side and added to the low side, the architects had to make trade-offs to determine the level for the pyramid base: what was the right level for the apron around the pyramid to minimize the cutting and movement of stone. The surface we see around the Pyramid today could have easily been several feet higher or lower.

Along the pyramid's west and north sides, the builders cut a wide, deep trough in the original sloping limestone surface to create a vertical quarry wall up to 25' high on one side of the trough and the stepped bedrock to be incorporated in the pyramid on the other side. The quarry wall parallels the full length of

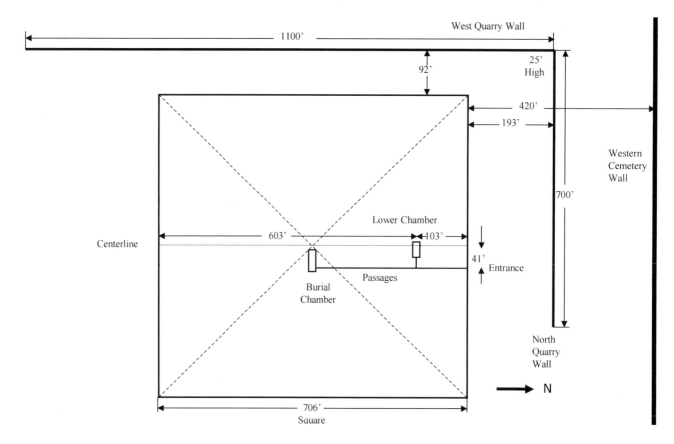

the Pyramid west side, forms a right angle northwest of the pyramid and then parallels the pyramid north face. Along the Pyramid west face the bed-rock incorporated within the pyramid can be easily identi-fied, shaped in steps to receive casing blocks, but without the horizontal and vertical seams that

A trough was cut between the quarry wall on the right and the fifth pyramid course on the left. The dashed line represents the approximate height of the original surface.

characterize laid blocks. The height of the bedrock incorporated in the pyramid is not uniform down the face but is anywhere from 14'3" high in five courses at the Pyramid northwest corner to 11'10" high in

The bedrock incorporated within the pyramid core shaped in five courses at the northwest corner.

three courses at the southwest corner. When covered with the casing, the bedrock appeared the same as any other part of the Pyramid. We do not know what volume of the Pyramid this upward projecting bedrock might form, but it is not insignificant since bedrock courses can be identified on all four pyramid sides.

Our eyes can connect the top of the west quarry wall and the highest level of bedrock incorporated into the pyramid west side and see the volume of limestone which was removed from the high side. Roughly, stone amounting to 4 million cubic feet[2] or more than 5% of the pyramid volume[3] was removed. Likely much of this quarried stone went to level the pyramid low east and southeast sides where extremely large blocks were added to raise and even the sloping surface. The size of these blocks is plainly visible to the pyramid southeast where a hole is

Charlie Rigano stands on one of many blocks used to level the pyramid southeast corner. This block is 24' long, 5' high, 5' wide and weighs almost 50 tons.

formed by three missing leveling blocks and to the northeast of the pyramid where the platform edge is plainly visible.

Quarry Wall

Just as we visit Giza today, ancient visitors also traveled to this even more ancient site. Around 1250 BCE when the pyramids were already 1300 years old, May and Pameniou, a builder and sculptor under Ramesses II, marked their visit to the pyramids by leaving inscriptions in sunken relief on the north and west quarry walls.

Along the base of the west quarry wall are about 30 rock cut tombs from Dynasty V and VI. Some have chambers cut into the quarry

Pameniou's inscription in 18" high glyphs on the north wall: "The Chief of Works in the (edifice) Brilliant is Ramesses, beloved of Amon in the Grand House of Prince, May, true of voice, son of the Chief of Works, Bakeamon, true of voice, from Thebes, (signed) the Chief of Sculptor, Pameniou, true of voice."[4]

face, a large number are small inclined passages cut at the wall's base. The tombs which are not sand filled are either blocked with stones to prevent entry or have such a horrible stench that visitors do not venture inside. For many years the tombs were used as homes to the people that inhabited the Plateau and anything of interest was removed long ago.

May's inscription on the west wall: "The Chief of Works in the Temple of Re, May."

The top surface of the vertical north quarry wall extends about 30' to the north where there is a straight east – west channel 2' wide and 800' long cut into the bedrock. From this main channel short channels were cut to the north to surround blocks which were being quarried. There is no evidence to suggest whether the plan was to remove the whole quarry wall. However, since some blocks were separated from the bedrock but never removed, the appearance is that quarrying was halted in the middle of the operation as if a sudden change in plan occurred.

Stone Base Field

A field of about 150 square stone bases runs from the quarry northwest corner to the east along the quarry wall. From the top of the quarry wall the full dimensions of the field can be studied. The field is six bases wide and touches the quarry wall to the north and west. The bases in the northern row vary in size which results in the field narrowing somewhat from west to east. To the east the bases disappear under the sand. Early Egyptologists thought the channels between the bases were the remains of an extensive system used to level the pyramid apron.

From the top of the west quarry wall looking down on the stone bases about 25' below. Khafre's Pyramid is just out of site to the right, the north quarry wall is to the left. Pameniou's inscription is at the arrow.

The theory was that the channels were filled with water and the flat water surface was used as a reference point from which to measure up or down to set the base of the pyramid. However, even a casual observation of the bases shows this view is obviously wrong and the bases are what remain from quarrying operations. If we estimate that each block removed

From Khafre's Pyramid entrance looking at the northwest corner of the quarry. The stone base field runs on the lower surface from the corner (arrow) to the right. A deep notch was cut at the top of the west wall (left of the arrow) and extends to the left.

was 5' high, then we can calculate that they weighed about 30 tons each.[5]

Why were bases left only in this one area and nowhere else around the pyramid? A field of similar bases must have covered the entire area between the quarry walls and the pyramid as a

Stone Base Field	Dimension
Field	70' Wide, 300' Long
Individual Base	9' Square
Channels Between Bases	24" Wide, 18" Deep

result of quarrying operations to form the flat apron around the pyramid. All of these bases were removed to form the flattened surface we see today except those along the north quarry wall. At this corner, there is a notch cut into the top of the west wall the width of the base field. Possibly, immediately after quarrying to form the apron was complete, a ramp with a 5^{06} slope was built along the north quarry wall, covering the bases and preventing their removal. This ramp could have been required to facilitate movement of mate-

rial around the pyramid. The route along the east side of the pyramid was blocked by the causeway, quarries north and south of the causeway, and the mortuary temple. The only available route was around the pyramid west side and a ramp would have been necessary to climb the 25' high quarry wall. When the ramp was removed after the pyramid was complete, cutting away the bases which were outside the enclosure wall may not have been important or the bases could have intentionally been covered and hidden.

As seen from the pyramid entrance, the outline of a possible ramp over the stone base field.

The "Barracks"

To the west of the Pyramid, just the other side of the modern road are the "Barracks" first described by Petrie. Though the area is large, almost 1500' by 275', there is nothing here to draw the tourist attention. The whole area is sand covered and littered with small, irregular stones. In aerial photographs the "Barrack" walls are easily identified but on the ground only low mounds are visible. The structure is composed

This small section of the "Barracks" top north-south wall is the most distinct. Other parts look like very low mounds.

of many individual long, narrow "rooms" in a comb like configuration. Shaped in the form of an L, 78 rooms run east-west and 19 rooms north-south[7] all of which are open to the side of the pyramid.

In 1837, Vyse made preliminary cuts through some of the mounds thinking they might be burials for common people but found only stone and sand.[8] Petrie was drawn to the site by what appeared to be lines of stone rubble and identified the sharp edges of walls. In a brief excavation he found the walls were built of rough limestone pieces imbedded in mud and covered with mud and lime.[9] Petrie proposed that the galleries were barracks which could house 4,000[10] people, possibly the permanent pyramid staff of masons.[11] Based on location, the "Barracks" were presumed part of the Khafre's complex, but a quick look at a map will show they are also close to Menkaure's complex. Possibly they were employed during the building of both pyramids.

Comb-like "Workmen's" Barracks just west (left) of the road. Khafre's pyramid on the right, Menkaure's pyramid at bottom, north to the top. While these low walls are only a few inches high on the ground and difficult to find, they are obvious on the satellite image. (Image: Digital Globe and Apollo Mapping Copyright 2014)

In barracks we would expect to find settlement debris such as ash, bones, charcoal, and fiber. Instead, Petrie found Old Kingdom pottery shards, alabaster and diorite statue fragments, pieces of quartzite, and a part of an unidentified statue head.[12] In 1988 - 89, Zahi Hawass and Mark Lehner opened eleven "rooms" to sample the site. They found the rooms, which were about 9' wide, 93' long, and at minimum 11'10" high, filled with windblown sand. They found a large number of quartzite, diorite, basalt, and granite fragments; some minor statue pieces; and small flint tools. These findings reinforced the idea that the galleries were not barracks but may have served several functions including the storage of food, raw craft material, and items related to the royal cult. Additionally, the galleries and areas in front of them may have been used for sculpting and stone working.[13]

The Pyramid Exterior

While the length of Khafre's Pyramid sides are somewhat shorter than Khufu's Pyramid, the steeper incline established by Khafre's architects produced a height almost identical to the Great Pyramid and the builders obtained accuracies similar to those found in Khufu's Pyramid.

The face angle of 53°10' was determined from measurements of inclined surfaces. While today we measure angles in degrees, minutes, and seconds of arc, recall that the ancient Egyptians measured the angle of inclined surfaces in sekeds. As we did with Khufu's Pyramid, we can also identify the face angle intended by Khafre's architects by determining the seked employed (lateral displacement in palms for a drop of 7 palms[18]) and translate that into our modern terms. We can determine that the builders

Pyramid Comparison[14]	Khufu	Khafre
Side Length	756' 440 cubits	706' 410 cubits
Difference Between Longest and Shortest Sides	1.8"	5"
Mean Error of East and West Sides[15]	5'30"	5'26"
Height	481'	472'
Face Angle	51°52'	53°10'
Ratio Run to Rise[16]	11 to 14	3 to 4
Face Seked[17]	5 ½	5 ¼

intended a seked of 5¼ which results in a slope of 53°7'48".[19] This is a very common slope used in six other pyramids.[20]

By applying the base length in a ratio using the seked we can determine the architects intended a height of 470'10"[21]. While this made Khafre's Pyramid 10' shorter then Khufu's Pyramid, the position of Khafre's Pyramid 33' higher on the Plateau set the top of Khafre's Pyramid 20' higher than the top of the Great Pyramid. We wonder how much thought Khafre and his architects gave to this subject.

When Herodotus reported that the "basement" of Khafre's Pyramid was built of the *"many colored stone of Ethiopia"*[22] he was referring to the red granite blocks which formed the lowest course of the casing, the rest being limestone. The Pyramid may have appeared to Herodotus to be built on a base of granite; however, we can easily see today that behind the granite casing are either limestone blocks or the shaped limestone bedrock. Vyse reported that the bottom two courses were granite cased.[23] While he must have seen something to support this conclusion, today there are no granite casing blocks in place above the bottom course. But more significantly, when granite is used to face a limestone core in temples and pyramids, the softer limestone is always cut to accept the shape and dimensions of the harder granite block. The limestone backing stones on the first course of Khafre's Pyramid show the irregular cut limestone surface for the fitting of the granite blocks. However, the surface of the second course is straight and does not display the irregularities which would indicate a granite casing. As a result, it is doubtful the granite casing was placed above the first course. The purpose of the granite is not clear since a single exterior course provided no structural benefit and the pyramids built immediately before and after (Djedefre and Menkaure) had a number of courses of granite casing.

The limestone backing blocks on the first course were cut to different depths to accept the harder granite blocks. Course 2 has a flat face. The darker granite casing bocks litter the area.

The construction quality applied to Khafre's Pyramid core was inferior to the construction of the Great Pyramid. Khafre's builders took shortcuts by creating wide vertical joints which are generally devoid of the mud filling common in other pyramids. With the well-laid protective casing gone, these wide joints permitted rain water to penetrate deep into the interior and there are indications that water had run through the passages and stood in the chambers.[24]

The limestone cap, while intact, is heavily damaged. The top courses are missing, similar to the Great Pyramid.

The limestone casing is in place on the top 140' of the pyramid. This stone is of fine Mokattam limestone but somewhat grayer and harder than used in Khufu's Pyramid. As in Khufu's Pyramid, the course heights generally decrease from 41" at the bottom to 21" at the top.[25] Though several archaeologists measured each course of the Great Pyramid, similar information is not available for Khafre's Pyramid. While it is generally believed that the casing blocks of the Giza pyramids were removed in the 14th century, Khafre's casing was reported to be in-place by Palerma in 1581 and by Albinus in 1591 but Sandy in 1611 reported seeing only the cap.[26] We might have thought that the best way to remove a pyramid casing would be to climb to the top and pry the top most stones out, and slide them down the flat casing face. However, the evidence here and at the Bent Pyramid is that the stone robbers actually started at the bottom, probably at the corners, in what must have been a tough, dangerous job.

---

1. Maragioglio and Rinaldi, L'Architettura Delle Piramidi Menfite, Parte V Le Piramidi di Zedefra e di Chefren, p44.

2. North side avg. 17' high x 700' long x 193' wide plus west side avg. 17' high x 1100' long x 92' wide = 4,017,100 cubic feet.

3. 4 million cubic feet divided by pyramid volume of 78 million cubic feet = 5.12%.

4. Swelim, "The Pyramid Court and Temenos Wall of Khafre" *Etudes sur l'Ancien Empire et la necropole de Saqqara dediees a Jean-Philippe Lauer*, p406.

5. Calculation is 9' wide x 9' long x 5' high x 155lbs per cubic foot = 62,775lbs = 31.4 tons.

6. Ramp 25' high and 300' long would have a tangent of .083 resulting in an incline of 4.7°.

7. Lehner, The 1988/1989 Excavation of Petrie's "Workmen's Barracks" at Giza, *Journal of the American Research Center in* Egypt, Volume XXXVIII, 2001, p25.

8. Vyse, *Operations Carried on at the Pyramids of Gizeh in 1837, VolII-A, p88.*.

9. Petrie, *Pyramids and Temples of Gizeh*, p102.

10. This would have allowed about 20 square feet per person, about enough to lie down. A permanent staff would have likely required better "accommodations."

11. Petrie, op. cit., p102.

12. Ibid.

13. Lehner, op. cit., pp 28-60.

14. Petrie, op. cit. pp 39, 43, 97, 98.

15. Arnold, *Building in Egypt*, p15.

16. Khufu's Pyramid ½ (Base) to Height = ½ (756) to 481 = 11 to 14.
    Khafre's Pyramid ½ (Base) to Height = ½(706) to 472 = 3 to 4.

17. Robbins and Shute, *Rhind Mathematical Papyrus, p15.*

18. Ibid..

19. Tangent Intended Angle based on the seked was = 7/5.25 = 1.333
Angle with a tangent of 1.333 = 53°7'48.

20. Userkaf, Neferirkare, Teti, Pepi I, Merenre, and Pepi II

21. Petrie's measurements have been accepted as accurate and are used in the following calculation of intended height:
$$\frac{5.25}{½ (706.25)} = \frac{7}{\text{Intended Height}}$$

5.25x Intended Height = 2471.875"
Intended Height = 470.83' or 470'10".

22. Herodotus, *The History of Herodotus,* Book 2.

23. Petrie, op. cit., p96.

24. Maragioglio and Rinaldi, op. cit., p46.

25. Maragioglio and Rinaldi, op. cit., p50.

26. Petrie, op. cit., p98.

Chapter 7
Khafre's Pyramid Interior

Looking at Khafre's Pyramid today, unencumbered by rubble, all four sides clean down to the pavement, and the entrances obvious to the eye; it is difficult to imagine how the interior passages and chambers could have ever gone undiscovered. But when Herodotus visited the pyramids 2,000 years after they were built, he likely found the casing intact and the entrances sealed and hidden. He reported there were *"no subterraneous apartments in Khafre's pyramid,"*[1] likely repeating what he was told by the locals. In the early 1800's explorers found the pyramid sides covered high with debris left by the removal of the casing and 200 years of windblown sand. With this later picture in mind we can understand the difficulty the explorers of that day had in penetrating the pyramid. But before Herodotus and before the modern explorers, robbers had entered and emptied the pyramid of its contents.

Belzoni Finds the Entrance

Giovanni Belzoni originally came to Egypt to demonstrate and sell a hydraulic device. When this venture failed, he turned to archaeology for a living and attempted to be the first person in modern times to penetrate Khafre's Pyramid. In 1818, Belzoni found limestone rubble piled high against the pyramid sides, hiding any openings. Knowing that pyramids generally had entrances on the north side, Belzoni put 40 men to work clearing the rubble in the center of the north face. Here he uncovered a forced entry and explored it for a distance of 100' before the fall of a large stone deep in the pyramid nearly killed one of his men. Having avoided a disaster, Belzoni abandoned this tunnel and reconsidered the situation.

Belzoni studied the entrance to Khufu's Pyramid. After realizing the entrance was not in the center of the north face, but east of the center, he moved the operation at Khafre's to the same relative location. Here he found the debris to have a slight concavity and was less compact. Belzoni quickly found the

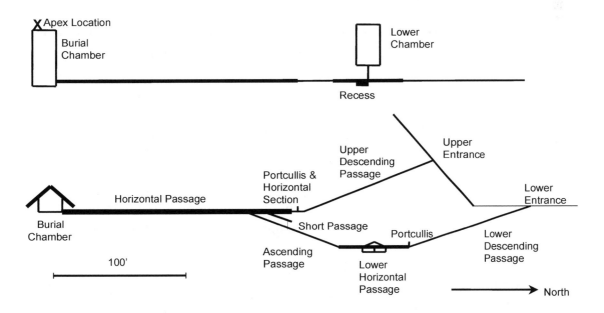

The interior arrangement of Khafre's Pyramid. The plan (top) looking down from above shows the upper passages lie in the same vertical plane as the lower passages. The cross-section (bottom) is the view from the east. There are no standard names for the features as in the Great Pyramid so we have chosen descriptive names for the purposes of this discussion.

original Upper Entrance high above the pavement. That entrance opened to the Upper Descending Passage which he found filled with stone rubble and debris that had fallen into it over the years.[2] After clearing this debris, at the lower end of the passage Belzoni's way was blocked by a 4-ton granite portcullis still in the lowered position.[3] Fortunately there was an 8"

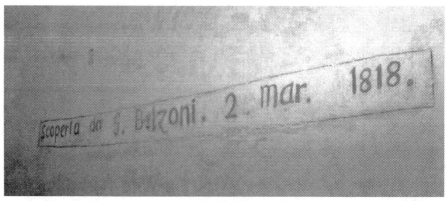

Belzoni's inscription on the south Burial Chamber wall "Scoperta da (Discovered by) G. Belzoni. 2. Mar. 1818".

gap between the portcullis bottom and the passage floor permitting the use of a lever to raise the stone. In this narrow, low passage it was difficult for even two men to work side by side and the passage height restricted the lever's length. However, in very small increments, Belzoni's men raised and supported the portcullis until there was enough space for him to pass underneath and gain access to all of the pyramid major spaces. Belzoni found the Burial Chamber but it was already robbed and emptied. He wrote that the sarcophagus was sunk in the floor; the lid broken off at one end (Note – our examination found the lid whole, chipped at one end but not broken, see the later description and pictures), and the sarcophagus interior half filled with stones and rubble. At the west end of the Burial Chamber he discovered Arabic writing which was translated to say that the pyramid had been opened in the time of King Ali Muhammad, approximately 1200 AD.[4] [5] As was typical of the early explorers, Belzoni inscribed his name at the Upper Entrance and in the Burial Chamber where they can still be seen today.

From the burial chamber, Belzoni returned to the northern end of the Horizontal Passage where he found many stones blocking access to the Ascending Passage. After removing these stones he was able to pass down the Ascending Passage to the lower substructure. The Lower Chamber contained many small stone blocks, some not more than 2' long. Continuing on north to the foot of the Lower Descending Passage, he discovered the lower portcullis already broken and pieces of it lying on the floor. The Lower Descending Passage was clear for the bottom 48', then blocked by stone plugs which he did not attempt to remove.[8]

Entrance

From a position 100' north of the pyramid, four entrances are visible: the original Upper Entrance on the pyramid face, the original Lower Entrance directly below in the pavement, and two forced entries in the center of the face. These forced entries are not comparable to the wide, high Al Mamun entry into the Great Pyramid; these are difficult holes cut irregularly through Khafre's pyramid core.

The Upper Entrance on the pyramid face is east of the north-south center line. There are no inclined gable blocks as over the entrance to Khufu's Pyramid, but instead a large granite block forms a lintel over the passage entrance. The entrance itself is not visible from the ground but a depression in the pyramid face and the granite lintel identify the spot.

The Lower Entrance is cut into the pavement directly below the Upper Entrance. The two forced entries are in a vertical line separated by five courses near the center of the north face, one slightly higher than the original entrance, one slightly lower.

Original Entrances	Dimension[6]
Original Upper Entrance position	42' 8" above the pavement 40'10'" east of center[7]
Lower Entrance	33' north of pyramid in the pavement

North face of Khafre's Pyramid.(left) The two robber entrances are the dark holes in the center of the face. The original Upper and Lower Entrances are marked by arrows. A closer view of the upper entrance and robber holes.(right) The Upper Entrance is immediately below the flat granite block marked by the arrow.

There are no indications as to whether they were created at the same time, or if the lower forced entrance was hidden by debris when the upper forced entry was cut. From the lower forced entry, a rough passage runs to the south for a distance, then bends to the east and turns downwards finally exiting in the ceiling of the Horizontal Passage, behind the blocking Upper Portcullis. This was the robber's entry Belzoni tried to use, but found too dangerous.[9]

Upper Descending Passage

The Upper Descending Passage is lined with granite blocks down to and including a short Horizontal Section at the bottom. The Horizontal Section has an unusual rounded torus in the ceiling and contains the vertically-operated granite Upper

The upper entrance found under debris by Belzoni. The passage is composed of inclined granite blocks forming the floor, walls, and a large lintel. Though they appear on the surface today, these granite blocks were originally located well inside the pyramid.

Portcullis which Belzoni had such a hard time rising. The portcullis, still in place today, was damaged by John Perring in an attempt to search for spaces hidden above its seating.[11] A slot 1.5" deep was cut in the granite floor to seat the portcullis bottom and prevent a pry bar from being inserted underneath.

Descending Passage	Dimension[10]
Descending Length	104'
Size	47" high, 39.4" wide
Passage Slope	26°30'
Horizontal Granite Passage	8'5" long
Portcullis Slot	1'3" thick

Past the Horizontal Section, the passage height rises to a comfortable 5' 11" and, after passing over the entrance to the lower passage system, continues straight to the Burial Chamber. Since the bottom of the Upper Descending Passage is about 10' below the outside pavement,[12] at some point, hidden behind the granite lining, the passage descends below the level of the limestone knoll. A trench must have been cut into the knoll and the Upper Descending Passage,

Looking down at the bottom of the Upper Descending Passage (top left). The horizontal section (top right) contains a wooden ventilation unit. The portcullis Belzoni found raised 8" above the floor is in the raised position and is supported by blocks in the side walls. Some damage can be seen at the lower edge of the portcullis. In the granite floor is the shallow grove for seating the portcullis. Looking up at the passage ceiling (bottom) is the torus, its purpose is unknown.

Horizontal Section, and the portcullis system built inside the open trench.

There is no evidence that the Upper Passage was ever filled with plug blocks. The destruction and removal of the blocks should have left marks in the passage side walls, but the walls are generally undamaged. Since Old Kingdom thieves did not have the means to cut through granite, the hard granite passage walls, ceiling, and floor acted as a barrier to intruders. This protected the passage from entrance through the side, or if the thief was able to find the entrance and get inside the passage, the granite kept the thieves from tunneling around the portcullis.

Lower Entrance, Passages, and Chamber

In 1837 Colonel Howard Vyse spent two weeks removing debris from the pavement to the north of the pyramid before finally discovering the Lower Entrance. He found the passage closed for the upper 36' with limestone blocks 6' to 10' long, fitting closely and mortared in place.[14] While the local Egyptians in Vyse's employ tried to break-up the

The bottom of the Lower Descending Passage as seen from within the Lower Horizontal Passage. The granite portcullis sits to the left side in a recess.

blocks, ultimately they required the help of Mokattam quarrymen to blast and remove them. At one time, similar blocks likely filled the entire passage, the lower blocks having been cut away from the inside by robbers in a search for additional chambers.

The Lower Descending Passage is cut entirely through the bedrock. At the upper north end the entrance is open to the sky for 10', but marks along the sidewalls indicate that part of the ceiling was cut away by Vyse in his attempt to force the passage. The granite Lower Portcullis, which originally blocked the passage bottom, today sits with one end broken in a small recess just inches from its original position. The builders had to excavate a wide space in the bedrock ceiling of the Lower Horizontal Passage to maneuver the 2 ton portcullis up and between the guides. Normally, 25 to 40 men would be required to lift this weight; however in the confined passage this was not possible. Great skill and planning was necessary to place the portcullis with the few people that could work in the passage. Just as Belzoni used levers to raise the upper portcullis, likely the ancient builders used

Lower Substructure	Dimension[13]

Lower Descending Passage
    Length
    Size
    Slope
	112' to the portcullis
	47" high, 41" wide
	21°40'

Lower Portcullis	12" thick, 46 ½" wide, present 4' high

Lower Horizontal Passage
    Length
    Size
	51'6" long
	5'11" high, 41" wide

Recess	10'4" long, 5'7" deep, 5'4" high

Passage to Lower Chamber
    Length
    Size
    Slope
	22' Long
	47" high, 42" wide
	20°30'

Lower Chamber
    Size
    Height
	10'3" wide, 34'3" long
	6' at sides, 8'7" at center
	of gabled roof

Ascending Passage
    Length
    Size
    Slope
	80'
	47" high, 41" wide
	21°40'

levers to raise and place the lower portcullis. As in the Upper Passage, there was a slot cut in the floor to receive the bottom of the portcullis. However, since the floor here was made of limestone instead of granite, the slot provided minimal protection from a pry bar.

Looking north down the Lower Horizontal Passage (right) towards the Lower Descending Passage. The Recess is to the right, the gated entrance to the Lower Chamber on the left. The gated entrance (left) leads to the Lower Chamber. The Recess was used as a turning space for long objects to make the turn from the Lower Horizontal Passage to the Lower Chamber.

The Lower Chamber from both ends. Charlie Rigano kneels(left) in the entrance at the east end. The chamber west end(right). While the ceiling appears to be laid granite blocks, it is actually cut entirely into the limestone bedrock.

Beyond the portcullis, the Lower Horizontal Passage ceiling rises to a comfortable height for walking upright. This long passage has a rising inclined passage at both ends while at the midpoint in the west wall is the entrance to a low descending passage. Immediately across from the entrance a Recess in the east wall is 7" lower than the passage height. The Recess was used to turn equipment up to 9' long around the right angle corner from the Lower Horizontal Passage into the short passage leading to the Lower Chamber. The Lower Chamber is cut entirely in the bedrock but has a pitched ceiling typically used for weight relieving purposes. Recall however, that the Great Pyramid Subterranean Chamber, also cut entirely in the bedrock, has a 55' by 30' flat ceiling with no significant cracks. Since Khafre's Lower Chamber has a ceiling area only 20% the size of the Subterranean Chamber, there is no reason to believe that architects determined a pitched ceiling was required for weight relieving reasons. Finding no functional reason for the ceiling shape, we might anticipate a religious or symbolic purpose. The chamber has the long axis oriented east-west, the standard arrangement for burial chambers. The Chamber floor is neither smoothed nor paved. We observed three plaster coats on the south wall and on the ceiling indicating the chamber was finished at one time. Sitting on the floor in the northeast corner is a granite block 35" long and 12" thick, most likely broken from the Lower Portcullis.

Refer back to the plans for Khufu's subsidiary pyramids GI-a, GI-b, and GI-c and compare them to the Khafre's lower substructure. We find the four have in common a descending passage connecting to a horizontal passage which incorporates a turning space. Across from the turning space a short descending passage leads to a chamber oriented east-west. These four interior constructions were likely built within a period of 15 years and the similarities might show the same architect's hand or the application of a standard design.

Ascending Passage

At the southern end of the Lower Horizontal Passage the ceiling abruptly drops 24" at the opening to the Ascending Passage which connects the lower and upper passage systems. Inclined at the same angle as the Lower Descending Passage, the Ascending Passage

At the south end of the Lower Horizontal Passage, the ceiling drops to enter the Ascending Passage.

emerges through the full width of the Horizontal Passage floor. The Ascending Passage was finished in the typical manner with squared corners and smoothed sides.

When Giovanni Caviglia was clearing the Horizontal Passage just south of the upper portcullis, he found the floor composed of small blocks instead of the bedrock which formed the rest of the floor. On removing the blocks, he discovered a Short Passage paralleling the Ascending Passage and connecting to the Ascending Passage by a small roughly cut hole. This rough hole can be seen in the Ascending Passage ceiling though it is easily missed since visitors typically climb this passage with their heads down. The walls of the Short Passage are squared and well worked but terminate in a roughly formed lower northern end. Maragioglio and Rinaldi hypothesize that this passage represents a construction mistake. They propose that the Ascending Passage was excavated starting from both the north and south ends. During the excavation, the builders realized the two cuttings were offset and would not meet.[15] The connecting hole may have been cut to see how far apart the excavations were. Since the upper excavation became unnecessary, it was abandoned, filled in with small blocks, and covered. The lower tunnel was completed to form the Ascending Passage.

The Ascending Passage does not appear to have been part of the original plan. In the next section we will see that the Horizontal Passage has a ceiling which is flat for the full length of the passage and the portion over the Ascending Passage was cut through the bedrock. Therefore the Ascending Passage had to be excavated after the Horizontal Passage was in place or it would have extended up through the ceiling of the Horizontal Passage. When the Ascending Passage was cut, the likely intent was that it would

Horizontal Passage	Dimension[16]
Length	129' from Ascending Passage to Burial Chamber 181'11" from Granite Passage to Burial Chamber
Size	41" wide, 71" high

interrupt the Horizontal Passage for about 10'. However, the mistake caused by cutting the Short Passage from the top, resulted in an opening 29' long. The evidence indicates that the Ascending Passage was cut purposely as a connecting passage between the upper and lower substructures.

Horizontal Passage

The floor of the Horizontal Passage would be level from the Upper Portcullis to the Burial Chamber if not for the interruption caused by the Ascending Passage emerging from below. Assuming the burial party came in through the Upper Entrance, there is no evidence to indicate how they maneuvered over the long gap caused by the Ascending Passage. Recall that Belzoni found the Ascending Passage clogged with large stones, but he did not describe them any further. We could consider that the Ascending Passage was plugged to the extent that the Horizontal Passage floor was made level or near level over the area and the plugging material removed by early intruders to gain access to the lower substructure. But that raises the question of to where the intruders disposed of the plugging material. There are no reports of a large amount of debris found in the pyramid which could have been the removed plugging material and it is unlikely that the intruders took the trouble of removing the material to the outside of the pyramid. Therefore, it seems unlikely that the Ascending Passage was plugged. So we should consider that the burial party did not have to cross the Ascending Passage gap; more on this later.

In the ceiling above the Short Passage is the end of the forced entry from the lower robber hole seen on the Pyramid north face. There is no record of who forced this passage, but it was an intrusive route from the center of the north face, around the granite-lined passages and portcullis, to the easily-penetrated limestone-lined Horizontal Passage and on to the Burial Chamber. We should not attribute enormous good luck to the robbers in hitting this narrow passage ceiling. Instead they must have used some knowledge gained during the excavation to change the direction of the forced passage 41' to the east (left) to hit this spot.

The Horizontal Passage has the same high ceiling as the Lower Horizontal Passage which allows a comfortable upright walk to the Burial Chamber. Why the architect determined that the horizontal passages could be 5'11" high while the inclined passages are only 47" high is difficult to imagine. This is certainly not the case in the Great Pyramid where the horizontal passage leading to the entrance to the Subterranean Chamber is so low that the visitor actually has to crawl. The Queen's Chamber Passage and the short passage between the Antechamber and the King's Chamber are only 46" and 44" high respectively. However the height change Khafre's architects made was carried forward into Menkaure's Pyramid where again the inclined passages have low ceilings but the two horizontal passages are 5'10" high.

The Horizontal Passage ceiling is slightly more then 3' below the level of the exterior pavement but is not cut entirely through the bedrock. Starting from the north end of the Horizontal Passage, the first 31' was cut through the bedrock as indicated by the lack of joints in the walls, ceiling, or floor. However, for the next 33' joints appear indicating the passage was constructed with cut blocks. Then for the final 65' the passage is again cut entirely through the bedrock. This central constructed section might indicate either an area of poor quality bedrock as evidenced by a gap in the blocks along the east passage wall revealing a very friable earthy material which would not allow tunneling, or a dip in the natural stone formation which necessitated block construction of the passage at that point.[17]

From just beyond the portcullis looking over the wide gap were the Ascending Passage cuts through the floor of the Horizontal Passage as indicated by the slotted floor boards, then down the long Horizontal Passage towards the Burial Chamber. The robber's hole is the open space in the ceiling (at arrow).

From the single portcullis at the bottom of the Upper Descending Passage, the Horizontal Passage runs straight to the Burial Chamber without the presence of additional blocking or antechambers. While Khufu's Pyramid had a triple portcullis protecting the immediate entrance to the burial chamber, in Khafre's, and later in Menkaure's Pyramids, the portcullis protection is distant from the burial chamber.

Burial Chamber

The Burial Chamber was cut into the bedrock as an open pit then covered by a gabled ceiling of finely finished limestone beams. This chamber is enormous, the largest chamber of its type in any pyramid. It measures 23% larger in floor area and 40% greater in volume than the Great Pyramid King's Chamber, is twice the size of both the Bent and Red Pyramid burial chambers, and has a ceiling supporting the greatest weight of pyramid core.

The limestone bedrock forms all four walls. Rather than having a granite or Tura limestone lining as found in the Great Pyramid and its subsidiary pyramids and as we will later find in Menkaure's Pyramid, the walls were simply plastered. The ceiling is similar both in appearance and construction to

The Burial Chamber east end (left) with the entrance (lower arrow) from the Horizontal Passage to the raised platform. The lower area was filled with granite blocks to form a level floor. The hole (upper arrow) was cut by Perring to see how far the ceiling beams penetrated behind the wall face. Looking west (right) towards the sarcophagus. Four of the granite pavement blocks remain.

the Great Pyramid Queen's Chamber ceiling. A gabled roof composed of 34 limestone blocks, 17 on each side, rests directly on top of the bedrock walls. The ceiling blocks have been finely worked and are very smooth, having the appearance of cement. Sitting on top of the short walls at the east and west ends are triangular shaped blocks.

We might wonder why Khafre's architects did not employ relieving chambers above the Burial Chamber as we found above the Great Pyramid King's Chamber. We will recall that every horizontal granite ceiling block in the King's Chamber was cracked. Based on the presence of an inspection tunnel leading from the top of the Grand Gallery to the first relieving chamber and the cement dubbed into the cracks, we can conclude that the damage to the granite beams occurred before the Great Pyramid was closed and therefore before the construction of Khafre's Burial Chamber. Likely this failure with the first attempt at relieving chambers dissuaded the architects from repeating that mistake. On the other hand the gabled ceiling of the Queen's Chamber appeared to be a success. This successful method was repeated as a weight-relieving device not only for Khafre's Burial Chamber but also in all the pyramids which followed.

Burial Chamber	Dimension[18]
Length (East-West)	46'5" (27 cubits)
Width (North-South)	16'4" (9 ½ cubits)
Height (North and South walls) From Top of the Raised Platform	17'2" (10 cubits)
Height (Center and East and West Walls) From Top of the Raised Platform	22'5" (13 cubits)
Slope of Ceiling	Calculated 34°10' Based on Height and Width, Seked 11

Original granite floor blocks surround Khafre's red granite sarcophagus. The hole at left held the canopic packages

In the northeast corner at the top of the burial chamber Perring cut away part of the wall to see how far the roof blocks extend beyond the chamber limits, much as Vyse did in the Great Pyramid Queen's Chamber. Perring found that the gable extends 8'9" into the wall[19] while 9'9" is exposed within the chamber. This is unlike the Queen's Chamber where the greater length is within the wall. Whether additional gabled blocks lie above the ceiling is unknown but they likely exist based on the multiple levels above the Great Pyramid entrance and in the construction of later pyramids.

The Horizontal Passage does not enter the Burial Chamber at the northeast corner as in the three chambers in the Great Pyramid, but 8'8" from the east end. The bedrock floor from the Horizontal Passage is continuous and level into the Burial Chamber. The western two-thirds of the chamber was excavated 2' deeper and originally paved with large granite blocks to form one continuous, level floor. Belzoni's drawings show the whole floor level and at one height. The floor was still intact in 1837 when Vyse and Perring explored the pyramid. In Menkaure's Pyramid they found a similar chamber with a descending passage in the center of the floor leading down to the burial chamber. Thinking that Khafre's granite floor blocks might hide a similar descending passage, Vyse and Perring explored further. At first they removed just a few floor blocks but found nothing. In August 1837, Perring removed the whole floor. Again he found nothing and made a general mess of the chamber.[22]

Khafre's red granite sarcophagus sits at the customary western end of the chamber surrounded by large granite paving blocks which have been restored to their original position. Except for a few chips, the sarcophagus is intact,

Sarcophagus Comparison	Khafre[20]	Khufu[21]
Exterior		
Length	103.7"	89.6"
Width	42.0"	38.5"
Height	38.1"	41.3"
Volume	165,940 inch³	142,470 inch³
Interior		
Length	84.7"	78.1"
Width	26.7"	26.8"
Depth	29.6"	34.4"
Volume	66,940 inch³	72,000 inch³

The finely finished sarcophagus interior. The lid is whole.

unlike Khufu's heavily damaged sarcophagus. Khafre's sarcophagus was originally imbedded in the granite paving blocks up to its lid. Edwards reported the lid was found nearby broken in two pieces,[23] while Petrie said it was lying unbroken on the chamber floor.[24] Belzoni's report had the lid broken on one side leaving part of the sarcophagus open. We have found that different archeologists cannot agree on the measurements for the same feature. Here we find several descriptions that disagree on whether a large piece of granite was broken. To settle the question, we examined the lid carefully and found it completely intact except for some chips. Today the lid is nicely displayed just to the rear (west) of the sarcophagus with one side raised. When Perring removed the floor; he also moved the sarcophagus in the hope of finding a passage underneath. Instead he found the sarcophagus was sitting on a fine mortar laid on top of a large granite block. The granite block was also seated in fine mortar and he found no indication of a further passage.[25]

Petrie closely examined the sarcophagus in 1881. Unlike Khufu's sarcophagus, he found no saw blade lines visible on the sides and all interior and exterior surfaces, except the bottom, were polished.[26] This may indicate that the initial intent was for the sarcophagus to be freestanding rather than buried to its lid. While Khafre's sarcophagus could fit through the passages, it is too long to make the turns either at the bottom of the Upper Descending Passage or at either ends of the Lower Horizontal Passage. Therefore, like Khufu's sarcophagus, Khafre's sarcophagus had to be placed in the Burial Chamber before the Chamber ceiling was closed.[27] Since Khafre's Burial Chamber is at ground level the sarcophagus had to be ready early during construction. Additionally, since the sarcophagus has unnecessarily finely finished sides, we see the possibility that it was originally intended for someone else and usurped by Khafre.

The locking mechanism for the lid was very simple and is obvious today. The two-ton lid was slid horizontally from the rear and seated in grooves angled towards the interior at the top of the sarcophagus short sides. The grooves locked the top in place and kept it from being easily raised. There are two round holes cut into the bottom of the lid with matching round holes in the top of the sarcophagus west side wall. Resin was found in the lower holes. When the lid was slid into place, heated pins in the upper holes fell into the lower holes and seating themselves into the resin, locked the lid in place. The same pin and hole locking method was used for Khufu's sarcophagus. However, in both cases the lids were found removed and the interior emptied of any significant items. Given enough time robbers will find a way.

Perring found a pit measuring 28.75" by 30" against the Burial Chamber south wall. While nothing was found inside, the enclosed area suggests that it contained either a chest or was sectioned to hold Khafre's canopic packages or jars. Drawings of Belzoni entering the Burial Chamber show the pit but no cover. If a cover ever existed, it was already missing.

The Mysterious Holes

In the Burial Chamber north and south walls, 13' above the floor and 16' from the east wall are two holes opposite each other that are roughly 12" square and slightly more than 12" deep. Every published description of the Burial Chamber describes red vertical lines which extend from each hole 5' down to a painted red square of the same dimensions as the hole. We looked closely for these lines and squares but found them completely absent. The red markings are so often described that we do not doubt that they once existed. They may have been removed along with the salt and modern graffiti during a periodic cleaning of the chamber.

Edwards proposed that these two holes represent the start of shafts similar to the ones incorporated in the Great Pyramid King's and Queen's Chambers, but in the case of Khafre's Burial Chamber the "shafts" were quickly abandoned.[28] Shafts to the pyramid surface were unlikely the architect's intent. Khafre's holes are much higher on the walls and are only 12" deep. Since Khafre's Burial Chamber was sunk into the bedrock and capped by ceiling beams extending behind the walls, the builders would have had to cut the small shafts through many feet of bedrock before penetrating above ground and into the pyramid core, probably an impossible task for the time. If shafts were the intent, simpler construction methods were available.[29]

Opposing pairs of shallow holes high on chamber walls were fairly common in Old Kingdom pyramids. There are several pairs in the Maidum Pyramid; one pair has a wooden beam still between them. The Red Pyramid has two hole pairs high on the wall in the second chamber which apparently held beams associated with raising equipment to the burial chamber. Menkaure's Pyramid has several pairs of empty holes in the Upper Chamber. The Great Pyramid has five pairs of rectangular holes at the entrance to the Queen's Chamber Passage which almost certainly contained beams that supported a ramp. The Khafre holes bear a greater resemblance to these holes than to shafts.

The Burial Chamber entrance with the north hole (arrow) near the modern light. Note there is no indication of a line and lower box drawn on the wall.

Perring suggested that the holes supported scaffolding used in the construction of the ceiling or for maneuvering objects within the Burial Chamber. But since the Khafre's Burial Chamber was plastered, we would expect construction holes to be filled and covered. Since this does not seem to be the case, the holes may have had a function to perform in the finished chamber. Maragioglio and Rinaldi proposed that reed mats or a curtain hung from a beam spanning the distance between the holes. They note that the holes are above the point where the floor changes from a bedrock limestone floor to the paved granite floor. This curtain would have separated the funerary compartment at the west end from a possible anteroom or serdab at the east end.[30] Of course the builders could have easily inserted a stone wall here and not relied on a flimsy division. So in the end, while we find the idea of shafts lacking support, we do not find the other alternatives completely convincing.

The Mystery of the Lower Chamber and Passages

Having explored the pyramid in detail we can now step back and ponder one of its mysteries. Khafre's Pyramid has all the internal components found in Dynasty IV pyramids: an entrance high on the north face, a descending passage leading to a horizontal section, a blocking portcullis, and deep inside the pyramid a burial chamber and sarcophagus. But in addition to these standard features there are the Lower Chamber 240' north of the Burial Chamber and the associated Lower Entrance, Lower Descending Passage, Lower Horizontal Passage, and Ascending Passage. Why were these built? Over the years Egyptologists have offered a number of theories. We add another.

In considering the different proposals, there is one significant aspect of the pyramid for which every theory must account. The lower courses along the entire length of the pyramid west side are composed of bedrock cut in steps and formed into the northwest and southwest pyramid corners. All successful theories have to allow that this bedrock would not have been cut away at any time during construction. For instance, if the pyramid southwest corner was ever planned to be further north in the initial layout and the west side shorter, the bedrock at the southwest corner as we see it today and along part of the west side would not exist; it would have been cut away.

Several alternatives below describe the Lower Chamber as the burial chamber in the original plan when the pyramid was sited or sized differently. To avoid repetition, the evidence supporting this conclusion includes: plug blocks and a portcullis in the Lower Descending Passage to protect the chamber, the Lower Chamber is built as a long east-west room in the manner of a typical burial chamber, the chamber is on the pyramid north – south center line, the walls and ceiling were finished, it has a structurally unnecessary pitched ceiling, and there is a turning space immediately outside the entrance. Additionally, we previously described the layout of the lower passages and chamber as similar to the plans of pyramids GI-a, b, and c, built only 15 or so years earlier.

Alternatives as proposed by different authors/explorers can be briefly described as follows[31]:

1. Edwards – Initial plan for the pyramid to be 200 feet further north, Lower Chamber was planned as the original burial chamber.
2. Maragioglio and Rinaldi - Initial plan for a larger pyramid with an 800' base, Lower Chamber planned as the original burial chamber. Also in another alternative, Edwards proposed a larger initial pyramid.
3. Petrie - Lower Chamber planned as the burial chamber for person other than Khafre, no change in pyramid location
4. Our Proposal - Initial plan was for a smaller pyramid, Lower Chamber planned as the original burial chamber.

In the illustrations describing these proposals, the pyramid as located today is the gray square. The proposed initial location is the square marked by an "X" to indicate the faces.

Alternative 1: I. E. S. Edwards proposed that the original plan was to build the pyramid 200' to the north. This would have placed the entrance to the lower substructure about 50' high on the pyramid north face and Lower Chamber as the burial chamber in its customary position under the apex.[32] He likely determined 200' since either this is the

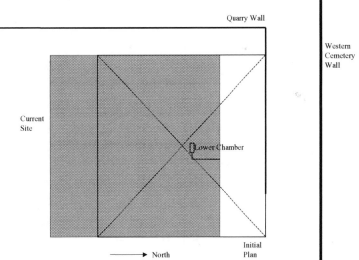

Alternative 1 – I. E. S. Edwards initial plan 200' north, same size pyramid. Note: Though the diagram shows the Lower Chamber slightly north of center, small alterations in size or location would move the Lower Chamber to the center.

distance to the quarry wall or this is the distance necessary to move the Lower Chamber near the pyramid center. Edwards proposed that after the initial siting and start of construction, better rock formations for the causeway were found concealed beneath the sand to the south[33] and the planned pyramid location was moved to accommodate the new causeway path. With the re-siting to the south, the Lower Chamber was no longer in the proper position for a burial chamber and was abandoned for this purpose in favor of a new burial chamber near the pyramid center.

If as Edwards' proposes the pyramid northern base was planned near the current North Quarry Wall, the plan would require removal of the North Quarry Wall to establish an apron around the pyramid. As we have already mentioned, quarrying operations were in progress on the "backside" of the North Quarry Wall, but abruptly halted. A decision to move the pyramid to the south would have made this quarrying operation unnecessary and it would have been discontinued.

However, Edwards' proposal fails for a couple reasons. It is unlikely that the original plan was for a causeway 200' to the north, since the path would have been through Khufu's quarry. And there is no provision for the mortuary temple to be sited further north. Additionally, the southwest pyramid corner would have been 200' north of its present location and the current southwest corner and bedrock which has been incorporated into the pyramid's west side would have been quarried away during site preparation.

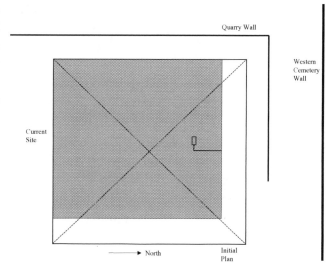

Alternative 2 – Maragioglio and Rinaldi 800' square pyramid.

Alternative 2: Maragioglio and Rinaldi offer evidence of an initial plan for a larger pyramid with the Lower Chamber intended as the burial chamber. They propose the south and west sides and the southwest corner were aligned as we see them today but each side was originally planned to be 30 meters (about 100') longer. This would have shifted the north and east sides creating a pyramid about 800' square. They propose the platform we see today built around the current pyramid is large enough to hold the 800' square pyramid plus an enclosure wall 34' from the pyramid.[34] Again for some unknown reason, the pyramid was reduced to its current size.

Maragioglio and Rinaldi suggest this change in plan would explain a number of facts such as the:
- Entrance 41' east of the current center line (larger size would have placed the entrance near the center line),
- Ground level entrance (Lower Entrance) which would have instead continued as a passage and exited on the pyramid north face,
- Current different distances to the quarry walls on the west and north sides would have been equalized,
- Current southwest pyramid corner would have been the same in both the original and final plans,
- The built-up areas on the northeast and southeast of the current pyramid which level the surface would accommodate a larger pyramid.[35] No other alternative accounts for the excessively sized platform.

This 800' square pyramid at the current inclination would have been 530' tall with a volume of 113 million cubic feet,[36] 22% larger than Khufu's Pyramid. The larger size may or may not have been out of proportion to the available resources in men and building materials. However, the plan places the lower burial chamber 200' north of the pyramid center; a very unlikely location. Additionally there is no surface physical evidence indicating preparations for a larger pyramid and there is no evidence the Mortuary Temple was planned to be in a different location.

Along the same lines, I. E. S. Edwards had a second proposal that a much larger pyramid was intended and was downsized by moving the north and east sides towards the center; however he does not suggest possible dimensions.[37] Since he does not mention how much larger the pyramid might have been, we can estimate a pyramid size which would place the Lower Chamber under the apex. With the

Lower Chamber currently 603' from the pyramid south side and 103' from the north side, to place the burial chamber on the pyramid center line would require enlarging the pyramid 500' to the north. This would place the northern side 80' inside Khufu's already built Western Cemetery. Additionally, this 700' tall, 1100' square pyramid, 3 times the volume of the Great pyramid was likely well outside of the resources and capabilities of the day.

Alternative 3: The two previous alternatives start with the assumption that the Lower Chamber was intended initially as Khafre's burial place. Petrie suggests that the recess opposite the entrance to the Lower Chamber was used to turn a sarcophagus from the Lower Horizontal Passage into the Lower Chamber.[38] He proposed that the Lower Chamber was a second burial place that could have been used separately from the primary burial chamber by blocking internal communication and using the Lower Entrance to gain access.[39]

There are several problems with this alternative. First, where would the plug blocks to close the Ascending Passage be stored? The only choice is the Horizontal Passage. The plugs would have been 47" high (the inclined height of the Ascending Passage[40]). If these were stored in the 71" high Horizontal Passage, there would have been a space of only 24" to pass over them. This is unlikely. Surely, if the intent was to store plugs in this passage, an obvious provision would have been made to store them as in the Great Pyramid where the Grand Gallery was specifically designed to store plug blocks. The other choice is that the Lower Chamber could have been closed not by sealing the Ascending Passage but by plugs placed in the short inclined passage between the Lower Horizontal Passage and the Lower Chamber. But again, there is no obvious place to store the plugs before use. The second problem with this proposal is it is highly unlikely that anyone else would have been buried inside the king's pyramid. There is no evidence in Khafre's Pyramid or precedents in other Old Kingdom pyramids for a double burial.

Alternative 4: We have debated the previous alternatives for hours without finding full support for any. As a result I have looked for an alternative which would better meet the existing physical evidence.

Consider that the height of power to command the resources required to build large pyramids came during the reigns of Snefru and Khufu. Snefru had four pyramids with a volume of 120 million cubic feet while Khufu constructed a pyramid of 91 million cubic feet plus a large burial complex. The next king, Djedefre, started a considerably smaller pyramid which, if completed,

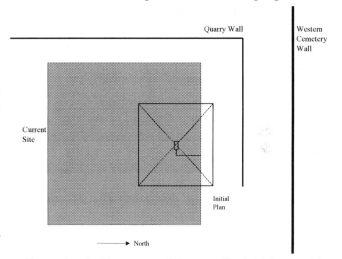

Alternative 4 – New proposal for a smaller initial pyramid.

would have been less than 12 million cubic feet. This decrease in pyramid size may be indicative of political or economic problems, a weakening of the central authority, or a diminished royal capability to command pyramid building resources. With the transition from Djedefre to Khafre, these conditions would have prevailed initially and forced Khafre to plan a pyramid similar in size to Djedefre. As a result, Khafre's initial plan may have called for a pyramid about 350' square (Djedefre's was 347' square). With sides inclined at the current 53°, the pyramid would have attained a height of 232' and a volume of 9.5 million cubic feet.[41] A descending passage entered from the north side 10' to 20' above the base would have led to the Lower Chamber as the burial chamber under the apex. With the Lower Chamber under the apex, the initial smaller pyramid would have a northern base about 75' north of the current location.

This smaller pyramid required a prepared site 15% the size of the final site and the west side quarry wall would not have been cut back very far from the small pyramid.[42] Additionally, the builders did not have to cut down as deeply into the original sloping surface to prepare this smaller site. Khafre's builders prepared the site for a small pyramid, excavated and finished the substructure, and started work on the pyramid. At some point, possibly even years later when the pyramid was well advanced, Khafre rid himself of constraints and became stronger and more ambitious. With changes in the political and economic conditions, he revised the plan for his pyramid and supplemental structures to the grand mortuary complex we see today. To accommodate the new pyramid plan his builders enlarged the site base, cut the west quarry wall back to the position we see today, and lowered the site removing any evidence of the original pyramid except for the Lower Chamber and supporting passages.

The Ascending Passage has to be explained. If the upper end of the Ascending Passage started at the surface, we would see it as part of the original plan for the initially smaller pyramid and it would go through the ceiling of the Horizontal Passage. However, it does not start at the surface, but at the Horizontal Passage floor which was added as part of the larger pyramid. So the Ascending Passage was cut purposely to connect the upper and lower substructures. We see a new possibility here. While the initial plan might have been for the funeral route to start at the Upper Entrance and through the Upper Descending Passage, the route was changed instead through the Lower Entrance with a stop in the Lower Chamber for a ritualistic purpose, then through the Ascending Passage and on to the Burial Chamber. This route would also negate the need to bridge the long opening in the Horizontal Passage floor.

1. Herodotus, *The History of Herodotus*.

2. Mayes, *Great Belzoni,* pp 200-202.

3. Evans, *Mystery of the Pyramids*, p88 indicates the portcullis is 6' high, by 5' wide, by 1.3' thick. This results in a volume of 39 cubic feet. Granite at 200 lbs. per cubic foot results in a weight for the portcullis of 7,800 lbs.

4. Mayes, op. cit, pp 203-204.

5. Two translations of the Arabic supply a slightly different reading. Each refers to "them" which should be read as "the chambers". One alternative contained in Belzoni's book translated by M. Salame reads "The master, Mohammed Ahmed Lapicide, has opened them; and the master, Othman, attended this (opening); and the king, Alij Mohammed, at first (from the beginning) to the closing up." Professor Lee in a letter dated October 24, 1819 provided the following version: "The master Mohammed, son of Ahmed, the stone cutter, first opened them; and upon this occasion were present El Melec Othman, and the master Othman, and Mohammed Lugleik." Professor Lee suggests this entrance was made during the period of the unsuccessful destruction of Menkaure's Pyramid in 1196-1197. Vyse, Operations Carried on at the Pyramids of Gizeh, Vol. II, p 116.

6. Maragioglio and Rinaldi, *L'Architettura delle Piramidi Menfite, Parte V Le Piramidi di Zedefra e di Chefren,* TAV 6.

7. Ibid., p 52.

8. G. Belzoni, Narrative of the Operations and Recent Discoveries within the Pyramids, Temples, Tombs, and Excavations, in Egypt and Nubia. P 253. The description of the upper entrance to the Ascending Passage is as described by Belzoni who does not mention the area until after exploration of the Burial Chamber. Mayes describes that Belzoni saw the Ascending Passage was "…half choked with earth and stones…" and that Belzoni noticed this on first passing the area. The question we are trying to answer is whether the Ascending Passage was originally filled in and closed. It is possible that the stones Belzoni describes were thrown down from the intrusive entrance in the ceiling above or they were the remains of a blockage of the Ascending Passage.

9. Ibid.

10. Ibid., TAV 7.

11. Ibid., p 52.

12. Ibid., p 54.

13. Maragioglio and Rinaldi, op.cit., TAV 6, 9. Portcullis measurements by the author.

14. Vyse, Vol. I, p 185.

15. Ibid., pp 60, 114.

16. Ibid., TAV 9, 10

17. Ibid., p 108.

18. Ibid., TAV 10, Maragioglio and Rinaldi apparently did not measure the height themselves. They show heights as measure by Petrie 17.18', 20.37'; Perring 19.25', 22.40'; and Vandier 17.18', 22.44'. In their drawings Maragioglio and Rinaldi show Vandier's measurements, probably as a good compromise to all three sets.

19. Maragioglio and Rinaldi, op. cit., p58.
20. Petrie, op. cit., p107.
21. Petrie, op.cit, p86.
22. Vyse, op.cit., Vol. I, p 196.
23. Edwards, *Pyramids of Egypt*, p 135.
24. Petrie, *Pyramids and Temples of Gizeh*, 1883 Edition, p 106.
25. Vyse, op.cit., Vol. II, p 99.
26. Petrie, op cit.,p106.
27. Petrie suggested, (op cit., p108) that the sarcophagus at 42" wide could not be moved through the passages since the passages were not that wide though he did not consider placing the coffer on its side which would have fit through the passages. Since he believed the sarcophagus could not fit, he did not evaluate whether it could make the turns.
28. Edwards, *Air Channels of Chephren's Pyramid*, pp 55-57.
29. Such as cutting a slot down each wall, building the shaft within the slot, and lining the chamber with pink plaster to hide the blocks placed in the slot.
30. Maragioglio and Rinaldi, op.cit., p 110.
31. We have left out as a non-starter Fakhry's proposal in *The Pyramids*, p 138. He proposed that the upper entrance and passage was reserved for the king while the lower entrance and passage was intended for workman. This explanation does not address the Lower Chamber and turning space, there is no precedent for such a well constructed workman's access, and the magnitude of the effort is well out of proportion to the purpose.
32. Edwards, op.cit, p 136.
33. Ibid.
34. Maragioglio and Rinaldi, op.cit., pp 116-118.
35. Ibid., p 118.
36. 1/3 x 800' x 800' x 530' = 113,066,666 cubic feet.
37. Edwards, op.cit., p 136.
38. Petrie, op.cit., p 36.
39. Petrie, *Pyramids and Temples of Gizeh*, 1885 Edition, p 108.
40. Maragioglio and Rinaldi, op.cit., p60.
41. 1/3 x 350' x 350' x 232' = 9,473,333 cubic feet.
42. The prepared site around the final pyramid is roughly 1,275' north-south and 1,085' east west resulting in an area of 1,380,000 square feet. The prepared site required for a 350' square pyramid would be about 450' by 450' resulting in an area of 200,000 square feet or 15% of the final. Additionally, the prepared site for the smaller pyramid would have extended 225' north from the center line. The northwest corner of the final pyramid is about 350' north of the center line, well outside of any space that required preparation.

Chapter 8
Khafre's Mortuary Complex

In front (to the east) of Khafre's Valley Temple and the Sphinx Temple are the fast food places[1] and tourists shops of Nazlet el-Simman, similar to those which surround virtually every major tourist attraction in the world. If we could dispose of the last 4500 years, on this spot with the rising sun to our backs we would be standing on the deck of a boat, before us would be Khafre's granite cased Valley Temple, the Sphinx Temple, and Sphinx, and high on the Plateau the great white bulk of Khafre's Pyramid. The harbor or canal under our feet served for the transportation of building materials and the transport of Khafre's body to the site.

All the Mortuary complex features are present in Khafre's Complex. The Valley Temple, the best preserved Old Kingdom example, served as the entry point for Khafre's body. The Causeway, which connected the Valley Temple and Mortuary Temple, today is not much more than a path. The Mortuary Temple is largely ruined but enough remains to understand the floor plan. From the Mortuary Temple, entry was made through the now almost entirely destroyed Enclosure Wall to the base of the pyramid. Boat pits, both covered and open to the sky, were clustered around the Mortuary Temple, and the bare remains of a subsidiary pyramid lies to the south of the main pyramid.

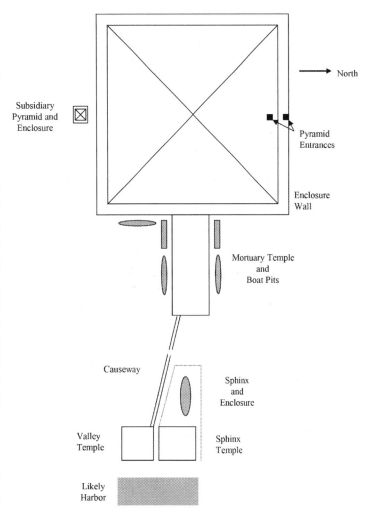

Valley Temple

Seeing the Valley Temple today free of debris, standing tall and broad in the open; it is difficult to think in terms of it being discovered. However, several thousand years ago, no longer used as either a religious site or quarry, the Valley Temple disappeared under the blowing sand. An early map identified the site as a mound with *"pits, probably unopened."*[2] The temple remained hidden until 1853 when Auguste Mariette rediscovered it and excavated the interior. In 1909 Uvo Holscher removed the sand and debris surrounding the exterior and completely freed the Temple.[3] Against the temple east façade, he found a Dynasty XVIII private house with a floor 18' above the Temple base. Above the south side of the house he found a mud brick building with limestone paved rooms which Selim Hassan excavated in 1938 and suggested it was the Temple of Osiris, Lord of Rosetaw, as mentioned on the Inventory Stele.[4]

The Valley Temple is 144' square[5] with interior open spaces of somewhat less then half the temple footprint. Originally the Temple was about 40' tall, but much of the top portions are now missing and the east front is now closer to 25' to 30' high. The Temple core was built of large blocks of local limestone with the exterior originally covered by finely dressed red granite, most of it now missing. However, some blocks remain at the lower east front, either in-situ or restored, and a number of individual blocks found in the debris have been placed along the temple north and south sides.

The Temple has two 20' tall entrances representing Upper and Lower Egypt. Holscher found "beloved of Bastet, giving life" inscribed beside the north entrance while

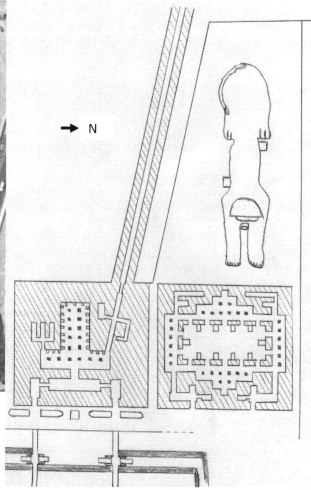

The Sphinx sitting in the Enclosure with the Sphinx Temple in front. Khafre's Valley Temple to the south, fronted by walkways and mud brick walls (shaded lines). The Causeway exits the Valley Temple and runs along the Sphinx enclosure to the Mortuary Temple.

The Valley Temple core was built of massive limestone blocks; note their size compared to the men. The north entrance (at right where men are standing) and south entrance (left) are still partially cased in granite. The Sphinx Temple is just out of the picture to the right. Khafre's Pyramid rises in the background.

"beloved of Hathor" was found beside the south entrance.[6] Four elongated depressions with rounded ends suggest sphinxes sat on each side of the entrances. At the center of the Temple face, a square depression may have held a statue of Khafre. When viewed in-person, these depressions are difficult to discern in the eroded surface and owing to a slight south-to-north rise in the limestone surface in front of the Temple, are not now all at the same level.

From either entrance a short passage leads to the Antechamber. In a pit in the Antechamber northeast corner, Mariette found a large diorite statue buried upside down[7] which was identified as Khafre by the cartouche inscribed on the base. The statue is now prominently displayed in the Cairo Museum. While other fragments were found in this room, none formed a complete statue. From the Antechamber a short passage to the west enters a large, high T-shaped hall now open to the sky. The hall contains 16 enormous red granite pillars that once supported 18 granite cross beams on which rested a ceiling enclosing the hall at a height of 18'. All of the pillars are in place today along with 12 of the cross beams but the ceiling is completely missing. We can be confident that the space was roofed since inward sloping slits were cut into the top of the granite walls through which

The temple south entrance is at the arrow. The depressions in which statues likely sat are barely discernible on either side of the entrance. The depressions at the north entrance are less distinct.

Charlie Rigano stands in one of the slots (left) along the temple north wall of the T-shaped hall. The south wall (right) is similar. The granite wall blocks are more than 5' tall. Angled spaces at the wall tops (above) let light into the temple.

sunlight illuminated the interior.

On the floor along the walls of the T-shaped hall are 23 rectangular slots with limestone bases cut into the Temple alabaster floor. These slots likely at one time held the bases of Khafre statues. Statue fragments were found in the room, evidence that the statues were not removed but destroyed in-place.[8] Presumably the diorite Khafre statue found in the pit once sat in this room and the general belief is that the priests saved this one statue by hiding it in the pit. This statue has a base measuring 37 ½" by 21 ¾", the bases of two other Khafre statues in the Cairo Museum measure 31" by 16 ½". In measuring all the slots in the Temple, we found that while the widths would accommodate the statues, the slots were significantly longer than the statue bases.[9] Possibly this difference between the slot and statue

135

lengths is evidence that these statues once stood in another location and were moved to the Valley Temple.

At the south end of the "T" a short passage, originally closed by a door, leads to six storerooms arranged in two stories, three rooms per story. At the "T" north end, a rising inclined passage leads out of the temple to the Causeway. Be-

The Khafre statue Mariette found, about 5' tall, now in the Cairo Museum. Horus sits behind the head.

A raising passage exits the temple.

fore exiting the Temple, a short side passage to the south leads to a small room probably for storage, while a passage to the north makes two turns and likely provided access to the roof. This exit passage is not squared to the building but is angled to form a straight line from the interior of the Valley Temple to the Mortuary Temple entrance.

The Temple interior granite walls are uninscribed. With the exception of the few words found around the doorways and the crowns cut into the granite blocks found along the Temple exterior south wall, the evidence indicates that the walls, both inside and outside, were largely bare. The hard granite likely discouraged inscribing the king's titles and deeds on the walls and religious requirements may have made it unnecessary. The Bent Pyramid Valley Temple is the only contemporary example which can be used as a basis for comparison. Here Fakhry found the softer limestone walls heavily inscribed with names of nomes and Snefru's estates, and scenes of Snefru performing ceremonies.[10]

There are not many other good examples of valley temples since other valley temples located at the waters edge provided convenient sources of finished stone for later builders. Khufu's Valley Temple and the temples belonging to the Maidum and Red Pyramids have not been found. The valley temples belonging to Sahure, Neferikare, and Unas have been found but are in a ruined condition and the extent of wall inscriptions, if any, cannot be determined. Menkaure's temple was hurriedly finished in mud brick and there was likely no time to complete inscriptions.

In Front of the Valley Temple

In 1995 a stage in front of the Valley Temple was removed and the space, which was partially excavated in the early 1930's by Selim Hassan, was re-cleared and the excavation extended in all directions.

An area 100' wide (east – west) extends across the face of the Valley Temple and slopes upward towards the Valley Temple ending in a step 2' high. Two parallel 7' wide raised limestone walks emerge from the un-excavated rubble in the east and slope upward first steeply, than more gently, straight to the two Valley Temple entrances. Bridges along each walk span a 7' deep channel cut in the bedrock. There is no evidence that the walks were enclosed, however doorpost holes cut into the

Looking at the site towards the south (top) and north (bottom), the two walkways rise steeply from the debris and lead to the Valley Temple entrances. At the top of the steep rise, the remains of a north-south mud brick wall with a door at the walkway may have crossed and hidden the site.

The 7' high channel under the bridge with mud brick walls on both sides. Note the area between the bridges could not have been filled with water without covering parts of the walkways.

bridge limestone surface and semicircular scratch marks on the stone floor provide evidence of swinging doors. Just east of the bridges, wide mud brick walls span the area in front of the Valley Temple between the walks. Both north and south of the walks, walls 10' to 15' apart and perpendicular to the walkways, composed in parts of mud brick and in other parts of fieldstones, were laid on the sloping surface and created a channel leading north and south from the bridges.[11] The ends of the mud brick walls do not simply meet the vertical sides of the walkways, but the walkway sides were roughly hacked away for a depth of several inches to receive the mud brick walls indicating the walls were later additions. Possibly the builders thought this would create a better bond. In all of Khafre's Mortuary Complex, this is the only mud brick. The presence of mud brick may indicate either hurried work to complete construction at Khafre's death or a change to the Temple plan well after his death to suit some other purpose.

We are tempted to see the channels as canals feeding water from the harbor to a basin between the walkways in front of the Valley Temple forming a "sacred lake". However, because the walkways are inclined for their full length, if the basin was filled, much of the walkways would be underwater. Additionally to the north of the northern bridge, there is a high point in the bedrock surface in the channel which would stop the water from flowing into the basin.

Our inclination is to see the mud brick added either in anticipation of Khafre's death or shortly thereafter to complete the area for the burial rites. The mud brick wall between the walkways was probably high and hid the area in front of the temple, and with sidewalls formed an enclosed area in front of the temple The door holes found in the walkway would position the doors within the walls and provide access from the harbor or canal area, through the wall, and into the enclosed Temple area. The channels under the bridges could have provided a corridor for access to the courtyard from the sides for the royal family members and court to either view or take part in some of the rites in preparing Khafre's body.

The Causeway

We can easily follow the path of the 1622' long Causeway as it rises 150' from the Valley Temple to the Mortuary Temple.[12] While the path is obvious there are few blocks left in place to identify its construction, except for the lower (eastern) end. As a result, we cannot determine directly if the Causeway was roofed and had walls inscribed with Khafre's feats and titles. However, we anticipate that Khafre's Causeway was comparable to Herodotus's description of Khufu's Causeway and the partial reconstruction of the Unas Causeway. Based on these comparisons we would expect both a roof and inscriptions.

About midway between the temples a passage is cut under the Causeway, similar to the passage under Khufu's Causeway, to permit north – south transit without going all the way around the Pyramid. At the south end of the passage a later period shaft, known as the Tomb of Osiris, descends 90' in three levels.

If the Causeway was constructed on a direct east – west line from the Mortuary Temple, the Valley Temple would have been located just north of the Sphinx Temple, instead of just south. Since this was

A partial reconstruction of the Causeway where it exits the back of the Valley Temple (left). Further up the Causeway (right), only blocks forming the base remain.

not the case, existing site constraints likely caused Khafre's architects to angle the Causeway 13°41'[13] which determined the placement of the Valley Temple. The constraints which confronted the architect are obvious today. About 300' south of Khufu's Pyramid lies a large quarry (north quarry) trapezoidal shaped 500' by 1500'[14] and filled with construction debris. Further south, starting 1,000 feet from Khufu's pyramid is an extensive quarry 100' deep (South Quarry), now largely free of debris. The Causeway was built on a ridge between these quarries. If Khufu's builders had quarried both fields, then there would not have been a strip left for the Causeway. Therefore, the existence of the Causeway ridge leads to the conclusion that one quarry was used primarily for Khufu's Pyramid, and Khafre's builders cut the other quarry, leaving the ridge. Mark Lehner proposes that stone from the North Quarry may have been used for the lower portions of Khufu's Pyramid, but as the pyramid reached higher levels and the supply ramp became longer, quarrying operations moved from the North Quarry to the South Quarry.[15] However, the situation is somewhat more complex and we find the opposite more likely. If Khufu's builders started quarrying operations close to the pyramid and moved these operations southward as the ramp extended, the Causeway ridge would have been at least partially cut away. Additionally, if the north quarry was largely untouched by Khufu, Khafre's Causeway could have instead taken the direct east-west line.[16] We should also consider that there is no archeological evidence for long supply ramps in pyramid construction to raise blocks to high levels. These ramps would have required enormous resources to build and maintain, and less resource intensive methods for raising stone were available.[17] If long supply ramps were not used, Khufu's builders would have used the closer North Quarry, the southern boundary of it defining the path available for Khafre's Causeway. Khafre's builders would have then reserved this path, which defined the angle of the Causeway and location of the Valley Temple, and started a quarry to the south.

Mortuary Temple

During Dynasty IV, mortuary temples increased in size from the 900 square foot enclosures at Maidum and the Bent Pyramid; through Khufu's less modest 24,000 square foot temple and Djedefre's 32,000 square foot temple; to Khafre's massive 54,500 square foot temple, much of it solid masonry.[18] From this time on, even when the pyramid sizes shrunk to only 4% the volume of the Great Pyramid, the mortuary temples remained comparably very large, often exceeding 30,000 square feet.

Khafre's Mortuary Temple[19] is entered from the Causeway, not in the Temple center but near the southeast corner, through a narrow passage which leads into an enclosed vestibule. On either side of the vestibule are storage rooms. A short passage to the west leads to a pillared hall. From the corners of

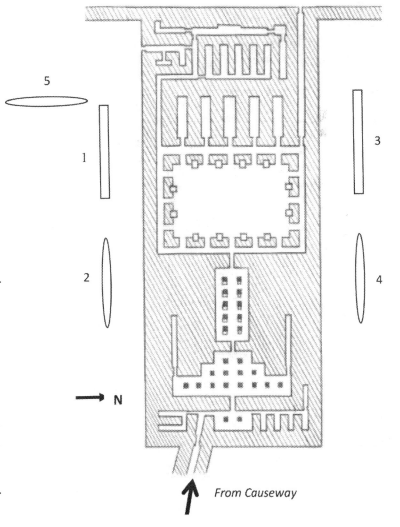

From Causeway

Not much remains of the Mortuary Temple. Both pictures were taken from the same spot near the back (west end) of the temple. One of the deep statue niches is outlined on the floor (top) immediately to our front. Across the open Court is the Hall of the Great Ones between the large constructions. At the back of the temple (bottom) are the five smaller niches and the Shrine against the back wall.

this hall run long narrow passages, possibly identified to Upper and Lower Egypt. What was at the end of these passages is uncertain: possibly large statues, carved granite blocks, or models of day and night boats. While the Temple exterior walls are generally intact in this area, at the end of each passage, enormous holes were cut through the exterior walls apparently to remove the objects whole. From the center of the pillared hall, a short passage leads west to a long narrow hall known as the "House of the Great Ones." Here pillars are fronted by slots which probably contained statues of Khafre.

Another short narrow passage provides access to a large open courtyard, the Hall or Court, which probably contained a central altar called "The Royal Offering of the Court." Surrounding the court was a cloister of 16 red granite pillars. Slots in front of 12 of the columns probably once held large statues of Khafre. To the rear (west) of the court are five deep statue niches, each with its own door. In Neferirkare's temple similar niches held statues of the king: in the central niche in Osirid form, two others as the King of Upper and Lower Egypt, and in unknown forms for the remaining two. From the southwest corner of the open court a passage leads to the back part of the temple probably accessible only by priests. Back here was another set of five niches, possibly replicating the public niches. In this area side rooms were used for storage and a library. In the center of the back (west) wall a sanctuary called the Booth or Shrine likely contained a false door and altar for daily offerings. Priests also could enter this part of the Temple from the exterior through a door at the Temple southwest corner. At the open court northwest corner, a 115' long passage led through the North Door and into the pyramid court.[20]

Boat Pit Dimensions[22]			
Pit	**Length**	**Widest**	**Depth**
1	82'	12'	25'
2	72'	13'	20'
3	90'	12'	23'
4	77'	16'	16'
5	123'	9'	23'

Boat Pits

Selim Hassan uncovered the boat pits around the Mortuary Temple during the 1934 - 1935 season.[21] He found five boat pits cut into the bedrock and a natural depression to the north that has been mistaken as the start of a sixth boat pit. Four of these pits lie parallel to the Temple walls on the north and south sides while the fifth is to the south and perpendicular to the temple. These five boat pits are not just long, deep holes cut into the bedrock, but each is cut into the

Boat Pit 2 (right) and 5 (left) show a lip likely for covering blocks.

shape of a boat with prows, sterns, hulls, cabins, and ribs. The four paralleling the Mortuary Temple walls were placed prow to prow. The impression is not so much that the boat pits were built around the Temple, but that they were actually moored to it.

Pits 1 and 3 closest to the pyramid are covered with two layers of large limestone blocks while pits 2 and 4 furthest to the east and pit 5 are uncovered and open to the sky. Each of the three uncovered pits has a lip around the inside roughly one cubit

The entrance (top) to Boat Pit 1 with two layers of covering blocks which are significantly smaller then the blocks over Khufu's pit. From inside (bottom), the entrance is above the ladder. Ribs cut into the bedrock simulate the hull and the deck. Cut above the ribs and deck is a cabin.

wide and deep. Hassan interpreted the covered pits as night boats and the uncovered pits as day boats with the lip as a base for a protective wall.[23] However, based on the construction of the other boat pits, it seems clear these lips were a base for blocks which once spanned and closed the pits. These covering blocks are now missing though the area is littered with broken limestone pieces.

While the open pits can be examined easily from above, covered pit number 1 is assessable through a hole at its southwest corner. This boat pit is in an excellent state of preservation. Clearly visible cut into the bedrock is the boat shaped hull interior composed of stone ribs and sides flaring upward to the deck and continuing towards the prow and stern. Sitting on top of the hull, the outline of a cabin was cut into the bedrock. Thousands of 4500 year old chisel marks are still plainly visible. The roofing blocks are blackened from torches, and it is possible that at some point people actually lived in this boat pit.

Inside of pit 1 Hassan found the forelegs of a limestone sphinx and a basalt roller used for moving heavy objects. He described the area around pit 2 as littered with fragments of diorite and alabaster, coming from as many as 300 to 400 statues. In pit 4 there were fragments of alabaster statues, one was the top of a head wearing the royal uraeus. In addition, spread among the pits were miscellaneous pottery, incense burners, and ox bones. However, there was a complete lack of wood, any means to connect wood to the pit walls (peg holes or plaster), or anything that could be interpreted as boat parts.[24] We should not read the lack of wood as firm evidence that no boats were placed in the pits. However, with the pits already cut into the shape of boats, also building boats in the pits would seem superfluous. Considering all twelve Giza boat pits, ten were cut into boat shapes and contained no wood, while two rectangular pits contained wooden boats. These data points indicate that wooden boats may not have been actually constructed in boat shaped pits and they were purely symbolic.

The Enclosure Walls and Courtyard

There were not one but two enclosure walls. The inner wall surrounded the Pyramid on all sides about 34 feet, 20 cubits, from the pyramid base. Between the wall and pyramid was a courtyard paved with white limestone blocks. As around the Great Pyramid, the irregular shaped limestone blocks were laid on the bedrock which was cut to receive the shape of the individual paving blocks. The Enclosure Wall base was estimated at 6 cubits wide, or slightly more than 10' thick, with a rounded top about 26' high.[25] The wall is continuous with the Mortuary Temple west side. Remnants of the wall base can be found but they are not extensive or easy to identify.

An outer wall 420' from the pyramid has been identified along all but the eastern side. To the north the wall runs along the south side of Khufu's Western Cemetery and may have initially been a feature of the cemetery instead of Khafre's Complex. The west wall runs along the edge of the "Barracks" area. The south wall appears to have been partly finished then makes a right angle turn to connect with Menkaure's outer enclosure wall.[26] The outer wall does not seem to have been built to a single plan and the timing of its construction is uncertain.

The Subsidiary Pyramid GII-a

About 90' south of the Pyramid, there are a few very large limestone blocks littering the surface, one apparently standing on end, and an inclined passage cut into the bedrock. This is all that remains of Khafre's subsidiary pyramid. There was a separate enclosure wall surrounding the pyramid but no evidence of a mortuary temple. As discussed previously, the interior arrangement and overall dimensions and volume are similar to the subsidiary pyramid (GI-d) southeast of Khufu's Pyramid.

Originally the inclined passage opened from the pyramid north face and descended to a rectangular room cut completely, including the ceiling, into the bedrock. The descending passage is partially blocked by a limestone block through which a hole has been cut in the top east side just large enough to allow a person to crawl through. It is unknown if the block was original or part of an intrusive burial.

The passage enters the center north side of the rectangular chamber 2' above the chamber floor. A short ramp extends the passage to the chamber floor. The chamber walls show the remains of plaster and reference lines drawn by the builders.

Holscher was the first to investigate this chamber and as typical, found it robbed. Inside he discovered pieces of wood, fragments of jar or vase stoppers, two carnelian bead necklaces, and ox bones. On one of the stoppers an inscription reads *"The eldest royal son of his body, beloved by him, the sole friend."*[30] This stopper could have been originally placed in the pyramid indicating either the burial of Khafre's son or an object from a son placed in his mother's tomb. There was no evidence of a stone sarcophagus,[31] and it is unlikely that robbers broke one up and removed the pieces through the small robber hole in the entrance passage. But the evidence does not preclude a wooden sarcophagus.

There is disagreement among Egyptologists as to whether this structure was a burial place for one of Khafre's queens or a cult pyramid. Hawass notes that two of Khafre's queens, Khamerernebty I, Khafre's main queen, and Meresankh III have known tombs, while tombs for his queens Hedjhekenu and Persenti have not been located.[32] This pyramid could be the tomb of one of these

To the south of Khafre's Pyramid (top) the vertical arrow points to the demolished Subsidiary Pyramid and the other arrow points at the shaft which contained the disassembled wooden box. On the bottom are close-up views of the Subsidiary Pyramid entrance (left) and the inclined passage entrance (right) with the three plug blocks removed from the passage. The arrow points to the Subsidiary Pyramid entrance.

Subsidiary Pyramid Comparison[27]		
Feature	GII-a (Khafre)	GI-d (Khufu)
Base	69' square	71'
Height	Estimated 46'[28]	45'
Incline	53+° likely matched the main pyramid	51°+ likely matched the main pyramid
Descending Passage	41" square, originally about 38' long, now 13'	39" wide, height unknown
Passage Incline	Average 31°	32°
Chamber	25'9" long, 8'8" wide, 6'11" high (15 by 5 by 4 cubits)	27' long, 10' wide, 9' deep
Volume	73,000[29]	76,000

queens or another yet unidentified queen, the stopper referring to one of her sons, and the wood part of her coffin.

In 1960 when clearing the area just a few feet to the west of the subsidiary pyramid, Abdel Hafiz discovered an inclined passage cut into the bedrock descending from west to east. There was no evidence for a superstructure over the passage; the absence of which likely saved the contents from robbery. The passage, sealed by three undisturbed limestone plugs, led to a niche in the south wall.[33] In the niche was a disassembled wooden box tied with string. When reconstructed, the 73" high object took the form of a cornice supported by four columns sitting on a 25" by 29" base. Based on parallels in other tombs, Mark Lehner and Peter Lacovara concluded that the box was used to carry Khafre's ka statue which was placed in the cult pyramid, the purpose of the Subsidiary Pyramid. The box could also have carried a statue of the queen buried in the subsidiary pyramid.[34] Whatever the case, we can be sure that either the box or its association with the subsidiary pyramid were significant since religious protocol required the box to have its own sealed burial.

1. Here you can eat in a Kentucky Fried Chicken or a Pizza Hut and look out the store window at the Sphinx and pyramids.

2. Lehner, *Archaeology of an Image: the Great Sphinx of Giza,* p35, map was drawn by Wilkinson before Mariette's excavation.

3. Edwards, *Pyramids of Egypt,* 1993, p124.

4. Lehner, op. cit.,, pp.39-40, 77. Lehner also included a previously unpublished 1829 plan drawn by Borchardt which shows the floor plan of this house, the outline of the Valley Temple, a small part of the Causeway, the southwest corner of the Sphinx Temple, and the Sphinx forward paws, pp 49-50, figure 2.3.

5. Maragioglio and Rinaldi, *L'Architettura Delle Piramidi Menfite, Parte V Piramide di Zedefra e di Chefren,* Plate 14.

6. Hawass, *Funerary Establishments of Khufu, Khafra, and Menkaura,* pp194-195.

7. Ibid., p199.

8. Maragioglio and Rinaldi, op. cit., p82.

9. While two of the bases measured 17 ¾" by 40 ¼" and 17 ¼" by 43", and one in the center of the west side which apparently held a standing statue measured 35" by 43", the rest had lengths between 49" and 52 ¼ ", well longer than the statue.

10. Fakhry, *The Bent Pyramid of Dahshur,* p522.

11. These channels are described by Fakhry (The *Pyramids,* p132) as being a canal which runs north and south. He says the south end disappears under massive limestone blocks, apparently the south bridge, and the north end under a mound of sand in front of the Sphinx Temple. At the time Maragioglio and Rinaldi considered the site, the area in front of the Valley Temple was covered, probably by a stage. They picked up Fakhry's description, and erroneously assumed a wide canal which made this temple, and possibly Menkaure's and Khufu's Valley Temples, assessable by boat,*(Parte V Piramide di Zedefra e di Chefren,* p78).

12. Maragioglio and Rinaldi, op. cit., p74. The Causeway cannot be literally followed for its full length since the part along the Sphinx Enclosure is fenced and can only be accessed from within the Valley Temple.

13. Lehner, op. cit., p164. However, Maragioglio and Rinaldi, op. cit., Plate 11, show the angle at the Mortuary Temple as 16°.

14. Lehner, op. cit., p157.

15. Lehner, Development of the Giza Necropolis, pp121, 124.

16. We do not know the original shape of the Giza Plateau, but likely the original limestone surface was higher then we see today; an unknown depth of the top layers stripped away in the initial quarry operation. This layer of hard stone only remains in the Sphinx head and near Khentkawes' tomb. This layer was likely first exploited before deep quarries were cut for stone of somewhat lower quality. However, the basic flow of the discussion remains the same.

17. For a more detailed discussion for building methods and the lack of evidence for ramps, see my article "*How Pyramids Were Built, Where the Evidence and Lack of Evidence Leads Us"* in the Spring 2006 issue of the Ostracon. For now we can say there is no archeological evidence supporting long supply ramps built against pyramid sides or ramps which encircled pyramids. Ramps as the primary method for raising stone have only been envisioned and to some degree tested as a likely method. Building and dismantling these long ramps would have taken enormous resources in terms of men, time, and material. The changing plans for the Step and Maidum pyramids (and possibly the Bent, Khafre's, and Menkaure's) would have required several building, dismantling, and rebuilding of the ramps. While ramps were likely used to raise blocks for mastabas and the low levels of pyramids, the builders would have looked for alternate means when the blocks had to be raised to higher levels. Several are discussed in books dealing with the subject; none of which are supported by archaeological

evidence. Since there is no evidence to show how blocks were raised, I looked for a means which would leave no evidence. In the article mentioned earlier in this note, I suggested that blocks were pulled up the pyramid sides.

18. Maragioglio and Rinaldi, op. cit., Plate 11.

19. In 1893 scavengers uncovered papyrus in the mortuary temples at Abu Sir written in Old Hieratic. These papyrus soon found their way to the antiquities market and into the hands of Egyptologists, but it was not until 1956 after many changes of hands that they were studied in detail. The papyrus dated from the time of Djedkare (Dynasty V, 2414 – 2375 BCE) and concerned the administration of Neferirkare's (Dynasty V, 2477 – 2467 BCE) Mortuary Temple: schedules of priestly duties, inventories, and accounting documents. From the information contained in these papyrus we learned much about how the ancient mortuary temples were run, including the names for the temple parts and something about their purposes.

20. The temple part names from Hawass, op. cit., pp. 476-480.

21. Hassen, *Excavations at Giza, Vol VI-Part 1*, p56.

22. Pit sizes are in both Hassan's op. cit., pages 59 –64 and Maragioglio and Rinaldi, op. cit, Plate 11. A comparison shows the sizes are significantly different. We have used Hassan's measurements, since he was the original excavator, for all but the width of pit 5.

23. Ibid pp. 60-64.

24. Hassan, op. cit., pp59-64

25. Maragioglio and Rinaldi, op. cit., p72.

26. Hawass, op. cit., pp159-160.

27. GII-a per Maragioglio and Rinaldi, op. cit., pp88-90. GI-d per author's measurements.

28. Tangent 53.1° = X/34.5, X=46'.

29. 1/3 x 69' x 69' x 46 = 73,002 cubic feet.

30. Hawass, op. cit., p164.

31. Maragioglio and Rinaldi, op. cit., p90.

32. Hawass, op. cit., pp164-168.

33. Edwards, op. cit., 1993, p132.

34. Hawass, op. cit., pp168-171.

Chapter 9
The Sphinx Complex

The Sphinx body cut from soft limestone is heavily eroded while the harder stone from which the head was cut holds the original detail. At the left the lion's tail curves from behind the body; the paws positioned against the haunches. The front legs extend forward. The top of the Tuthmosis IV stele can be seen between the front legs. The Great Pyramid is behind the Sphinx head.

At the eastern base of the Giza Plateau sits the world's most famous statue, the Sphinx. Facing due east, the Sphinx sits in an unfinished rock cut enclosure. Limestone walls rise on three sides while immediately to the front is the incomplete Sphinx Temple. Though great planning and enormous labor went into building the Sphinx Complex, indications are that the Sphinx Temple was never used and the Sphinx was not employed as a religious symbol until more then 1,000 years after its construction. During the New Kingdom, the Sphinx, as Hor-em-akhet or Hor-akhty, Horus of the Horizon, was paid homage to by the famous rulers of that day: Amenhotep I, Tuthmosis I, Amenhotep II, Tuthmosis IV, and later by Tutankhamun, Seti I, Ramesses II, and Merneptah.

Sphinx

The form is of a recumbent lion, front paws outstretched and hind legs nestled under the body. The tail curls to the south side and lies against the body. The head is of a man; the nemes headdress, remnants of the uraeus, and the beard identify a king.

Of all the ancient visitors, only Pliny the Elder who visited Egypt in the first century AD[1] mentions the Sphinx. After briefly describing the three Giza pyramids, he writes:

"Before these is the Sphinx, an object still more worthy of being recorded, as it seems to give evidence of their venerating something of a mixed nature, like our rural deities. They suppose King Amasis to be buried therein, and assert that it appears

to have been brought thither. It is smooth and made out of natural stone. The circumference of the head of the monster, across the forehead, is 102 feet; the length is 143 feet; the height from the stomach to the crown of the head, 62 feet."[2]

Since Pliny was able to accurately determine the height of the statue, at least the front part must have been free from the sand. The King referred to is possibly Ahmose II of Dynasty XXVI; Amasis was his Greek name. The inaccurate information on the burial was probably supplied by the descendants of the self-appointed local "guides" who provided Herodotus with much of his inaccurate information.

Sphinx	Size[8]
Length - Front paws to tail	238'
Width - At rear haunches (widest)	62'8"
Height – Base to back	40'7"
Height – Base to top of head	66'4"
Face Width – less headdress	14'7"
Face Width – with headdress	33'9"
Face Height	19'4"

While the Sphinx was cut from the bedrock, most of it is in extremely rough condition today; the original shape has been restored with layers of blocks. Only the head shows the smooth surfaces of the face, the details of the ears and eyes, and the lines on the headdress. Some red paint on the face can still be easily seen; the nose and part of the mouth are missing. The popular, but erroneous, story is that Napoleon's soldiers used the face for rifle target practice. But the 15th Century Arab historian El Makrizi recorded that Saim-el-Dahr disfigured the face for religious reasons.[3] Chisel marks at the bridge of the nose and from below indicate the nose was actually cut from the face providing evidence for the second explanation.[4]

In 1837 Howard Vyse had William Perring drill into the Sphinx body just behind the head to determine if the body was solid. After drilling down 27' the boring rods broke and could not be extracted. Vyse then used explosives in an attempt to reach the rods but without success. After already cutting and blowing holes into the Sphinx, Vyse wrote, *"...but being unwilling to disfigure this venerable monument, the excavation was given up, and several feet of the boring rods were left in it."*[5] Vyse found the Sphinx solid and there is no reason to believe any different today.

There are two other holes, passages if you like, in the Sphinx. In 1926 Emile Baraize found and then covered a crudely cut passage at ground level on the Sphinx rump. We cannot be sure of exactly what he discovered inside since he did not document the passage. In 1980 this passage was reopened by Zahi Hawass and Mark Lehner. The passage leads in two directions. One arm angles down very steeply to a point 16' below the level of the Sphinx base. Footholds were cut in the shaft sides to assist with the descent.

The full Sphinx body after completion of a 10-year restoration. For much of its history the Sphinx was covered up to its neck with sand. Khafre's Causeway runs along the far side of the enclosure.

The hard stone still holds detail. Red paint remains on the front and side which is visible in person or color photographs.

They found the bottom filled to a depth of 4'9" with modern debris including metal foil and two shoes apparently left by Baraize. The other passage is cut between the Sphinx body and the ancient veneer ending 13' above the Sphinx base. Footholds were again cut into the passage sides. Nothing of significance was found in this upper part except some small pieces of charcoal, ceramics, and minor pieces of cement and limestone. Who cut these passages cannot be determined, but candidates range from the ancient quarriers who were preparing the Sphinx body to Vyse who probed the Sphinx in several places, not all of which were completely documented.[6]

Three photographs from Baraize's 1926 excavation show another possible passage in the middle of the north side, but more likely this was a recess and not a passage. The pictures show a workman standing in the space with another outside at base level. Baraize recovered this area and it is no longer accessible today.[7] Likely there is nothing of interest in the space and while it was known during the recent Sphinx restoration, no attempt was made to uncover and enter it.

The Sphinx body was much repaired in both ancient and modern times. Blocks from a number of different restorations cover the sides to about half its height. The Sphinx was abandoned by the Old Kingdom builders and became sand covered for 1100 years until freed by Tuthmosis IV. Not only did he remove the sand and build protective mud brick walls but he filled in the recesses eroded into the Sphinx body, probably with blocks from Khafre's Causeway.

At the rear of the Sphinx is the entrance (arrow) to the passage initially found by Baraize and reopened by Hawass and Lehner.

The second restoration occurred some 800 years later during Dynasty XXVI. This was a time of rebuilding the old monuments and venerating their builders. Possibly these ancient restorers had much in common with the modern Egyptologist in their awe for the Sphinx and restored it for the benefit of future generations. During this period, they repaired the south side upper part and worked on the tail and nemes headdress. During the Roman Period (30 BCE to 200 AD) the Sphinx was again freed from the sand, the enclosure floor paved, and blocks added to protect the paws and sides.

In modern times the Sphinx received additional attention. Between 1925 and 1936, Baraize cleared sand from around the Sphinx and accomplished extensive restorations to the head and sides. Most of these were later removed. The Egyptian Antiquities Organization made sporadic restorations in 1955, 1977, 1979, and 1982-1987. This work was undertaken without an overall plan and with minimal supervision; it resulted in more harm than help to the monument.[9] May 25, 1998 marked the completion of a 10-year restoration by the Supreme Council of Antiquities which addressed all of the previous shortcomings.[10]

Stone Quality

The fine detail in the Sphinx head, the rough surface of the lion's body, the rounded forms on the side (south) and rear (west) Enclosure walls, and the pitted appearance at the Enclosure base provide ready evidence that the stone from which the Sphinx and Enclosure were cut has not eroded uniformly. Even a casual look around the Enclosure will reveal that these differences are caused by the presence of several stone strata or layers, each with different properties.

In 1980 Lal Gauri, a geologist from the University of Louisville, named the layers from the bottom up as Member I, II, and III. Member I rises to a height of 12' at the Sphinx rear and 2' to 3' at the front. This layer is resistant to weathering and forms a bumpy, hard, brittle surface. The softer stone of Member II forms most of the Sphinx body and the majority of the side and rear Enclosure walls. This Member is divided into seven different beds of alternating hard and soft stone. These beds eroded differently into an uneven wall on which the harder stone protrudes while the softer beds recede.

The Sphinx (left) head was cut from the hard Member III stone which has resisted erosion. The body was cut primarily from Member II, the higher levels show a very rough surface, transitioning to the more rounded profile of the lower bed, most hidden behind the blocks enclosing the lower Sphinx body. The south Enclosure wall (right) shows four of the seven Member II beds with the rough surface at the top and the rounded profile below. At the wall bottom the brittle, pitted Member I stone emerges from the surface and angles upward.

At the highest level, Member III is a hard stone that is very resistant to deterioration and still shows the 4500 year-old fine details carved into the Sphinx head. On the Plateau, Member III only remains in the Sphinx head and shoulders and near Khentkawes' tomb.[11] [12] The top of the Sphinx may represent the original level of the Plateau surface. Likely the Plateau was originally covered by an extensive field of Member III stone which was stripped away and used to build parts of the pyramids; this one piece reserved for the Sphinx.

Stone Quality Summary		
Level	Characteristics	Location
Member III (Top)	Hard, weather resistant	Sphinx head and shoulders
Member II (Middle)	Soft, weathered	Sphinx body, enclosure walls
Member I (Lower)	Bumpy, hard, brittle, weather resistant	Sphinx and enclosure base

Enclosure

The architects intended the U-shaped Sphinx Enclosure to be bounded on the Sphinx right side (south) and rear (west) by quarry walls, to the Sphinx left side (north) by a bedrock wall cut parallel to the Sphinx, and to the front (east) by the Sphinx Temple (see drawing and satellite image in Chapter 8).

The eroded surface of the Enclosure walls to the Sphinx's right and rear appear in most Sphinx photos. The right side wall starts near the Sphinx Temple. For the first 100' this Member II wall is flat with relatively little erosion and slopes back at a slight angle. This flat surface transitions to a heavily eroded wall having a roughly textured upper surface below which the surface takes on a rounded profile. Along this wall near the Enclosure rear, the Member I layer emerges from the floor and angles upward. This Member I along the right side wall at the back of the Enclosure protrudes a few feet and generally is in alignment with the flat un-eroded Member II surface at the front of the Enclosure near the

The Sphinx sits within a quarried enclosure and rises well above the quarry walls. North is to the right. The large blocks forming the Sphinx Temple are in the foreground. The Enclosure wall parallels the Causeway on the left, turns 90° behind the Sphinx, and continues well past the Sphinx to the north (right). The stone strata rises from the photo front left, through the Sphinx body, to the back right. The Member III Sphinx head sits well above the current Plateau level and provides some evidence that originally this hard strata covered the Plateau and was stripped away.

The Enclosure from the Sphinx rear (top left) shows the wall to the Sphinx left was still being cut when construction was halted. The ledge at the top of the wall was excavated by Lehner and Hawass. The south wall (top right) was once smooth and was inclined slightly away from the Sphinx. The wall is flat at the front and erosion patterns increase towards the back end. The rear wall (bottom) continues the same rounded profile as the south wall. The unquarried Member I at the Sphinx rear is visible.

Sphinx Temple and represents the original position of the wall surface. The Enclosure wall to the Sphinx rear has a large mass of Member I limestone which had not been removed when work terminated. Along the rear Enclosure wall the eroded Member II stone with its rounded profile extends well north past the Sphinx and the original intent may have been to build something in this area.

The wall along the Sphinx left flank near the left forepaw has a ledge 3'7" high that shows quarry marks where blocks were in the process of being removed when work was halted. Hawass and Lehner cleared this ledge in 1978 and found channels up to 16" deep which were typical of an ancient quarrying operations. In the compacted sand and gypsum which filled the channels they found half of a Dynasty IV beer or water jar and pieces of quartzite, chert, and dolerite tool fragments used by the Old Kingdom builders. Also found in this area were crude brown and red jars and bowls, and other Old Kingdom vessels.[13]

Sphinx Temple

The Sphinx Temple remained hidden under the sand for most of its 4,500 years until the winter of 1926-27 when Baraise uncovered the walls and started clearing the interior.

Like Khafre's Valley Temple, the Sphinx Temple has two entrances. Each entrance leads to a short passage; on one side is a small room, on the other a long room or wide passage. After a turn to the west, a short passage leads to the main courtyard. The courtyard was surrounded by 14 large pillars, 10 of which were fronted by rectangular recesses cut into the floor. These pillars and slots, similar to the ones in Khafre's Valley Temple and Mortuary Temple, likely once held statues of the king or small sphinxes. Outside the large pillars were 24 square granite pillars, 6 on each side. To the front (east) and back (west) of the courtyard, centered on the walls were two niches, fronted by two additional granite square pillars, which may have been intended for rituals to the rising and setting sun. While the 28 pillars could have had some symbolic meaning, they were also required to support the roof surrounding the courtyard.

From the back of the courtyard, two passages led to rooms, possibly magazines for cult objects, the northern ones lined with granite, the southern ones lined with alabaster. These rooms were partially cut into the bedrock below floor level and have a lip around the edge, possibly for a facing. There was no access from the Temple interior directly into the Sphinx Enclosure. This provides evidence that ceremonies were not intended to be performed directly

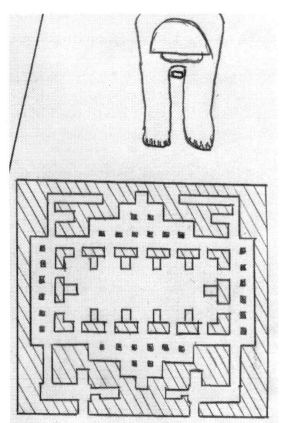

The Sphinx Temple is not centered on the Sphinx. North is to the right.

in front of the Sphinx but in the Temple niches and courtyard. The Temple interior seems to have been completed with a granite wall casing and an alabaster floor. The exterior was still under construction with only the granite casing around the Temple entrances in place when work was halted. The casing around the rest of the Temple was never finished.[14]

The form of the Temple with its east-west orientation, central court, and niche locations strongly suggests the Temple and whole Sphinx Complex were dedicated to the worship of the sun. The intent may

The center of the Sphinx Temple with the courtyard surrounded by large pillars fronted by statue slots. The niches are to the left and right. To the rear of the photo is a high wall of Khafre's Valley Temple; the Sphinx is out of the photo to the right. People are standing on the Causeway.

have been for the King in the form of Horus as represented by the Sphinx to be presenting offerings to the rising sun. This may have been an early attempt at a sun temple which became a standard construction of the Dynasty V kings.

The 200-ton blocks composing the Sphinx Temple can be traced to the Sphinx enclosure. A yellowish band of clay like marl has been identified in both the Temple blocks and in the natural bedrock of the Enclosure.[15] While these blocks seem enormous, their size may be another indication that moving large blocks the short distance from the Enclosure required fewer resources than cutting and finishing many smaller blocks.

Oddly, the Sphinx Temple is not centered on the Sphinx, but is offset 24' south. Since there is no reason the Temple could not have been built centered on the Sphinx, the placement must have been intentional and with purpose. However it is difficult to determine the purpose intended by the architects.

The Small Temple and the Tuthmosis IV Stele

In 1818 Giovanni Caviglia found the Sphinx body covered by sand with the head and neck sticking

A photograph from about 1880 shows the Sphinx mostly reburied after it was excavated by Caviglia.

The temple between the paws as found by Caviglia (left). The Tuthmosis stele is at the back and flanked by two Ramesses II steles, one of which has fallen; the small lion sits at the entrance. The temple area today (right), only the Tuthmosis stele remains.

154

out of the sand. He first dug a trench on the north side near the shoulder but had great difficulty with the loose sand. These difficulties forced him to move his dig to the front of the Sphinx where he employed 60 to 100 laborers for 4 months. In the sand he discovered fragments of what appeared to be pleated hair which he identified as pieces of a beard. On each side of the fragments were inscribed kneeling figures and hieroglyphics. He confirmed the beard hypothesis later when he found three steles depicting the Sphinx with a beard.

Digging deeper Caviglia found a small 10' long chapel filling the width of the space between the outstretched paws. The chapel consisted of the Tuthmosis IV granite stele in the center, flanked by two Ramesses II limestone steles standing against the Sphinx legs. He found a small lion at the entrance facing the larger Sphinx. Of some minor significance here we should notice that Ramesses II neither recarved the 140-year-old Tuthmosis stele with his name nor did he replace the Tuthmosis stele with one of his own. Generally Ramesses II was not this kind to his predecessors. [16]

The story of the Tuthmosis stele, commonly called the Dream Stele, is well known. About 1420 BCE, Prince Tuthmosis was hunting in the desert and rested in the shade of the Sphinx. Re-Harakhte, the Sphinx, appeared to him in a dream and promised the Prince would become King if he cleared the

sand from around the Sphinx. The sand was cleared and the Prince became King Tuthmosis IV. The Dream Stele, which is the earliest known reference to the Sphinx, commemorates the event. Possibly the dream never occurred, but Tuthmosis used the dream as evidence that he was chosen by the sun god to rule Egypt.

On the stele the Sphinx is shown sitting on a pedestal in the side of which appears to be a door. This pedestal does not actually exist but could represent a view of the Sphinx from the east where it is fronted by the Sphinx Temple and might appear to be sitting on top of the Temple. On the top left of the stele Tuthmosis offers a libation, on the top right he offers burning incense and pours a libation on an altar. The stele was copied by Henry Salt, British Consul, and sent to Samuel Birch of the British Museum to be translated. While the stele was already heavily eroded and the lower registers missing, the drawing showed most of 13 lines of characters and a couple

Tuthmosis IV Stele as it appears today (right). Compare this to Henry Salt's drawing in Appendix I; the lower registers have flaked off. To appreciate the stele's size, Charlie Rigano stands next to it (left).

additional spots. Not all of the lines were clear, but Birch interpreted what remained. See the translation in the Appendix.

Of significance was line 13, which has since flaked off and is lost. There was a partial cartouche which said *"Khaf"* followed by some additional hieroglyphics. The context of the statement is lost but this one piece reads *"Khafre, a statue made for Atum-Re-Horemakhet."*[17] This is the only textual evidence which relates the Sphinx to Khafre, even though the reference was written more then 1,000 years after Khafre ruled.

Thuthmosis IV did not choose a granite block from the Aswan quarry for this stele but instead went just up the hill to Khafre's Mortuary Temple. The granite block into which the stele was carved can be identified as a lintel by its shape and the sockets and pivot-holes cut into the back for a standard double leaf-swinging door. With a bit of detective work the lintel was tracked to either the entrance from Khafre's Causeway to his Mortuary Temple or to Mortuary Temple doors leading to the statue niches and magazines. Likely the workmen moved up the Causeway, removing blocks to use for restoration of the Sphinx body, then on reaching the top, removed the Mortuary Temple entrance lintel which was recarved into the form of the stele.[18]

Other Temples

The New Kingdom pharaohs clearly identified the statue as an object of importance. During the reign of Amenhotep I the Sphinx was referred to as Horemakhet, Horus in the Horizon. Tuthmosis I was the possible owner of a ruined mud brick chapel. Amenhotep II built a mudbrick temple which has been partially restored. Tuthmosis IV cleared the enclosure, patched the Sphinx body, and erected the stele between the paws. To the southwest of the Sphinx the names of Tutankhamun and his wife Ankhesenamun were found inscribed on a limestone door frame built into an 11 room rest house.[19] Ramesses added to this house, covered the previous occupants' names with his own, and likely had other buildings around the Plateau. Other Egyptian kings were found with connections to the site including Ay, Horemheb, Seti I, and Merneptah.[20]

At the northeast corner of the Enclosure a small section of the Amenhotep II mudbrick temple was built on original debris piled at the north side of the Sphinx Temple. Lehner excavated this undisturbed area and found in-situ three large limestone blocks left by the Sphinx builders when work was stopped in Dynasty IV. Under one of the blocks he found a large number of Dynasty IV pottery shards. The other blocks rested on a layer of tafla which was used as a lubricant to help move the blocks. These were the last blocks that were in process of being moved to the Sphinx Temple.[21]

Work Stopped

The Sphinx Complex was not completed. Work was probably terminated by Khafre's death and the complex never achieved its original purpose. Evidence for this is:
- A large amount of Member I stone remained in place to the rear of the Sphinx.
- The ledge on the north side of the Enclosure was unfinished.
- Limestone blocks were still being moved at the northwest corner of the Sphinx Temple.
- The granite casing on the Temple exterior was only completed around the two entrances.

Excavation of individual burials at Giza, Saqqara, and Abusir uncovered 115 people identified as connected with Khufu's cult, 31 people associated with Khafre's cult, and 25 with the funerary cult of Menkaure's.[22] However, no burials have been identified to people who were in the service of the Sphinx. While the lack of evidence does not prove a point, we can take this lack as an indication that services in the Sphinx complex did not occur during the Old Kingdom.

Who Built the Sphinx Complex

This has been a much-debated topic. Geological evidence has been presented to portray the Sphinx as being many thousands of years older than the Giza pyramids. Other geologists dispute this evidence. Without a firm geological basis, we can turn to the archeological record for an answer which points to the Old Kingdom.

- The Sphinx Temple aligns with Khafre's Valley Temple and is architecturally similar to it in the use of two entrances, square similar sized columns, recesses for statue bases, the size of the core limestone blocks, alabaster floors, and granite cased interior and exterior.
- Blocks for the Sphinx Temple were cut from within the Sphinx Enclosure making the Temple and Enclosure contemporary.
- Lehner found Old Kingdom pottery pieces under blocks still being moved into position during construction.
- Lehner and Hawass found Old Kingdom jar and bowl fragments in the incomplete cutting on the north ledge.
- While many artifacts date to the Old Kingdom and later, no artifacts have been found which can be attributed to earlier periods.
- The stele erected by Tuthmosis IV contains a partial cartouche which can only be identified as Khafre.

We can add to this, evidence which conclusively ties the Sphinx Complex to a time no earlier than Khafre.

- A Causeway runs in a straight line from Khafre's Mortuary Temple to the interior of his Valley Temple.
- The Causeway was built on a stone bridge probably reserved just for this purpose between two deep quarries.
- Khafre's Valley and Mortuary Temples and the Causeway are tied together and had to be contained in a single plan.
- The Causeway does not run directly east – west but is angled $13°41'$[23]
- The Sphinx Enclosure south wall forms this same angle, and lies within feet of the Causeway.

This coincidence of the Causeway and Enclosure angles not only ties the two structures together, but also provides that the Enclosure wall and the rest of the Sphinx Complex can date no earlier than Khafre's reign. With this evidence we can confidently reject the idea of a Sphinx which predates Khafre by thousands of years. The evidence indicates that the Sphinx and Sphinx Temple were built by Khafre as part of his mortuary complex.

While we tie the Sphinx Complex to Khafre, possibly the Sphinx Head and maybe the shoulders were carved slightly earlier. When Khufu's pyramid was started early in his reign, there was no plan to build other pyramids at Giza. So all advantage would have been given to Khufu's pyramid and nothing reserved for later building. So if we theorize that virtually all the top, hard Member III stone was removed and used in the lower levels of Khufu's pyramid, the part forming the Sphinx head would likely have also been removed. As others have noted, the Sphinx face does not resemble Khafre's face on the statue now in the Cairo Museum. We do not have any representations of Khufu's face, the one tiny statue of Khufu was from a later period. So we consider the possibility that the Member III stone now forming the Sphinx head was purposely not removed and carved to be a large Khufu head and surrounded by possibly a temple or other constructions at the then surface level forming the first sun temple. We see a possibility that the area was repurposed by Khafre and the original constructions destroyed when the Sphinx Enclosure, Sphinx body, and Sphinx Temple were built by Khafre. There is no physical evidence for this; we are just bothered by this piece of Member III stone remaining when virtually all the rest was removed and we look for a reason.

---

1. David and David, Biographical Dictionary of Ancient Egypt, p 107.
2. Vyse, Operations Carried on at the Pyramids of Gizeh in 1837, Vol. 2, p 189.

3. Fakhry, Pyramids, pp 158-159.

4. Lehner, *Archaeology of an Image: The Great Sphinx of* Giza, p180.

5. Vyse, op. cit., Vol. 1, p 274-275.

6. Hawass and Lehner, *Hommages a' Jean LECLANT,* <u>The Passages Under the Sphinx</u>, pp 201-210.

7. Nova Web Site, <u>www.pbs.org</u>.

8. Lehner, op. cit., pp 171-172.

9. Hawass, *Secrets of the Sphinx, Restoration Past and Present*, pp 24-34.

10. Hawass, *World Celebrates Successful Restoration of the Sphinx,* Press Release.

11. Lehner, op. cit., pp 159-163.

12. Hawass and Lehner, <u>The Sphinx, Who Built it and Why</u>, Archaeology, pp 33-34.

13. Hawass and Lehner, op. cit., pp 35-37. Hawass, *Funerary Establishments of Khufu, Khafra, and Menkaura, pp 207-208.*

14. Lehner, op. cit., p 88.

15. Hamblin, <u>A Unique Approach to Unraveling the Secrets of the Great Pyramids</u>, Smithsonian, April 1986, p91.

16. Vyse, op. cit., Vol. 1, p 109-110.

17. Lehner, op. cit., p 96.

18. Hawass and Lehner, op. cit., p 41.

19. Lehner, op. cit., p 54.

20. Lehner, op. cit., pp 114-115.

21. Hawass and Lehner, op. cit., p 37.

22. Hawass, op. cit., pp 560, 565, 568.

23. Lehner, op. cit., p 143.

Menkaure Pyramid Complex

Menkaure's Pyramid Exterior

Menkaure's Pyramid Interior

Menkaure's Mortuary Complex

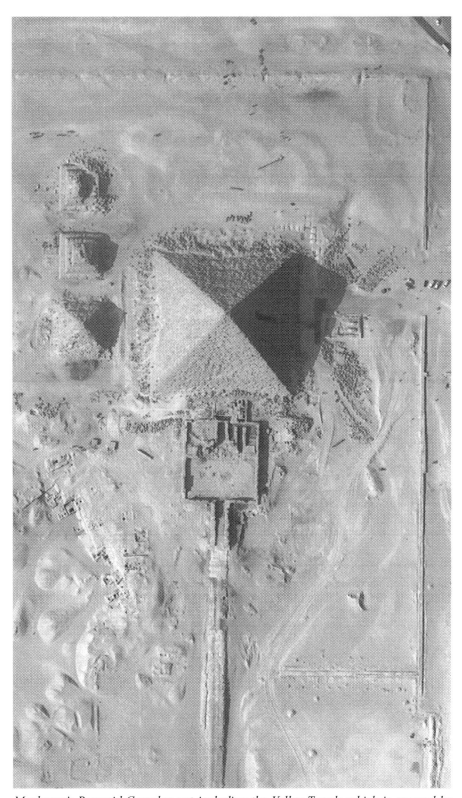

Menkaure's Pyramid Complex not including the Valley Temple which is covered by sand east of this image. Note the subsidiary pyramids are not centered on the main pyramid. Compare this image with the drawing at the beginning of Chapter 12 to identify specific features. North is to the right and east is to the bottom to match the orientation of the drawing. (Image: DigitalGlobe and Apollo Mapping Copyright 2014)

Chapter 10
Menkaure's Pyramid Exterior

The Menkaure's Pyramid west face (top) with the three subsidiary pyramids to the south. The north and east faces of the main pyramid (bottom) with the remains of the Mortuary Temple extending to the left. The gash in the north face and some of the remaining granite casing is visible around the pyramid base.

Howard Vyse and John Shae Perring completed the first modern investigation of Menkaure's Mortuary Complex in 1837. In addition to finding the entrance to the main pyramid and exploring the interior, Vyse entered the three subsidiary pyramids and cleared the Mortuary Temple offering room. Perring surveyed and prepared detailed plans of the main pyramid interior, Menkaure's sarcophagus, and the subsidiary pyramids. In 1881-2 Finders Petrie included the main pyramid and its subsidiaries in his survey of Giza. Between 1905 and 1924, George Reisner located the Valley Temple hidden under the sand and completely cleared both it and the Mortuary Temple. He prepared a detailed study of both structures. In addition he cleared the temples against the east face of the three subsidiary pyramids and the tombs in the quarry to the southeast of the main pyramid.[1] The Egyptian Antiquities Service cleared the Pyramid's south side, the subsidiary pyramids, and the tombs cut into the quarry walls.

The three main Giza Pyramids: Khufu and the white Boat Museum more then a mile away (right), Khafre (center), Menkaure with the three subsidiary pyramids (left). Menkaure main quarry is at the near center.

The Greek historians Herodotus and Diodorus Siculus credited this pyramid to Menkaure without providing evidence. Vyse was the first to confirm the owner. In July 1837 he found Menkaure's cartouche in red ink on the ceiling of subsidiary pyramid GIII-b and the next month found Menkaure's cartouche included on an inscribed wooden board in the main pyramid Upper Chamber.[2] Reisner found multiple references to Menkaure inscribed on statues, steles, and walls in the Valley Temple and adjacent tombs. The complex name, "Menkaure is Divine" was first identified in inscriptions from the tombs of funerary priests.[3]

Site

Menkaure probably grew-up spending time with his father, Khafre, and his grandfather, Khufu, on the Plateau. For Menkaure, building his mortuary complex at Giza may have been as much a personnel preference as a logic choice. The logical advantages the Giza Plateau provided were:

- Both his father and grandfather built their pyramid complexes here and the continued expansion of the royal cemeteries at Giza may have established this site as the primary royal necropolis for his family.
- As Khafre benefited from the infrastructure created to build Khufu's Mortuary Complex, so could Menkaure take advantage of the canals, harbors, warehouses, administrative buildings, royal residences, worker living quarters, food preparation areas, water sources, stone processing and manufacturing areas, pathways and roadways, and the procedures established over the last 50 years to build and support the Giza complex.
- High quality limestone was readily available within literally a stone throw from the pyramid site which minimized the size of the workforce.

There are opinions that the three main Giza pyramids were laid out to a grand plan, to mimic certain stars, or simply placed in a line. None of the theories is supported by a weight of evidence, or even common sense. Any theories which propose a grand plan for the site executed over an 85 year period (a period which matches the time from the beginning of World War I to the end of our last millennium) and through the reigns of five kings is not worthy of serious consideration. The individual kings simply picked the best location available when it came time to build their mortuary complexes. Each of the three Giza complexes were sited and laid out only with an eye to its own advantage given the constraints of topography and existing structures.

By the beginning of Menkaure's reign the locations suitable for a large pyramid were limited by the presence of the earlier monuments, the ever-expanding cemeteries for court official, and the quarries which formed vast depressions. In order to have a straight path to the east for his causeway and valley temple and possibly a clear view to the north, Menkaure was obliged to choose a position south of

164

The stone bases (top) to the northwest of the pyramid. The blocks added (right) to raise the surface just south of the pyramid. When first uncovered these blocks were thought to be covering blocks for a boat pit.

Khafre's Pyramid. A point high on the Plateau was also necessary to provide prominence. Directly south of Khafre's Pyramid was a basin. Therefore the logical place for Menkaure's Pyramid was southwest of Khafre's Pyramid along the north east – south west line perpendicular to the dip of the Plateau. This location placed the three Giza pyramids generally at the same elevation; the base of Menkaure's pyramid is 8' 5" higher than Khafre's which is 33' 2" higher than Khufu's.[4] With the building of this third large pyramid, the best sites at Giza were exhausted. Menkaure's son and successor, Shepseskaf, moved to South Saqqara for his tomb.

Menkaure's architects had to work within a set of physical constraints in placing the components of the mortuary complex. The surface sloped from the northwest to the southeast and had an east to west ridge through the site's center. There is a depression to the north of the planned pyramid location and a deep wadi immediately south. Leveling was necessary, but not to the extent required for Khafre's pyramid. Menkaure's Pyramid was set atop the ridge which also formed part of the Mortuary Temple foundation. To the northwest of the pyramid slightly raised square stone bases separated by trenches provide evidence that blocks were removed to lower the surface. On the north side of the Mortuary Temple two courses of very large blocks rise 10' to level the surface for the temple base.[5] To accommodate the wadi to the south of the Pyramid, large blocks were added to raise the surface between the main and subsidiary pyramids. The surface was then stepped down to the base of GIII-a.

Most of the limestone core blocks for the pyramid and its associated structures were extracted from a quarry to the southeast of the building site. Recently, when sand and debris were removed from this area, tombs of late Old Kingdom officials which were cut into the quarry walls were revealed. Other building materials not native to Giza were unloaded in the harbor and transported up the gentle Plateau slope westward towards the pyramid. The Causeway likely followed the same route.

Pyramid Layout

Based on Petrie's measurements, the architects intended a pyramid with a base length of 200 cubits,[6] or 343' 8", which produced a pyramid 9% the volume of Khufu's Pyramid. There is evidence (which will be discussed later) that the initial plan may have been for a pyramid with a 100 cubit base. This would have produced a volume of only 1.2% the size of Khufu's Pyramid, just slightly larger than Khufu's subsidiary pyramids.

While Menkaure's builders laid out his pyramid with great care, the base was not established to the same accuracy as the other two large Giza pyramids. There was an obvious degradation in the application of the methodology or new procedures were applied. It is unlikely that the builders were aware of this degradation and it can only be identified when we apply modern methods to more accurately determine angles and distances.

To determine the slope of the pyramid casing Petrie acquired 24 measurements from finished granite blocks in-situ, individual granite and limestone blocks, and two pyramid courses near the southwest corner. The result was a set of angles that varied by 1°16', from

Accuracy Comparison[7]	Khufu	Khafre	Menkaure
Difference Longest and Shortest Sides	1.8"	5"	8.6"
% Difference in Length	.02%	.06%	.2%
Mean Azimuth (minutes/seconds)	-3' 43"	-5', 26"	+14' 3"

50°42' to 51°58'. The differences can be attributed to either workmanship errors by the ancient builders or the difficulty and uncertainty in making measurements across a block face which has variation. Petrie concluded the best estimate of the angle as 51°0' ± 10'. But when we look at his measurements and if we consider just the nine blocks measured in-situ the average is 50° 50'.[8]

As previously discussed, the ancient builders did not measure angles in degrees and minutes but instead used sekeds (one seked equals the horizontal displacement for a vertical change of seven palms). Petrie's best estimate of the angle does not neatly match the value of a particular seked but falls between two values. Of course the height of the pyramid intended by the architects is dependent on the seked. The table identifies the likely sekeds

Side Angle	Theoretical Angle	Intended Height
Petrie's Estimate	51°0' ± 10	---
5 Palms 2 Digits	51°50'34"	218'8"
5 Palms 3 Digits	50°35'58"	209'2"

which the architects might have intended and the resulting impact on the intended height.

Pyramid Internal Construction

There is a large gash, 38' deep and 12' wide, on the Pyramid north face which is attributed to 12th century AD Mamluk efforts to either destroy or gain entrance to the pyramid. While the Pyramid exterior displays the typical flat, sloped faces, the gash provides a view of the Pyramid internal structure. Here, deep within the Pyramid core the flat, almost vertical faces of a step pyramidal structure are visible. Parts of two step faces are easily identifiable; one for its full height of seven courses and two courses of the step below. The step faces are composed of well-defined courses built of nicely squared and closely fitted blocks. Based on the height of the visible step face, there are likely six steps within the pyramid each seven or eight courses high and set back 15' to 17' from the step below.[9] Several courses of the lower visible step are missing, providing a view of the internal core. Behind the stepped faces the stones appear to be about half the size of the blocks which form the step surfaces and laid with only some minor efforts to fit the stones together and to square the stones. The blocks which fill in the steps to form the true pyramid are visible in the gash sides and above the step face. These fill blocks are roughly squared and laid generally in courses but set with wide spaces between blocks. The fill was then covered by the better prepared backing blocks we see exposed today on the pyramid surface over which was placed the final granite and limestone casing.

Without the gash, we would know little about the internal construction of the pyramid. The earlier Maidum Pyramid was originally built as a step pyramid; then the steps were filled in to produce a true pyramid. From that point forward, the final stepped form was abandoned in favor of the true pyramid. Likely, without benefit of the information provided within the gash, archaeologists would assume the internal construction of Menkaure's Pyramid was simply stone courses, laid one on top of the other. But within the gash we see instead that a step pyramid exists inside the true pyramid. Every pyramid built after Maidum, in which the internal construction is visible has a stepped interior: all three of Khufu's subsidiary pyramids which in their final form were true pyramids, all of the Dynasty 5 pyramids at Abu Sir which also were completed as true pyramids, and two of Menkaure's subsidiary pyramids.

The pyramid north face (left) with the gash above the entrance. From the edge of the gash (right) seven closely fitting courses of a step vertical face are clearly visible. Above are four loosely fitting courses of blocks which fill-in the steps. At the bottom of the vertical face was a flat horizontal step surface which connected to the next lower vertical face of which two courses are visible in the foreground. Above these two courses, several courses of this face are missing providing a window into the loosely fitted core and the hole in which Vyse cut a long passage.

We anticipate that the internal construction of Snefru's two Dahshur pyramids and the pyramids of Khufu and Khafre also have a stepped internal core.

Pyramid Casing

The pyramid was cased with both granite and Tura limestone. Khafre's Pyramid had one course of granite casing and Djedefre's had several. On Menkaure's Pyramid granite casing blocks remain on all four sides with pieces of granite found up to course 16 on all four sides[10] but none above this level. Granite casing blocks today rise five courses high at the back of the Mortuary Temple and seven courses high near the Pyramid entrance. While no limestone casing blocks remain on the Pyramid, the Tura limestone blocks found in the rubble surrounding the pyramid all have smoothed inclined surfaces[11] providing evidence that some part of the pyramid was cased with limestone and that limestone received the final dressing. The obvious conclusion is that the pyramid had a granite casing up to course 16, which at 54' above ground represents about ¼ of the total pyramid height, with a limestone casing covering the upper ¾'s of the pyramid. This conclusion is supported by the observations of Diodorus Siculus, who in 59 BCE recorded that the first 15 layers were of black stone – granite – and the rest finished with stones like the other pyramids – limestone.[12] Probably, at least one granite course was buried in the rubble at that time and he was not aware of its existence.

From the accounts of visitors to Giza we can estimate when the casing was removed. The casing was intact and no entrance was visible in 1618 when visited by M. De Villamont. In 1638-39 Graves reports "it was as perfect as when it was built." In 1647 M. De Monconys reported that the pyramid was so "dilapidated that it could not be ascended." Apparently the sides were no longer perfect; likely a general mess resulted from removal of a significant amount of casing. Then in 1655 M. Thevenot wrote that the third pyramid appeared to be cased with the same type of stone which lined the chamber in the Great Pyramid – granite – "as a number of the blocks were lying around." Based on these descriptions, most of the casing was likely

The bulbous unfinished casing face just west (right) of the pyramid entrance.

taken away during the first half of the 17th century. However, removal of stone probably continued over a longer period. According to Vyse, only a few years before his excavation, granite from the Menkaure's casing was used to build the arsenal at Alexandria and later there was a plan to dismantle the whole pyramid for building material.[13]

In preparing the granite casing blocks, the builders cut a very thin finished strip along all four of the front edges and left a bulbous center face. The other surfaces - sides, top, and bottom - where the blocks would come into contact were worked smooth, and at least the top and bottom faces were slightly

hollowed to receive mortar.[14] While the blocks were of standard heights for each course, the other dimensions depended on the shape of the original stone. Many of the joints between casing blocks were not vertical, but met at varying angles. Most assuredly the stone masons specifically selected adjoining blocks based on their shape and the amount of effort required to fit them together. Then the blocks were finished and aligned in the work yard before being moved to the pyramid and set in their final place.

There are many indications within the Mortuary Complex that it was unfinished at Menkaure's death and finished quickly by his son Shepseskaf in preparation for the burial rites. The most obvious indication is the granite casing was left with a rough surface. Only two small areas, probably critical to the burial, were smoothed to a fine finish. At the rear of the Mortuary Temple there was a 24' long granite platform which contained an altar and a stele against the Pyramid east face. The granite pyramid casing along the platform length was finished to at least the height of course five, above which the casing is missing. On the north face around the pyramid entrance the casing was finely finished in a squarish space to a height of five courses. This finished area may indicate that a temporary structure was built around the pyramid entrance for the internment.

Charlie Rigano sits on casing blocks on the west face. Granite casing blocks thrown down are in the rubble below.

The slope of the lowest casing course did not extend to the ground, but stopped anywhere from 6" to 18" above ground level. The bottom of this course was probably intended to be finished with a vertical section against which pavement blocks would be set, similar to the way the pyramid casing and courtyard pavement joined around the base of Khafre's Pyramid.[15] This work was also interrupted by Menkaure's death. The bottom vertical surface was never finished and the pavement was never laid.

Maragioglio and Rinaldi note that the pyramid shape as described by the backing stones up to the height of the granite casing forms a flat surface. Above this level where the limestone casing was laid, the backing stones form a concavity in the center of each face similar to the indentation in the faces of Khufu's Pyramid. They offer the same explanation here as they applied to Khufu's Pyramid; while the pyramid cased surface was flat, the limestone casing blocks placed in the center of each course were of greater thickness (front to back) than those laid

The small area around the entrance (top) and on the pyramid east face at the rear of the Mortuary Temple (bottom) were finely finished.

near the corners to bond the casing to the pyramid core. With the whole casing in-place each face would appear flat. However, with the casing removed the concavity in the center of each face became visible.

Some theorize that the Pyramid was intended to be cased completely with granite, but Menkaure may have become sick for a prolonged period or died with the pyramid casing in place up to course 16. In order to complete the pyramid quickly, the casing material was changed from granite to limestone which was easier to work and readily available. Others suggest that the architect always intended the pyramid to be cased with granite in the lower part and limestone in the upper part.[16] Additionally, not only the casing material changed at course 16, but the underlying pyramid shape was also revised. Most likely if the concavity was part of the original plan, it would have started at the pyramid base. Our view is that with both the underlying pyramid shape and the casing material changing at the same point, there was apparently a basic architectural adjustment made to address a problem that is not yet obvious to us today.

Entrance

The single entrance to Menkaure's Pyramid lies in the center of the north face filling the full height of the fourth course, 13' above the ground. This location is unlike the entrances to Khufu's and Khafre's pyramids which both lie east of center. Menkaure's entrance was likely closed with a granite block to make it inconspicuous. However, the finished granite casing surrounding the entrance would have had exactly the opposite effect.

While the smooth casing on the pyramid's north face would draw the attention of anyone looking for the entrance, it was hidden under mounds of debris in the early 1800's when Vyse was trying to penetrate the pyramid. Diodorus Siculus recorded that Menkaure's name was inscribed on the Pyramid north side.[17] After Vyse uncovered the

The inscription just below the level of the entrance at upper right.

Pyramid entrance in 1837 at course 4 (detailed in the next chapter), he did not dig any deeper and left debris piled against the north side up to the level of the entrance. Since no inscription was visible in the mid 1960's when Maragioglio and Rinaldi investigated the site, they assumed that the inscription was on the now missing limestone casing.[18] However, in 1968 when the Antiquities Department cleared the north face, they found five lines of hieroglyphic text just below and to the east of the entrance cut into the smoothed granite surface. The inscription was badly eroded and has only been partially translated. It says Menkaure was buried on the twenty-third day of the fourth month of the winter season, about March, with all his possessions. The year was either not present or eroded away. Four cartouches are barely visible, the names in three cannot be read, the fourth contains Menkaure's name.[19]

1. Reisner, *Mycerinus: The Temples of the Third Pyramid at Giza*, p4. In 1902 the concessions for Giza were split among the Americans, Germans, and Italians. The Germans were given Khafre's Pyramid, the Italians Khufu's complex, and the area including Menkaure's complex was given to the American Hearst Expedition of the University of California for which Reisner was the Director. In 1905, the Hearst Expedition ended and the work was taken over by the Joint Egyptian Expedition of Harvard University and the Boston Museum of Fine Arts also led by Reisner. The Italians also gave-up their concession which Reisner took over. Work on the Menkaure temples continued on and off until 1924.

2. Vyse, Operations Carried on at the Pyramids of Gizeh in 1837, Vol II, pp 48, 93.

3. Reisner, op. cit., p5, Appendix A.

4. Vyse, *op. cit*, p106.

5. Maragioglio and Rinaldi, L'Architettura Delle Piramidi Menfite, Parte VI, pp32-34.

6. Petrie, *The Pyramids and Temples of Giza*, 1883, p111. Petrie identifies 4153.6" as the mean measurement of 3 sides. This equates to 201.4 cubits. Since the architects likely planned to even numbers of cubits, the intended base length was probably 200 cubits, or 343'8".

7. ibid, Khufu measurements p 39, Khafre measurements p97, Menkaure measurements p111.

8. ibid, p112. Petrie measured seven finished granite blocks in situ, the first and fourth courses at the SSW, six single granite blocks which were shifted, and nine limestone casing blocks brought to England. He considered the in situ dressed granite block surfaces to be very irregular and likely they were hurriedly finished after Menkaure's death. One of the courses at the SSW may have been misestimated. And since the moved granite and limestone blocks were not measured in situ, it is unknown if they sat on a horizontal surface. Additionally, one of the granite blocks was found to have two surfaces which differed by 1°40'. As a result, the best that can be hoped for is a rough estimate.

9. Maragioglio and Rinaldi, *op. cit.*, p 34

10. Petrie, *op. cit.*, p113.

11. Maragioglio and Rinaldi, *op. cit.*, p 36

12. Vyse, *op. cit.*, p186.

13. *ibid.*, pp. 203-221, 120.

14. Maragioglio and Rinaldi, *op. cit.*, p36.
15. Petrie, *op. cit.*, p111.
16. Maragioglio and Rinaldi, *op. cit.*, p36.
17. Vyse, *op. cit.,* p186.
18. Maragioglio and Rinaldi, *op. cit.*, p98.
19. Notes on Archeological Activities in Egypt, American Research Center Egypt Newsletter, vol 66, July 1968, p18.

Chapter 11
Menkaure's Pyramid Interior

Today, even from a distance, the rectangular flat area of smoothly finished granite around the Pyramid entrance immediately draws our attention by its contrast to the surrounding unfinished casing. Since the Pyramid north face is clear of debris, the entrance 13' above the ground is easy to identify. This was not always the case.

In 1836 and 1837 Colonel Howard Vyse carried on extensive excavations all over the Giza Plateau: simultaneously exploring the three large pyramids, their subsidiary pyramids, the Sphinx, and Campbell's Tomb. With Khufu's and Khafre's Pyramids already open, the prize would be to open and enter the third pyramid. He found this pyramid in much the same state that Belzoni found Khafre's Pyramid just 19 years earlier. Due to debris around Menkaure's Pyramid, created by the removal of the limestone and granite casing, the Pyramid sides were covered to a point higher than the top of the granite casing and the entrance was hidden.

Vyse Enters the Pyramid

Though Vyse knew that the entrances to the two other major Giza pyramids were near the center of the north face, he did not believe that would be true for Menkaure's Pyramid. He presumed that the Mamluk[1] examined the north face and only after failing to find the entrance did they expend an enormous effort to create the breach.[2] With that belief and no other obvious location for the entrance, in November 1836 Vyse tunneled into the Mamluk breach; his intent to break into the spaces located within the Pyramid core the same way the Arabs obtained access to the interior of both Khufu's and Khafre's Pyramids. Using gunpowder, he tunneled in two stages 70' horizontally and down 79' intersecting the center of the pyramid. But he reached bedrock without finding any passages or chambers before giving up on July 26, 1837.[3]

A month earlier, probably out of frustration with the lack of results from the tunneling, Vyse started clearing the north face. On July 28 the workman uncovered the top of the finished granite casing which Vyse assumed indicated the entrance was nearby. He concentrated the work below the breach where his workmen removed the rubble and a large number of blocks thrown out of the breach. The next day under this debris they uncovered the

Howard Vyse used diary like entries to record the results of his explorations. (By Richard William Howard Vyse [Public domain], via Wikimedia Commons)

entrance. Vyse found the entrance passage open and accessible to just below the point where it entered the bedrock, from here the passage was clogged with rubble. While clearing the rubble, he found Arabic characters beyond the blockage which were similar to characters in Khafre's Pyramid, one of Menkaure's subsidiary pyramids and over the entrance to two of Khufu's subsidiary pyramids indicating they were all entered about the same time.[4]

Upper Passage System

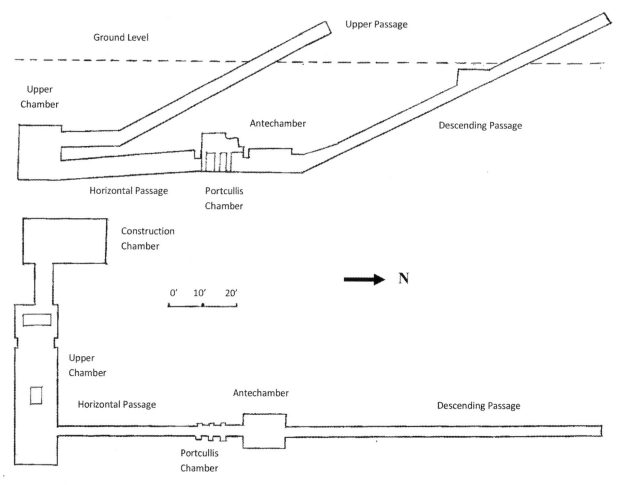

N

0' 10' 20'

Lower Passage System

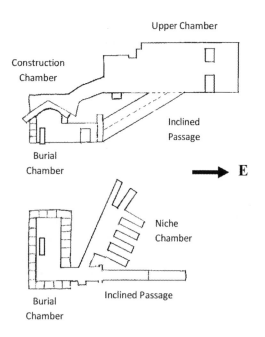

E

The layout of the pyramid substructure looking from the side and above. The Upper Chamber, likely intended to be the original burial chamber, has an area set off at the western end with a lowered ceiling and hole for a sunken sarcophagus. A change in plan resulted in the Construction Chamber and Lower Passage System accessed through the Inclined Passage cut into the floor of the Upper Chamber. Here was the final granite lined Burial Chamber. The location of the sarcophagus as found by Vyse is shown.

Descending Passage	Dimension[5]
Entrance Height	13' above the pavement, in the center of the north face
Passage Length	104'0" inclined, 4'3" horizontal
Passage Dimensions	Inclined Section - 41" wide, 47" high Horizontal Section – 41" wide, 68" high
Passage Slope	26°2'

The limestone block top and limestone bedrock where the Descending Passage enters the bedrock.

Descending Passage

For the first 28' the Descending Passage is lined with granite and travels through the pyramid core. Where the passage enters the bedrock, there is a large limestone block in the ceiling which may either fill a fault, or possibly form the foundation of the Pyramid internal first step. At this point the height of the bedrock is very close to the height of the exterior pavement and there is no evidence that the Pyramid was constructed around an internal bedrock knoll as the pyramids of Khufu and Khafre. From here the passage is cut through the bedrock and is neither lined nor plastered. The chisel marks left by the workman are still visible.

If the lower part of the passage was filled with granite plugs, the first robbers would have tunneled through the softer limestone walls rather than try to break-up the harder granite plugs. Since there is no tunneling, we can safely assume there were no granite plugs. If limestone plugs were inserted, the thieves may have damaged the walls in removing the plugs. While there is some damage to the passage walls, this seems mostly due to natural flaking.

The ceiling in the bottom 11' slowly rises 21" until it connects with the ceiling of a short horizontal section. The higher connecting ceiling may have been necessary to maneuver the large beams which we will later find form the Burial Chamber ceiling.

Antechamber	Dimension[6]
Length (N-S)	11'11"
Width (E-W)	10' 6"
Height	7'0"

Antechamber

The Descending Passage enters through the north wall of the Antechamber; a small rock cut room with a flat ceiling and a doorway to a passage in the opposite (south) wall. The north and south walls are divided into thirds by the doorways and flanking sidewalls. The entrance (northern) doorway is surrounded by a shallow cut frame which is replicated around the restored exit (southern) doorway. A false door façade, often called the "palace façade," covers all four walls.

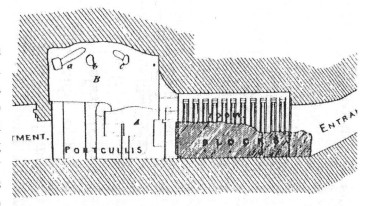

The blocks in the Antechamber filled the length of the Chamber but were only as wide as the Descending Passage (from Vyse).

The bottom of the Descending Passage enters the Antechamber (top left). The opposite wall (bottom left) has been restored. Black 1' ruler in both pictures. The granite block at right was likely part of the portcullis. The false doors (right) cut into the Chamber side walls.

The façade was cut directly into the coarse bedrock surface then covered with a thin layer of plaster.[7] In earlier pyramids the descending passage connected to either another passage as in the Bent, Khufu's, and Khafre's pyramids; or off-centered spaces as in the Maidum and Red Pyramids. Here is the first example of the Descending Passage entering a symmetrical chamber. In pyramids which followed, this type of antechamber became a standard feature.

When Vyse first entered this chamber he had to climb over two large blocks placed end-to-end spanning the chamber length, filling the south wall doorway and on the north side extending the length of the Descending Passage horizontal section.[8] In the horizontal section the blocks did not reach the ceiling so entrance could be made over them. The only information available on the blocks is two sentences from Vyse and two of Perring's drawings. These blocks were apparently broken-up when Vyse removed the sarcophagus (see later). On the chamber south side Vyse found the lintel and jamb of the doorway were torn out by earlier intruders.[9]

Perring concluded that during construction, the builders cut open the entire width of the Antechamber south wall to permit the introduction of the granite portcullises into the chamber beyond.[10] After the portcullises were placed, the Antechamber wall was built on each side of the doorway with limestone blocks, covered with plaster, and the false doors carved. The doorway was completed with a pink granite rounded lintel and jambs resembling a false door. Today the southern wall and doorway, which were destroyed by thieves, has been restored to its original condition.

176

From the floor of the Portcullis Chamber (left) looking towards the Antechamber (see 1' ruler on left). Above the architrave a high ceiling was cut into the bedrock to make room for the raised portcullis. On the sides, wall slots held three portcullises. At the chamber opposite end (right) thieves cut away part of the architrave to gain access over the last portcullis.

Portcullis Chamber and Horizontal Passage

Directly beyond the Antechamber is a section which contained three granite portcullises. In Khufu's Pyramid three granite portcullises were contained within the granite Antechamber; in Khafre's the upper granite portcullis was placed at the end of a granite passage. In both pyramids, the surrounding granite provided an extremely hard material which would be difficult for all but the most determined and well equipped thieves to penetrate. However, in Menkaure's Pyramid, even though granite was liberally employed in the Mortuary Temple, pyramid casing, and burial chamber, the granite portcullises were placed within a limestone walled space. The soft chamber walls provided little protection and represented a serious design flaw if the architect's intent was to actually protect the burial.

The Portcullis Chamber walls were formed in part by bedrock, and in part by laid limestone blocks. While the chamber contains no remnants of the portcullis, the three sets of grooves cut in the east and west walls identify the Chamber purpose. Since the space is contained entirely within the bedrock, a high ceiling was necessary to permit initially raising the portcullis into position. Above each groove a set of holes once held beams that spanned the Chamber width and were used to raise and set the portcullis in the grooves and later assisted in lowering the blocks. Once the portcullises were placed in their grooves, the builders likely placed supports below rather than rely only on ropes to hold the blocks in a raised position for years. Today, the high-ceilinged space is empty. But either a ceiling was constructed as the portcullis were set or the space was packed with blocks after the portcullises were lowered to keep the opening from becoming an easy route around the portcullis.

Feature	Dimension[11]
Portcullis Chamber	
Length (N-S)	13'10" (including 1'6" thick wall at the south end of the Antechamber)
Width (E-W)	42"
Height	9' 10" to 11'5"
Portcullis Grooves	13" Wide
Horizontal Passage	
Length	41'3"[12]
Width	41"
Height	5'10"
Incline	4°

Looking from the Upper Chamber down the Horizontal Passage to the lit Antechamber at the far end. A black 1' ruler sits in the hole above the chair.

After gaining access to the Antechamber, thieves apparently first tried to tunnel through the Antechamber south wall as a means to circumvent the portcullis and the two large blocks lying on the Antechamber floor. Vyse's description of the robber excavations which he found around the portcullis is contained in one sentence and one diagram, both difficult to interpret. Additionally, the Antechamber wall and space beyond have been reconstructed to their presumed original configuration, so analysis of how the thieves attacked the Chamber is no longer possible. However, they apparently failed in tunneling around the portcullis and instead removed the lintel over the Antechamber's south doorway and the ceiling packing blocks which were placed above the portcullis. Making their way to the south end of the Portcullis Chamber, they cut through the limestone lintel, successfully by-passing the portcullis system. Since Vyse found the Pyramid entrance open, only covered by debris, likely the Pyramid interior was accessible for much of its existence since robbed during the First Intermediate Period. Possibly, the robbers or someone in the years that followed destroyed the portcullises so as to remove large objects from the chambers.

Beyond the Portcullis Chamber, a straight, slightly descending Horizontal Passage leads to the Upper Chamber. Fine pointed chisel marks on both sidewalls for the full passage length show by their arc that the passage wall were finely finished starting from the inside (the Upper Chamber) towards the outside (the Portcullis Chamber). Both Vyse and Petrie believe these marks provided evidence that the passage was cut from the interior of the pyramid,[13] however, at best, we can say the walls were finished in this direction, the chisel marks provide no evidence in what direction the passage was initially cut.

Upper Chamber

The floor remains level and unbroken as the Horizontal Passage enters the Upper Chamber. This chamber appears to have been initially planned for the burial before a change in plan created a lower level. The Upper Chamber was excavated entirely in the bed rock. The Chamber was lined with a pink plaster which still largely covers the ceiling and can be found in spots on the walls.

Holes in the chamber walls and floor likely once held beams used in moving the sarcophagus and the granite blocks used in the Burial Chamber. In the north and south walls are three pairs of holes positioned across from one another, two sets about 6' high and one near the entrance a few inches lower. There is a single hole low on the south wall across from the Horizontal Passage and there are three holes in the floor: one near each corner at the Chamber east end and the third in line with the Horizontal Passage and Descending Passage.

The architect's initial plan was to place the sarcophagus at the chamber's western end which

Upper Chamber	Dimension[14]
Full Chamber	
Length (E-W)	46'7"
Width (N-S)	12'7"
Height	16'0"
Western Section – Burial Section	
Length (E-W)	8'8"
Width (N-S)	12'7"
Height (Above Missing Floor)	12'0"
Floor Below Ground Level	34'8"

The framing pilaster and architrave separate the chamber west end (left) which was initially intended for the sarcophagus. The gated hole behind this section leads to the Construction Chamber above the Burial Chamber. Looking back to the long chamber (right) the entrance is at the left. Hole pairs are visible in the walls. The fenced Incline Passage leads to the lower chambers.

was separated from the rest of the chamber by a framing pilaster and architrave. This section contains a rectangular hole 32" deep sized to accommodate the sarcophagus with only the lid above floor level, similar to Khafre's burial. A limestone block floor was laid around the sarcophagus; a few blocks remain at the Chamber far western end.

The Upper Chamber and Khafre's Burial Chamber are very similar. They were constructed less than 20 years apart and possibly we are seeing the same architect's hand or initially Menkaure just wanted a burial chamber fashioned after his father's.

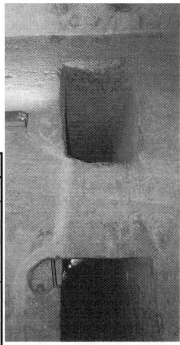

High on the wall above the entrance from the Horizontal Passage is an opening which leads to the Upper Passage. This passage, cut through the bedrock, has a short horizontal section, then inclines upward and comes to a blind end within the pyramid core at a 50 ton

Upper Passage	Dimension[17]
Entrance Height Above Floor	9'10"
Horizontal Section	
Length	16'10"
Width	41"
Height	54"
Inclined Section	
Length	63'7"
Width	41"
Height	47"
Angle	27°34'

The Upper Passage enters the Upper Chamber 1'7" from the ceiling.

Chamber Comparison	Menkaure Upper Chamber[15]	Khafre Burial Chamber[16]
Entrance Passage	Horizontal (slight down slope) 41" wide, 5'10" high, bedrock floor continuous into chamber	Horizontal 41" wide, 5'11" high, bedrock floor continuous into chamber
Entrance Position	8'8" from east end	8'8" from east end

Chamber
   Length
   Width
   Height
	
	46' 7"
	12'7"
	16'0"
		
		46'5"
		16'4"
		17'2" (north and south walls)

Floor Step Down	16"	16"
Sarcophagus from West Wall	32"	43"

Sarcophagus
 	
   Length
   Width
   Height
	(Based on the space cut in the floor; the sarcophagus is missing)
	
	103"
	40"
	32" (16' hole, 16" surrounding floor)
		(Actual sarcophagus)
		
		103.7"
		42.0"
		38.1"

limestone block; similar to blocks placed as the lintel over the entrances to smaller pyramids.[18] The passage was plugged with limestone blocks which were largely destroyed by plunders who forced the passage from the inside and cut tunnels at the upper end looking for additional chambers.[19] Since this passage does not lead to additional spaces built within the pyramid core, it must have been the entrance passage leading from the surface of an initially planned smaller pyramid downward to a simple burial chamber. When the pyramid was enlarged, this passage was abandoned, plugged, covered at the top end, and possibly closed at the bottom end.

Inclined Passage, Lower Horizontal Passage, Niche Chamber

From the middle of the Upper Chamber floor, an Inclined Passage descends and provides access to the lower substructure. This Passage was probably plugged and filled to the level of the Lower Chamber floor, but since the chamber floor is bedrock, the filling would have been immediately obvious and the Passage opened by robbers. The Passage today appears much different than its original construction or as found by Vyse.

Inclined Passage	Dimension[20]
Passage Length	32'6" at floor
Passage Height	65"
Passage Width (at ceiling)	51"
Ramp Height above Floor	35"
Width Between Ramps	37"
Passage Angle	28°

The Passage is composed of two vertical sections, a lower part 35" high by 37" wide and an upper portion 30" high and 51" wide. Total height of the space is 65". There is evidence at the lower end for a vertical sliding space which held a 10" thick portcullis to close the bottom end of the Inclined Passage.

Considering the odd passage construction we see a few possibilities on how it was built:

- The full 65" passage height (lower 35" high plus upper 30" high) was required to move large objects into the Burial Chamber, but inclined passages typically have lower heights than

Looking up the Inclined Passage (top). The right side ramp is intact, the left side ramp was cut away by Vyse. Originally, blocks were laid across the passage on the ramps producing the final passage below the side ramps. From the granite lined Burial Chamber entrance (right) through the Lower Horizontal Passage to the bottom of the Inclined Passage. With the limestone ceiling blocks in place, the Inclined Passage would have a about half the present height and the lower end closed by a portcullis. A very ineffective arrangement. The entrance to the Niche Chamber is behind the bars at left.

horizontal passages. So the builders first cut a high downward sloping passage with side ramps through the limestone bedrock. Once the extra height was no longer needed, blocks were set on top of the side ramps, spanning the distance between them to form a ceiling leaving only the lower part as the final passage 35" high and 37" wide.

- The builders first cut the small 35" by 37" lower part of the passage. The sarcophagus and Burial Chamber side walls were not moved down the Inclined Passage but instead were lowered into the Burial Chamber through its ceiling (see later section). After the Burial Chamber ceiling was closed and the only access was through the small Inclined Passage, they decided to cut the Niche Chamber and needed a larger passage to remove the resulting debris, or they needed to move more large objects (burial goods?) into the Burial Chamber or new Niche Chamber. To accommodate the new requirement they cut the upper part of the passage and when the high passage was no longer needed, they inserted the ceiling blocks returning the Inclined Passage to its original height.

- The original passage was the small 35" by 37" lower passage. Again, the sarcophagus and Burial Chamber side walls were lowered into the Burial Chamber through its ceiling. The small Inclined Passage was closed with granite plugs. The first robbers into the pyramid found the Inclined Passage blocked with granite plugs. Rather than dealing with the hard granite, the robbers tunneled through the softer limestone ceiling. At some unknown later time, the pyramid was used for intrusive burials and the roughly cut robbers passage was finished with a limestone ceiling. The upper limestone ceiling could have again been removed by still later robbers.

In considering these possibilities, we note that the lower portion of the Inclined Passage at 35" high by 37" wide is very small. This Descending Passage in Menkaure's Pyramid is 12" higher and 4" wider. The only comparable passage in any pyramid from this period is the Lower Horizontal

The roughly cut Niche Chamber looking towards the entrance (left) and looking from the stairs (right).

Niche Chamber	Dimension[24]
Chamber (Less Niches)	6'7" high, 17'1" long, 6'2" wide
Niche (Average of Six)	4'8' high, 8'5" long, 2'7" wide
Floor Below Ground Level	54'

Passage in Khufu's Pyramid which is 36" high and 33" wide and that passage is so small it has to be crawled through. It is hard to imagine why Menkaure's architects would want the final dimensions of the Inclined Passage to be so small.

When Vyse entered the Pyramid, he found the plug blocks (type of stone not mentioned) still in place but the ceiling blocks missing, removed by robbers to gain access to the Burial Chamber.[21] Since the thieves attacked the ceiling blocks rather than cutting a passage around them, the ceiling blocks were likely limestone. When Vyse brought the sarcophagus up from the burial chamber, he removed the plug blocks and cut away the northern side ramp.[22] The plugs were likely the granite blocks found at both ends of the Upper Chamber.

From the bottom of the Inclined Passage the short (12'6" long), high-ceiled (6'8" high) Lower Horizontal Passage continues directly to the Burial Chamber. From the Passage north wall a low opening leads down six steps to the flat ceiling Niche Chamber which has six low, long niches cut into the walls. This Chamber is not oriented to the cardinal points as typical of chambers in Old Kingdom pyramids but is angled 25° east of north. The whole space is crudely excavated with chisel marks readily apparent. There is no evidence that the walls were plastered or that a limestone or granite lining was intended. When Vyse first entered the chamber, he found it half full of rubble and identified several Arabic characters on the ceiling.[23]

Petrie believed the niches were intended to hold coffins.[25] We see two possibilities for this chamber:

- Because of the chamber odd orientation, the steps uncharacteristic of the period, and roughness of construction, we are tempted to assign the Chamber to a later period when it was excavated for intrusive burials.
- Similar niches, probably for the storage of burial goods, are found in the tombs of Shepseskaf (Menkaure's son) and the Khentkawes (possibly Menkaure's daughter). Since the other chambers in Menkaure's pyramid were decorated, plastered, or lined with granite, the excavation of the unfinished Niche Chamber might have been interrupted by Menkaure's death; or possibly it represents a hurried construction by Shepseskaf after Menkaure's death.

In the Lower Horizontal Passage, opposite the entrance to the Niche Chamber, a shallow space was cut into the wall with squarish corners and a similarly sized opening, but only 1' deep. Based on its location, the rough construction, and readily visible chisel marks, this space was probably cut at the same time as the Niche Chamber. This could represent the start of another chamber or cut so that long objects could be turned into the Niche Chamber.

The Burial Chamber as found by Vyse (left) with the sarcophagus against the west wall and how it appears now (center). Floor blocks have been removed since Vyse. The granite lined Burial Chamber opposite end (right) with the entrance. The ceiling arch was cut into ceiling blocks which meet in the middle with the opposite ends extending well beyond the walls.

Burial Chamber

The Lower Horizontal Passage opens directly into the southeast corner of the Burial Chamber. This Chamber was excavated in the bedrock, then lined floor, walls, and ceiling with finely finished granite blocks; the ceiling blocks cut to form a slightly pointed arch. Unlike most burial chambers which are oriented east-west, this chamber has its longer axis aligned north-south.

Burial Chamber	Dimension[29]
Bedrock Excavation	26'6" long, 15'7" wide (approximate)
Granite Chamber	21'9" long, 8'8" wide, 8'9" high at side walls, 11'3" high at center
Floor Below Ground Level	51'0"

When Vyse first entered the Chamber he found the basalt sarcophagus against the west wall, one end raised on a stone, the lid missing, and the interior empty.[26] The sarcophagus top had the standard provisions to hold the lid in place: an undercut groove around three sides which accepted a projection around the lid bottom, and two holes in the fourth side for pins dropped from the lid. While there were no inscriptions, the

Sarcophagus	Dimension[27]
Inside	6'5" long, 24 ½" wide, 24 ½" deep
Outside	8'0" long, 37" wide, 35" high
Weight	4 tons[28]

sarcophagus exterior was finely carved in what appeared to be architectural decorations. The exterior was finely polished to a brown finish but chips revealed the stone was blue.

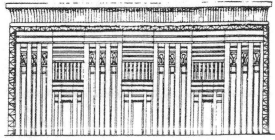

Perring's drawing of the lost sarcophagus side and end.

A cross section of the Burial Chamber and Construction Chamber. The space was cut out of the bedrock and the granite Burial Chamber build within that space.

The wooden anthropoid coffin top found in the Upper Chamber reads from top right "Osiris, King of Upper and Lower Egypt, Menkaure, living forever. Born of the sky, conceived by Nut, heir of Geb, his beloved. Thy mother Nut spreads herself over thee in the name of Mystery of Heaven. She caused thee to be a god, in thy name of god, King of Upper and Lower Egypt, Menkaure, living forever." An inscription from the Pyramid Texts.

Though both Khufu's and Khafre's sarcophagus remained in their pyramids for many years, Vyse believed that Menkaure's sarcophagus would be destroyed if left in the Burial Chamber. To get the sarcophagus out Vyse destroyed the plug blocks and a side ramp in the Inclined Passage and the large stones spanning the Antechamber. He sent the sarcophagus to the British Museum on the merchant ship Beatrice. Unfortunately the Beatrice sank in the Mediterranean somewhere between Malta from which it sailed on October 13, 1838, and Cartagena, Spain and the sarcophagus was lost.[30] All that remains are Perring's drawings.

Vyse found most of the stone sarcophagus lid among the debris in the Upper Chamber, near the entrance to the Inclined Passage. Why anyone moved the heavy lid or pieces of it over the plug blocks and into the Upper Chamber is hard to imagine. Close-by he discovered skeleton ribs, vertebrae, and leg and foot bones wrapped in a yellow coarse woolen cloth and an anthropoid shaped wooden top to a mummy case with an inscription that included Menkaure's cartouche.[31] The bones and top were not related since radiocarbon tests date the bones to the Christian period and the top is of a design not used before the Saite period (Dynasty 26) at the earliest.[32]

Entrance to the Construction Chamber (left) looking down at the top side of three of the blocks forming the Burial Chamber ceiling. From the bottom of the stairs and looking right, Charlie Rigano lays atop the blocks at the chamber's far end. The blocks come within inches of the rough ceiling and extend into the wall at his feet.

The Burial Chamber floor is placed between the sidewalls which rest directly on the bedrock. The sidewalls are four courses high; an additional course was added at each end to meet the arched ceiling. The blocks at the entrance and a hole cut in the chamber wall at the northwest corner show the granite lining is two blocks thick. When Vyse first entered the Chamber he found some of the floor blocks taken up but still in the Chamber. Today only half the floor remains, the other blocks removed entirely from the Chamber; some may have been placed in the Niche Chamber.

The Burial Chamber ceiling is formed by inclined blocks meeting in the center: nine beams on the west side and eight on the east side. An arch cut in the beam underside runs the length of the Burial Chamber. Above the ceiling is a Construction Chamber cut entirely in the bedrock. While inclined ceiling beams were used in both Khufu's and Khafre's pyramids, they were transported and laid in the open as the pyramids were being built. In Menkaure's Pyramid the 5 ton beams[33] were moved over 200' through the internal passages and chambers. The beams were then accurately placed in position in the underground Construction Chamber which has a ceiling only inches higher than the beams butted ends in the Chamber center.

The Construction Chamber is accessed by a short passage cut through the bedrock from the western end of the Upper Chamber. The passage entrance was originally closed by solid masonry and covered with plaster,[34] but it was forced by ancient robbers and found open by Vyse. Within the Construction Chamber two rows of inclined beams meet along the north – south center line. Their opposite ends lay in a groove cut along the length of each side wall, a limestone wedge closing the space between the beam and the groove top.

Changes in Plan

The Upper Passage near the ceiling of the Upper Chamber provides evidence that the initial plan was for a much smaller pyramid. If the 50 ton block at the passage end was intended to be a lintel over the pyramid entrance, the resulting pyramid would have been 172' or 100 cubits on a side, just slightly larger than the subsidiary pyramids to the east of the Great Pyramid. Based on the structure we can imagine two possibilities:

- The passing of a long reigning king, Khafre, could have produced a period of some unrest as different factions maneuvered for power. Following Khafre's reign several short lived kings ruled. When Menkaure ascended to power, a tentative power base and loyalties could have caused economic and political uncertainties which resulted in the initial plan for a much smaller pyramid. This initial plan had a simple descending passage, the Upper Passage, leading to a small burial chamber. After Menkaure consolidated his power, he planned a larger pyramid complex.
- The plug blocks found in the Upper Passage could indicate an earlier burial in a small pyramid that was usurped by Menkaure. Since the Upper Passage ended within the pyramid core, Menkaure's builders would have no reason to block it, therefore the plug blocks must have been placed when an earlier pyramid was closed.

We discount the alternative that the passage was used for ventilation or for construction access due to the presence of the plug blocks and it could have been used for only a short period before the top was covered as the pyramid was built.

Given either of the choices, the original plan was expanded. The Descending Passage, Antechamber, Portcullis Chamber, and Horizontal Passage were cut into the bedrock to provide access to the Upper (burial) Chamber. The Upper Chamber was enlarged and assumed much the form of Khafre's burial chamber. The western end was architecturally separated from the rest of the chamber by the framing pilasters and architrave and a space was created for a sarcophagus sunk into the floor. We cannot know if the sarcophagus was actually brought into the chamber.

Based on the apparent finished state of the Upper Chamber's western end (sarcophagus end), after this plan was complete, the plan changed to favor a lower, granite-lined, arched-ceiling burial chamber. The Inclined Passage in the center of the Upper Chamber was started and possibly at the same time, the Construction Chamber. The beams used in the Burial Chamber ceiling were too long to fit through the existing passages. The builders raised the ceiling at the bottom of the Descending Passage and cut a space 15" deep into the floor of the Antechamber to permit the beams to pass this junction. The granite lined burial chamber was constructed. The Niche Chamber was built last based on the roughness of construction.

1. There are a number of ways to spell this name. We have settled on this spelling as used in the Anchor Atlas of World History.

2. Vyse, *Operations Carried on at the Pyramids of Gizeh in 1837*, Vol II, pp.17,28.

3. Ibid, pp64, 121. This excavation was started by Caviglia in November 1836. Over a three month period he penetrated 6'. Vyse continued this excavation. The total excavation was actually horizontally 6' by Caviglia and 52' by Vyse. Then Vyse cut a first shaft down 29', horizontally 11'6", and a second shaft down 49'6" reaching bedrock. At the bottom he cut several side passages.

4. Ibid, pp69-74.

5. Maragioglio and Rinaldi, *L'Architettura Delle Piramidi Menfite*, Parte VI, *La Grande Fossa di Zauiet el Aryan, la Piramide di Micerino, il Mastabat Faraun, la Tomba di Khentkaus*, TAV 4,5, and 7. The passage width is shown as both 39" and 41".

6. Ibid, TAV 7.

7. Eleven on each of the east and west walls and four on each of the north and south walls for a total of 30.

8. Perring, *Pyramids of Gizeh, from Actual Survey and Measurements*, Third Pyramid Plate III.

9. Vyse, op. cit., p78 and figures on the following 2 pages.

10. Ibid, p78.

11. Maragioglio and Rinaldi, op. cit., TAV5 & 7 except as noted.

12. Vyse, op. cit., p121.

13. Petrie, *The Pyramids and Temples of Gizeh*, p118. Vyse, op. cit., p79.

14. Maragioglio and Rinaldi, op. cit., TAV 6.

15. Ibid.

16. See Chapter 8.

17. Maragioglio and Rinaldi, op. cit., TAV 5.

18. Petrie, op. cit. p120.

19. Maragioglio and Rinaldi, op. cit., p48.

20. Maragioglio and Rinaldi, op. cit., TAV 6.

21. Perring, op. cit., Third Pyramid, Plate IV.

22. Vyse, op. cit., p83.

23. Vyse, op. cit., p85.

24. Maragioglio and Rinaldi, op. cit., TAV VI.

25. Petrie, op. cit., p119.

26. Vyse specifically states that he found the sarcophagus "completely empty". (Vyse, op. cit., p84) We have seen reports which are apparently incorrect (for instance Clayton, *Chronicle of the Pharaohs*, p58) that a wooden anthropoid coffin with Menkaure's cartouche were found inside.

27. Vyse, op. cit., p123.

28. Outside dimension (8x3.083x2.917) - Inside dimensions (6.42x2.041x2.041) times 190 lbs/square foot = 8,588 pounds.

29. Maragioglio and Rinaldi, op. cit., TAV VI.

30. Edwards, *Pyramids of Egypt*, p143.

31. Vyse, op. cit., p86.

32. Edwards, op. cit., p143.

33. The beams were on the average 32" wide, 27" thick, 10 ½' long. Which equals 63 cubic feet times 155 pounds per cubic foot equals 9,777 pounds, about 5 tons.

34. Vyse, op. cit., p80.

Chapter 12
Menkaure's Mortuary Complex

Although Menkaure enjoyed a long reign, estimated at 28 years,[1] when he died his pyramid complex was far from complete:

- Mortuary Temple lacked the final granite casing and some rooms were only outlined.
- Causeway and Valley Temple were barely started.
- Pyramid was finished and cased, but the casing was not finely finished.
- Enclosure Wall and pavement around the pyramid were not started.
- One subsidiary pyramid was complete while the other two were in the form of step pyramids.
- The interior of one subsidiary pyramid was incomplete.
- Only one of the three subsidiary pyramid temple foundations was laid.

Menkaure's son and successor, Shepseskaf, used mud brick to complete the Mortuary and Valley Temples, all of the subsidiary pyramid temples, the Causeway, and probably the Enclosure Wall.

A stele found in eight pieces in the portico of Menkaure's Mortuary Temple reads:

"Under the Majesty of the King of Upper and Lower Egypt, Shepseskaf, the Horus, Shepsesy-khet, in the year after the first census of the large and small cattle, he made it as his monument for his father, the King of Upper and Lower Egypt [Menkauwra]."[2]

This stele provides proof of both the order of these two Dynasty IV kings as well as their relationship and some evidence that Shepseskaf completed his father's complex up to three years after Menkaure's death.[3]

It is possible that the work necessary for the burial was completed during the time Menkaure was dying and/or his body was being prepared. This would include finishing the granite casing around the pyramid entrance and in the Mortuary Temple, and using mud brick to at least preliminarily complete the Valley Temple and Causeway. The remaining work which included completing the Mortuary Temple, Enclosure Wall, and work at the subsidiary pyramids needed for the long term cult rites and to give a final finished appearance to the complex could have been completed after the burial.

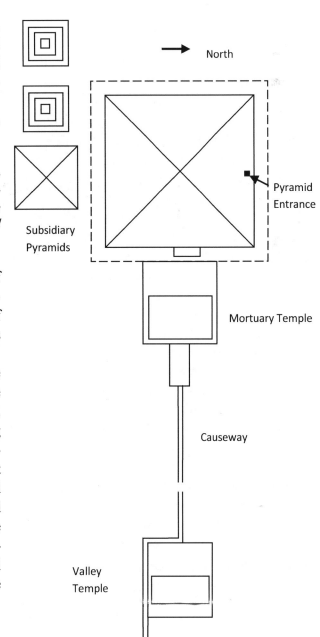

Shepseskaf ruled for only four years. During the time he was completing Menkaure's complex, Shepseskaf built his own tomb known today as the Mastaba Faraun. Although the superstructure of this tomb is in the form of a low mastaba and not a pyramid, it has an elaborate set of subterranean apartments lined with granite.[4] We wonder whether Shepseskaf, for all his apparent piety, diverted the granite blocks already intended for Menkaure's temples to his own tomb.

While Howard Vyse concentrated primarily on exploring the main pyramid interior, most of what we know about Menkaure's complex is as a result of George Reisner's excavations on behalf of Harvard University and the Boston Museum of Fine Arts. Having first excavated the mastabas to the west of the Great Pyramid, Reisner turned his attention to the Menkaure complex in December 1906. In the 1906 – 1907 season he cleared the Mortuary Temple and part of the quarry cemetery to the southeast. In the summer of 1908 he started work clearing the Valley Temple which he completed in the 1909 – 1910 season. During this season he also excavated the temple of GIII-a, the eastern subsidiary pyramid. After spending years working at other locations, in the summer of 1924 Reisner returned and completed his work with the clearing of the temples adjacent to GIII-b and GIII-c,[5] the two stepped subsidiary pyramids.

Mortuary Temple

The Mortuary Temple was started by Menkaure using limestone and granite blocks, finished by Shepseskaf with mud brick, and modified more than 200 years later during Dynasty VI by Merenre. To form a level surface, Menkaure's builders first laid a foundation of huge limestone blocks.[6] On top of the foundation they laid out the Temple walls with enormous limestone core blocks, which weighed up to 355 tons.[7] Since the core blocks were to be hidden behind a casing and since their large size was not needed to form a firm foundation, we again find this as evidence that the effort to cut these large blocks to more manageable dimensions was greater than the effort required to move the large blocks from the nearby quarry.

The original plan called for casing the limestone walls both inside and out with granite to match the pyramid casing. Some of this veneer can still be found today as it was set in place by the builders. In other places the space cut into the softer limestone core for the granite blocks is easily identifiable but the blocks themselves are long gone; removed during later periods and put to other uses. The granite temple casing was barely started at Menkaure's death. Since finishing the casing with granite blocks brought from Upper Egypt would have taken a long time, Shepseskaf instead cased the temple walls with mud bricks which were plastered and painted white.[8]

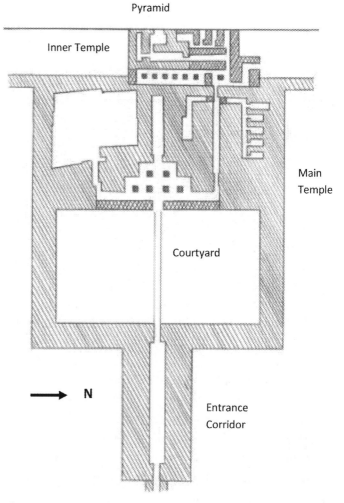

The Mortuary Temple as completed by Menkaure and Shepseskaf with still later changes identified by double crosshatch.

Mortuary Temple	Dimension[9]
Entrance Corridor	
Exterior	48' wide, 91' long
Interior	12' wide, 108' long
Exterior Dimension, Main Temple	177' north - south 185' east - west
Interior Dimension, Courtyard	143' north – south 78' east - west
Inner Temple (Adjacent to Pyramid)	77' north – south 36' east west

From the temple entrance through the Entrance Corridor. The remains of a thick mud brick casing is easily visible along the left side.

These walls covered and hid the granite blocks to provide a standard finish. While Reisner found some of these walls still rising to their original height approaching 10', after he uncovered the wall and exposed the mud brick to the elements, today they are at most 2' high. In some places the brick form is barely recognizable, in other places the bricks have been reduced to a layer of fine, dark silt covering the ground.

The Temple plan is not complicated. The Temple is entered from the Causeway through a long narrow Entrance Corridor which has no parallel in any previous Dynasty IV mortuary temple but became standard in later Dynasty V mortuary temples. At Menkaure's death some black granite facing blocks had been placed along the corridor, but Shepseskaf covered these and the corridor walls with a thick layer of plastered mud brick.

The Entrance Corridor opens to a large Courtyard formed of huge limestone blocks, three courses high. In some places the first course of granite facing blocks was placed, but none of the second course. Again, Shepseskaf covered the granite and limestone blocks with mud brick walls which he had decorated with alternating groups of two and three niches. The limestone paving blocks which form the courtyard floor are also attributed to Shepseskaf since they do not penetrate under the mud brick casing. The floor slopes slightly towards the Courtyard center where there are two holes to drain rainwater into the underlying foundation. A slightly raised walkway of yellowish limestone slabs crosses east – west through the Courtyard. At the Courtyard west end there are three exits. Originally, the three exits were accessed directly from the Courtyard, but late in the Old Kingdom, a mud brick wall was built across the Courtyard's western end, providing only one exit. The intent was likely to separate the area reserved for priestly attention to the rear of the Courtyard, from the secular space.

From the Courtyard looking back to the Entrance Corridor (left). The walkway of yellowish limestone slabs is at center. The Courtyard (right) with 18' high walls. Remains of the mud brick casing along the right (south) wall.

From near the pyramid looking at the unfinished space and beyond to the Courtyard (top left). The Portico and Offering Hall (bottom left) which was completely cased with granite. The North Corridor (top right) with entrance to the Inner Temple at the end. When Reisner uncovered this area, the mud brick went to the top of the stone walls and covered the granite blocks. The limestone wall was cut to accept the granite blocks which still have the protecting torus around the edges (bottom right).

To the Courtyard left (southwest) a short passage enters an area unfinished and undefined at Menkaure's death and not completed by Shepseskaf. In this space Reisner found two layers formed of rubble: one leading to the top of the first course of the north wall, the second layer to the top of the second course. These were apparently construction ramps used to raise blocks which formed the temple walls.

At the Courtyard center there is a recess which contained two rows of granite columns, forming a Portico, behind which was the Offering Room shaped as a long, wide hall. Menkaure completed the granite casing around the Portico and Offering Rooms but all of the blocks have since been removed by stone robbers. This Offering Room was built to house a significant object at its end, likely a statue of Menkaure, but all evidence of what stood at the end is missing. In the Portico Reisner found pieces of two steles. One, attributed to Shepseskaf, is quoted in the chapter introduction. The other stele dated to Dynasty VI King Merenre probably marked the Temple renovation.[10]

To the right (north) side is the long North Hall at the end of which a doorway passes through the Temple west wall and provides access to the Enclosure around the pyramid and to the Inner Temple against the pyramid face. This hall had several granite facing blocks in place when Menkaure died which Shepseskaf covered with a thick covering of mud bricks. Just before the doorway, short halls to both sides provided access to spaces which were initially defined only by their outlining limestone walls. In the northern space Shepseskaf built five small rooms and to the south he created a single room, all from mud bricks. Late in the Old Kingdom the halls leading to these side rooms were permanently bricked up and the rooms made inaccessible.

Immediately behind the Temple, against the pyramid and centered on its eastern face was a granite platform 24' square on which was probably a stele and altar. The pyramid casing above this platform was finely finished just as around the pyramid entrance. Originally the altar and stele stood in a fine limestone

Inner Temple. Shepseskaf finished the Inner Temple by adding several mud brick rooms. King Merenre removed what was left of the deteriorating mud brick and started rebuilding the space with crude limestone. Since the poor quality blocks were not worth the attention of the stone robbers, these rooms covered by a ceiling are still in place today. Reisner found construction platforms in five of the rooms indicating Merenre's did not complete the work. In a long, narrow, columned, sand filled room Reisner found 87 mummified bodies. Each was wrapped in cloth layers, a few were gilded or painted, some were in wooden coffins, others were wrapped in reed mats. The burials were dated by three small Roman coins, one of which was held in a hand, to between 50 and 150 AD. The bodies had been introduced through a break in the roof and covered by a deep layer of sand. In another room were the remains of a small campfire and some Arab coins dating to the 12th or 13th Century.[11]

An alter and stele stood in the Inner Temple against the finished pyramid face.(top) Merenre's addition to the right. Part of the granite floor remains. The finished pyramid casing is just out of the photo to the left (bottom), Merenre's spaces to the rear and the columned narrow space to the right where Reisner found mummified bodies.

Mortuary Temple After Dynasty IV

Through careful excavation, Reisner was able to identify not only the original Mortuary Temple plan but also to describe its subsequent reuse and decay. He derived important information from the stratigraphy (or layering) of the debris and an understanding of the way in which archaeological structures were affected by both human and physical agents of destruction.

Except in true sandstorms, wind will lift sand only a few inches above the surface. If the surface level remains constant for a long period, the continued scouring action of the windblown sand will eat into the limestone blocks and form an erosion band only slightly above ground level which can be used to estimate the surface level. Multiple erosion bands on the same rock face identify changes in ground level.

In the Mortuary Temple, Reisner identified three distinct horizontal erosion bands on the three courses which enclose the Courtyard. Reisner suggested the highest band was created when the Temple was nearly full of wind-blown sand leaving only the uppermost course of blocks exposed. At some unknown time several blocks were removed from the top course forming an opening which allowed the sand to be blown out to a lower level where it remained for an extended period forming the middle erosion band. Later removal of more blocks drained more sand and produced the lower erosion band.[12]

Combining these observations with the depth of mud layers, the location and dates of recovered artifacts, and construction details, Reisner was able to put together the following scenario:

- Menkaure built the Temple foundation upon which he constructed most of the Temple core walls; completed the granite casing and pillars in the Portico and Offering Room; and placed some granite casing blocks in the Entrance Corridor, Courtyard, and the North Hall.

- With the temple still under construction at Menkaure's death, Shepseskaf completed the Inner Temple partially with Tura limestone, then giving up the limestone, used the easier to work with mud brick to finish the rest of the Inner Temple. He added a mud brick casing in the Entrance Corridor, Courtyard, North Hall, and around the exterior, and in the process covered the existing granite casing blocks. He also added a stone pave-

From the back of the Offering Hall, a deep erosion band formed along the left wall when sand partially filled the temple.

ment in the Courtyard, mud brick dividing walls in a space at the Temple's north west corner forming five niches or storerooms, and added at least a partial mud brick Enclosure Wall around the Pyramid.

- During Dynasties V and VI the mud bricks walls began to decay, the storage rooms were plundered and some statues were shattered. Merenre in Dynasty VI replaced the mud brick rooms in the Inner Temple with rooms of crude limestone blocks.

- After the Old Kingdom, the Temple was abandoned, rain further dissolved the mud brick, and the roofs, probably wood, collapsed. The granite casing from the entrance corridor, courtyard, and offering room and the granite columns in the portico were removed, perhaps during the reign of Ramesses II.

- Drift sand filled the Temple. During the first or second century AD, the local Roman population used one of the rooms in the Inner Temple for burials.

- From the 11th through 13th Century AD, likely as part of the same operation which removed the pyramid casing, Arab stone robbers removed the fine limestone walls and part of the granite floor from the Inner Temple. During this same period, treasure seekers dug five large holes in the temple floor. These last operations caused the greatest destruction to the site.

With not much of value left, the Temple remained untouched by man but suffered the natural decay from wind and weather.[13]

Boat Pits

Khufu and Khafre each had five boat pits and Djedefre had one, so we expect Menkaure at least planned to have boat pits. In 1971 – 1972 Abdel-Aziz Saleh searched for the pits to the north of the Mortuary Temple. He cleared debris down to the large foundation blocks and found the joints between the foundation blocks filled with mortar. Since this mortar would provide little cohesive power to the multi-ton blocks, he thought the purpose would be to provide some protection to a space below. Additionally he found four illustrations on blocks of divine boats. He could not ignore this evidence and he removed foundation blocks in search of the boat pits but did not find any. He also searched to the south and west of the subsidiary pyramids without success.[14] Possibly the boat pits were planned, but their excavation had not started at the time of Menkaure's death.

Enclosure Wall

Menkaure's intention was probably to build a high stone wall surrounding his pyramid and to pave the resulting interior courtyard with limestone. Since this wall would have cut-off access to the pyramid which was still under construction, the Enclosure Wall would have been built last. Reisner found scant remains of a brick enclosure wall about 33' from the pyramid, probably built by Shepseskaf as an extension of the Mortuary Temple's west side. Likely this wall surrounded the pyramid, but no remains have been identified on the other three sides, and there is no evidence the courtyard was ever paved.

As with the other two Giza pyramid complexes, an outer boundary wall constructed of rubble, large chips, and mud mortar surrounds and encloses Menkaure's whole complex. This wall connects to a similar wall which surrounds Khafre's complex and is probably a later construction which identified each king's precinct.

Western Field

The Outer Boundary Wall forms the east side of a 523' (E-W) by 800' (N-S)[15] rectangular field to the west of Menkaure's pyramid. The field is defined by the low remains of a wall which on the north side is aligned with the Outer Enclosure Wall. While there are breaks in the Western Field wall, none are obviously entrances and a modern road has destroyed part of the wall. The area is relatively flat and there are no indications of demolished buildings. No excavation has occurred to determine the purpose or date of this field. However, if we assign Menkaure's outer boundary wall to a period later then Menkaure, the Western Field must also be so assigned. Excavation is required to determine what was being enclosed.

The Western Field forms a backward "E" to the west of the pyramid. (Image: DigitalGlobe and Apollo Mapping Copyright 2014)

Causeway

The Causeway is oriented along a direct east-west line connecting the two temples. From the Mortuary Temple, the Causeway foundation is visible on the surface for only 800 feet. Beyond that point, a gully carrying rainwater down the Plateau from near Khafre's pyramid had washed out the Causeway.[16] Whether there is a transit passage under the Causeway as in the case of Khufu's and Khafre's Causeways cannot be determined due to the engulfing sand. The Causeway does not connect directly to the Valley Temple interior, as in Khafre's Valley Temple. Instead the Causeway turns and runs along the Valley Temple south side, similar to the way Snefru's Causeway passed to the south of his valley temple, and provides two access points to the Valley Temple interior along this side. The Causeway continues past (to the east) the Valley Temple but a modern Moslem cemetery prevents excavation to determine how the Causeway terminates.

Menkaure completed the Causeway foundation of large limestone blocks on which Shepseskaf built the 7' thick Causeway mud brick walls. The walls were vertical on the inside and battered on the outside; both surfaces were plastered and whitewashed.

Nothing remains of the Causeway but the base. Reisner knew the Valley Temple was someplace in the distance.

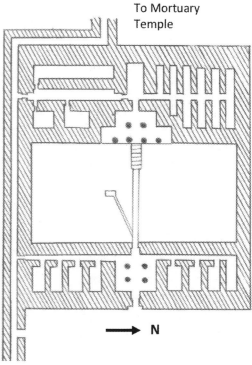

To Mortuary Temple

→ N

The gray smudge at bottom center is all that is visible of the Valley Temple. The Moslem Cemetery at the bottom. Khentkawes' tomb is to the immediate rear.

Reisner suggested that the Causeway interior passage, itself 5' wide, was roofed with wooden beams, but Maragioglio and Rinaldi believed that a barrel-shaped brick vault was more likely given the length of the Causeway and scarcity of wood in Egypt. They note that at Shepseskaf's own tomb, remains of a brick vault were found over his causeway.[17]

The Valley Temple as finished by Shepseskaf. The Causeway ran from a canal or harbor at the bottom left (east) around the Temple, than towards the Mortuary Temple at the top (west). There were three access points between the Causeway and Temple. Reisner found the slate triads in the passage inside the Temple southwest entrance. A modern Moslem cemetery prevented further excavation to the east.

Valley Temple

After the Old Kingdom, all trace of Menkaure's Valley Temple disappeared beneath the blowing sand. Before Reisner could excavate it, he first had to find the temple. By analogy with other Old Kingdom pyramid complexes, he expected to find the temple at the end of the Causeway

Valley Temple	Dimension[19]
Exterior Dimensions	161' north - south, 172' east - west
Interior Courtyard Dimensions	134' north – south, 49' east - west

close to the flood plain. However, most of the Causeway was also hidden under the sand. Reisner reasoned that the Causeway might continue straight east from the Mortuary Temple, so he had a series of posts set in a straight line to identify the Causeway's probable path. One after the other he had five trenches dug at right angles across this line. As expected, in the first four he found remains of the Causeway foundation confirming his thesis that the Causeways ran straight east. Finally in the fifth trench he uncovered the decayed remains of a mud brick building 11' below the surface. Working backwards between the last two trenches he discovered the end of the Causeway and the mud brick walls marking the Valley Temple, 1,994' east of the Mortuary Temple.[18]

Menkaure's plan was to build a large stone temple. The Valley Temple was apparently started after the Mortuary Temple, and was in an earlier stage of construction when Menkaure died and the initial intent abandoned. Only the foundation, formed of the same types of large limestone blocks used in the Mortuary Temple, was complete and some limestone wall blocks were laid for the north and south walls. Shepseskaf was not faced with casing an already partially completed temple, but with building almost the whole temple. As with other parts of the complex, Shepseskaf built the temple of mud bricks,

Statues Found by Reisner[25]				
Location	Quantity	Size	Material	Subject
Mortuary Temple	1	Over Life Size	Alabaster	Menkaure
	1	2/3 Life Size	Alabaster,	Seated Menkaure
	5	Fragments	Slate, Alabaster, Copper	Too small to determine
Valley Temple	5	Small to Minute	Slate, Alabaster, Copper	Various
	8 (5 intact)	2/5 Life Size	Slate (7), Alabaster (1)	Triads, most include Hathor and a nome god
	1 (intact)	Life Size	Slate	Dyad with woman, possibly Queen Khamerernebty
	6	Life Size	Alabaster	Menkaure
	1	Life Size	Alabaster	Queen
	1 (intact)	Life Size	Alabaster	Young man
	28 (13 intact)	4" to 24"	Diorite(14), limestone(3), granite (2), alabaster(2), reddish stone(2), ivory, wood, copper, slate, porphyry	Various

the walls were plastered and whitewashed, and the floor constructed of stone chips covered with mud rather than some higher quality paving.

In front of the Temple was a terrace beyond which was likely either a canal or harbor. The original entrance on the east face led to a vestibule that was flanked on north and south by four storage rooms. In the Vestibule Reisner found the alabaster bases of four round wooden columns.[20] To the west, the vestibule opened to a large open courtyard similar to the Mortuary Temple courtyard in that a paved east – west walkway ran across its floor and niches lined the walls. A channel crossed the court veering from the entrance end of the walkway slightly south to end in a basin sunk in the courtyard floor.

To the rear (west side) of the courtyard, a ramp led up to a columned portico which provided access to an offering room similar in layout to the same parts of the Mortuary Temple. The offering room was flanked by storage rooms. And as in the Mortuary Temple, in the Valley Temple during a later period, a mud brick wall was built across the face of the portico.

Reisner traced the temple's phases after Menkaure was buried.

- The Pyramid City which housed the people attending to the temple rites was initially east of the Valley Temple. It later encroached on the Temple proper and homes and silos were built within the courtyard.
- At some point during the Old Kingdom, possibly as late as Dynasty VI, flood waters broke through the Valley Temple mud brick western side and destroyed much of the temple interior.[21]
- As an inducement to continue temple services, pyramid city inhabitants were given privileges, like exemption from taxes. Possibly the desire to maintain these privileges provided some impetus for the people of Menkaure's Pyramid City to rebuilt the Temple and continue the rites.

Three of the four triads (top) in the Cairo Museum. All have Menkaure in center, Hathor on his right, and a nome god to his left. The nome gods from left to right are from Thebes, Diospolis Parva, and Cynopolis. The forth (not shown) has Hathor seated in the center with Menkaure on her right and the nome god of Hermopolis to her left. The dyad(right) has the headdress, hair, and kilt details unfinished.

- The Temple was rebuilt. Reisner found a badly preserved decree from the 50th year of Pepi II's reign, 280 years after Menkaure's death, which possibly renewed these privileges.
- With the end of the Old Kingdom at the end of Pepi II's reign, the privileges ceased to exist. With the incentives gone, Menkaure's cult disappeared and his Pyramid City and Valley Temple were abandoned. The ruined temple was soon covered with sand and forgotten.[22]

The abandoned Temple lay undisturbed and well preserved beneath the sand for 4,000 years until Reisner found and cleared the it. After Reisner finished his work, drifting sand again covered the Temple and the Causeway. Today nothing remains to mark the Valley Temple location but a grayish discoloration of the sand caused by disintegrated mud brick.

Temple Statuary

Since both of Menkaure's temples and his Causeway were finished with plastered mud brick instead of granite and limestone, there was little hard wall surface on which to inscribe permanent reliefs. While Reisner did not find inscriptions, he did uncovered pieces of 51 royal statues, either intact or in fragments, many more than attributed to any earlier king.

The most remarkable find occurred in the Valley Temple southern magazine corridor: five slate triads (four of which were intact) all finely carved. The members of each triad are clearly identified by inscriptions on the base. The original number of these triads is unknown, but there may have been as

GIII-a, GIII-b, and GIII-c. The main pyramid is just out of the picture at left.

many as forty-two, one for each of the Upper and Lower Egyptian nomes. Or there may have been as few as eight triads, one for each of the eight rooms flanking the entrance vestibule, representing only those nomes where Hathor had a special cult that enjoyed royal patronage. In these five surviving triads Menkaure wears only the crown of Upper Egypt; there may have been others in which he wore the Lower Egypt crown. [23]

In the same corridor in which Reisner found the triads, he also discovered a slate dyad of Menkaure and a woman. While both figures are complete, the detailed pleats in the King's kilt and headdress and the folds of the woman's hair were not cut, and there is no inscription on the base naming the pair. The woman is of equal stature to Menkaure with one of her arms around his waist and the other holding the King's arm. The identity of this woman is open to discussion. The queen's status in the Old Kingdom was not comparable to the rank of the king, and there are no other statues in which a female figure, assumed to be the queen, is shown at a scale equal to that of the king. If the woman is Hathor, the horns and sun disk which identifies this goddess are missing. These conditions might seem to eliminate both Menkaure's wife and Hathor. However, we notice that the face, hair, and torso carved for Hathor in the triads and this woman in the dyad are essentially the same person. This could lead to a conclusion that the dyad is the royal couple in which the woman is Menkaure's wife Khamerernebty, who as the goddess Hathor, is given equal status to the King. This style of representing a couple, with the wife at a normal size and affectionately touching her husband, became popular for statues of private persons in Dynasty V and VI

From these statue remnants, we may conclude that there was a great variety of statues in both of Menkaure's temples and likely the other Giza temples. Some statues were broken and reworked into small votive vessels or figures; many were destroyed by vandals during the First Intermediate Period. These few remaining pieces were hidden and protected by the sand which engulfed the Valley Temple.

Subsidiary Pyramids

There are three small pyramids located in an east-west row to the south of the main pyramid. Reisner designated these from the east as GIII-a, GIII-b, and GIII-c. As with Khufu's subsidiary pyramids, Menkaure's are also outside the main pyramid Enclosure Wall, physically separating them and their function from the primary burial. However, Reisner found a rubble wall enclosure which surrounded the subsidiary pyramids and a pathway leading from the enclosure northeast corner for several feet towards the northeast. He assumed this pathway connected to the main pyramid Enclosure Wall.[24]

While GIII-b and GIII-c have a stepped appearance, GIII-a is a true pyramid. But since the main pyramid has a stepped core, GIII-a probably does also. There are no indications that the steps of GIII-b and c were once filled in to form true pyramids. The distance at the base between the sloped side of GIII-a and the stepped side of GIII-b is 33' and between the stepped sides of GIII-b and GIII-c is 45'.[26]

The mortuary temples fill virtually this entire space leaving no room to complete the inclined sides of the pyramids. While the final form of both GIII-b and GIII-c are stepped pyramids, they were not necessarily designed from the outset to be stepped pyramids, but were more likely planned to be true pyramids with stepped cores. This is based on:

- It would have been 100 years since the last stepped pyramid; their re-introduction would have been unlikely.
- The final pyramids, in either stepped or true from, would have been cased yet there is no casing foundation around the two stepped pyramids.
- The temples were likely not intended to be placed on the pyramid east side of GIII-b and GIII-c since the view of the rising sun would be blocked by the bulk of the pyramid immediately to the east.
- If the temples were not located on the east face, there is enough space to complete both GIII-b and GIII-c as true pyramids

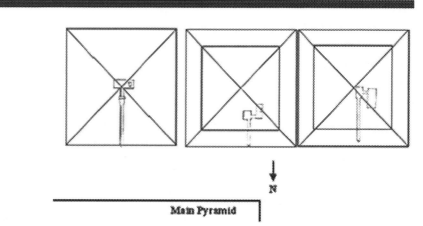

The three subsidiary pyramids as finished by Shepseskaf and their relationship to the main pyramid (top). Each pyramid has a mudbrick temple on the east side. However, there was enough room to finish the two step pyramids as true pyramids of equal size to GIII-a (bottom).

We will see later that the temples were built of mud brick. The original intent may have been to place the temples on the subsidiary pyramid north or south sides where the rising sun would be visible. Possibly these areas were not prepared at Menkaure's death and the most expeditious placement may have been on the east side.

Based on their degree of completeness, the three pyramids were likely started in order beginning with GIII-a and moving west to GIII-b and GIII-c. Possibly the original plan called for three standard pyramids but when Menkaure died only one pyramid was complete and the other two had only their inner stepped core built. Shepseskaf was likely faced with accommodating partially completed subsidiary pyramids into an acceptable final complex and he was forced to deviate from Menkaure's original plan.[27]

Subsidiary Pyramid GIII-a

At the pyramid base on the north, east, and south sides are the remains of one course of granite casing blocks. The blocks on the north and south still have rough faces, while to the east near the temple the granite faces are finished. On the north side near the entrance, two courses of finished limestone casing sit in-situ above the granite casing provides evidence that the granite casing was limited to one course.

Subsidiary Pyramids[28]	GIII-a (Eastern)	GIII-b (Center)	GIII-c (Western)
Estimated Height	93'3"	69'6"	69'6"
Face Angle	52°15'	4 Steps	4 steps
Base	145'8" (85 cubits)	102'6" (60 cubits)	102'6" (60 cubits)
Volume (cubic feet)	660,000	250,000	250,000
Descending Passage Length (at floor) Dimension Angle	56'9" 41" wide, 50" high 27°12'	36'5" 39' wide, 42" high 27°	60'4" (floor) 38" wide, 47" high 30°
Ante Chamber	None	10'3" wide, 13'8" long, 8'7" high	8'7" wide, 13'8" long, 7'6" high
Burial Chamber	10'5" wide 25'2" long 8'9" high	8'9" wide 19'2" long 10'4" high	11'4" wide 26'0" long 7'1" to 9'6" high
Sarcophagus (outside)	39" wide, 37" high, 96" long	31" wide, 31" high. 80" long	None

Vyse discovered the pyramid entrance at ground level in the center of its north face on June 30, 1837. The Descending Passage has limestone sides and was filled with limestone plug blocks. Rather than remove the plugs, robbers cut a narrow tunnel through the west side of the plug blocks. At the bottom in a high ceiling room cut entirely in the bedrock, he found a *"corroded"* granite portcullis in the lowered position. Thieves did not break the hard portcullis, but instead cut an access hole above it in the softer limestone bedrock. From here a short passage leads to the burial chamber which Vyse found almost full of rubble, nearly reaching the ceiling at the eastern end. The source of this rubble behind a closed portcullis is not obvious. The burial chamber is a long east-west room with plastered walls cut into the bedrock. In the chamber west end, Vyse found a granite sarcophagus embedded in the floor; the lid, as Vyse wrote, was *"forced off with great violence."* The pavement around the sarcophagus had been removed. On the south wall he found a chapter from the Koran scrawled in Arabic. Because the narrow robber's tunnel in the descending passage provided minimal ventilation, the air in the lower chambers quickly fouled and candles would not burn. As a result, Vyse did not completely clear the burial chamber.[29]

A mortuary temple, large by subsidiary pyramid standards, measuring 67' by 80', was built against the pyramid east face. The temple consists of mud brick walls built on a platform of limestone blocks. This indicates the temple was laid out during Menkaure reign but completed after his death by Shepseskaf. During excavation of the chapel, Reisner found alabaster fragments which once formed the statue of an unnamed queen and five alabaster offering cups inscribed with "king's son, Kay." Reisner believes the cups were a later offering by a pious descendant of the pyramid owner based on the way the cups were placed in the temple. The chapel showed signs of modifications, possibly as late as Dynasty VI, suggesting that

The east side of GIII-a. The mud brick temple remains are on the left. The pair statue (see later this section) is at the arrow at bottom right.

199

The GIII-a entrance, filled with small rocks, is below the large architrave which spans the passage ceiling. To the bottom right is one course of granite casing blocks with bosses still in place, above which are two courses of finished limestone casing.

mortuary rituals were performed there for a long period of time. While there is no direct evidence of the pyramid owner, Reisner believed that it belonged to Menkaure's chief wife, Queen Khamerernebty II.[30]

Looking down the 50" high entrance passage. Robbers cut away part of the plug blocks, on the left, to gain entrance to the pyramid interior

In 1996, workmen from the Inspectorate of Antiquities at Giza, while clearing around GIII-a, discovered an unfinished pair statue at the northeast corner of the pyramid foundation. The statue was carved from a large piece of red granite taken from the pyramid casing and depicts two males standing side-by-side with their hands touching. The left-hand figure wears a kilt, nemes headdress with uraeus, a royal beard, and a sun disk on his head. The figure on the right also has a sun disk on his head, a long wig, a uraeus and a long beard. While there are no identifying inscriptions, based on style, proportions of the subjects, and similarities to other pair statues, Zahi Hawass believes they represent Ramesses II and a solar deity, most likely Re-Atum, god of Heliopolis.[31] The stone block is cracked across the pair at waist-level. Since the statue top and bottom parts are aligned, likely the crack occurred during the carving and the statue was abandonment on the site where it was being roughed out.

Subsidiary Pyramid GIII-b

The exterior of the center subsidiary pyramid, features large, well squared blocks which are closely fitted and laid in regular courses. Vyse cut a horizon-

Looking down on the pair statue which is 11'1" high, 5'1" across, 1'10" thick, weighs 3.5 tons.

tal passage completely through the pyramid at base level in search of hidden chambers.[32] While he did not find any, this excavation provides a view of the construction. Internally, the core blocks are smaller and only roughly squared; the wide spaces between them are filled by mortar and limestone chips.

Vyse found the pyramid entrance, only three days after opening GIII-a, not on the pyramid north face but in the bedrock 13' north of the face and 12' west of the pyramid north-south center line. The whole substructure was cut into the bedrock under the pyramid north-west quadrant. The oddly located entrance and substructure led Vyse to search for a second entrance and additional passages and chambers, but he found none.

Vyse found the descending passage filled only with rubble but believed it once contained plug blocks. The interior is significantly different from GIII-a but similar in plan to the two chambered "L" shaped interior of Khufu's subsidiary pyramids. But in GIII-b the space holding the two chambers was excavated in the bedrock creating an open pit, then the chambers were built with blocks within the pit. The descending passage opens directly into a large antechamber which was unlined but coated with white stucco. From here a short passage descends at a shallow angle to the burial chamber.

The north face of GIII-b. The entrance is under the sand.

Midway down the passage Vyse found a granite portcullis forced out of place. This passage provided access to the burial chamber, oriented with its long axis north – south. The burial chamber was completely lined - walls, floor, and ceiling - with limestone blocks. Near the chamber western side, Vyse found a small plain granite sarcophagus with the lid off, and nearby a large quantity of decayed wood which had turned to dust. Inside the sarcophagus he found the bones of a young woman. Whether this was what remained of the original tomb owner or an intrusive burial is unknown. In the antechamber Vyse found two hieroglyphics which read *"giver of life"*, a statement which usually follows a cartouche. More importantly, in the burial chamber he found hieroglyphics in red paint, likely quarry marks, which contained Menkaure's cartouche.[33] The marks are thought to be the name of a work gang which translates somewhat literally *"Menkaure is drunk."*[34] This was the first evidence that the whole pyramid complex belonged to Menkaure.

The temple along the east face was built of mud brick. Reisner found the temple was built on the beginning of a base of large limestone blocks. Because of the minimal space available for the temple, it is entered from the north rather than the typical eastern entrance.

Subsidiary Pyramid GIII-c

The western most of the three subsidiary pyramids, is in the most ruined condition. While Perring's drawings show part of the top step was intact in 1837,[35] today the top step has disappeared. Vyse spent 18 days removing stones from the north face before he found the entrance in the bedrock 14' north of the face and 6' west of the pyramid north-south center line.

The layout of the GIII-c interior is very similar to GIII-b. Again the whole interior is located under the pyramid north-west quadrant. The descending passage leads to an antechamber from which a short level passage leads to the burial chamber. But unlike GIII-b, instead of the chambers being

The ruined GIII-c pyramid. The north face is to the right.

201

constructed in a pit, they were cut individually into the bedrock. Also GIII-c has no portcullis and no sarcophagus.

Vyse found the descending passage had not been plugged and excavation of the burial chamber was not complete. About half the burial chamber north end remains uncut, forming a platform 2 ½' high. He compared the state of this unfinished chamber to the Great Pyramid unfinished Subterranean Chamber. Additionally, chisel marks were readily apparent on the unplastered walls; construction lines were marked on the burial chamber ceiling, over the chamber entrance, and on the connecting passage walls; and the chambers contained round stones that were apparently used as hammers.[36]

The temple was not built on a base of laid limestone blocks; rather mud brick walls were placed directly in trenches cut into the bedrock. While the unfinished interior raises questions about whether the pyramid was used for an Old Kingdom burial, the temple was complete and the temple walls were replastered many times[37] indicating some use was made of this subsidiary pyramid complex.

It is difficult to determine who was buried in these three pyramids. Menkaure's wife, Khamerernebty II who appears with Menkaure on the statues found in the Valley Temple was probably placed in one, likely GIII-a. The presence of the sarcophagus in GIII-b provides evidence of a burial, judging by its size, a small woman. While GIII-c was not complete, the temple was used which indicates a burial did occur.

Industrial Settlement

Continued exploration at Giza proves that the sand and rubble still conceal many secrets. In 1971-2, archaeologists from the University of Cairo directed by Abdel-Aziz Saleh found the remains of buildings belonging to an Old Kingdom settlement in the depression south of Menkaure's Causeway. The buildings did not seem to be grouped into a compact, planned village. Instead they flanked both sides of an enormous 9 ½' wide foundation wall or embankment running for 678' in a north-south line, with shorter arms extending to the west at both ends. The wall was built of chunks of limestone mortared together with clay. Dating of the settlement to the Old Kingdom was based primarily on potsherds found in debris that are characteristic of this period and a Carbon-14 date, on ashes and charcoal from the last fires in an oven, of 2660 BCE ± 150.

Fifteen buildings of different sizes and styles were spread over an area of three acres, and Saleh believed that further excavation would reveal more buildings. Like the embankment, the buildings were made of random rubble set in mortar. Inside walls were plastered white, but the excavators found pieces of crimson plaster and patches of red, grey and black paint. Several were finished with plastered walls retaining traces of painted horizontal bands. Floors were gravel and topped with clay; a few were paved with a smooth white stone, possibly alabaster. In one of these buildings, the bases of two pillars were found which suggests a high roof, possibly over an administrative center. A few of the buildings may have been temporary homes, since they contain a single room with raised platforms that likely served as beds. However, the usual household debris were absent from the buildings.

Menkaure's pyramid and temple at top left with the Causeway extending to the right. The Industrial Settlement is along the wall at right. The main quarry is in the center. North is to the top. (Image: DigitalGlobe and Apollo Mapping Copyright 2014)

Traces of recesses for water or storage jars were found in some buildings along with a large number of unroofed, barrel-like ovens. Saleh concluded that while some people may have actually lived here, the primary purpose was for some essential industrial activity. Possibly, based on a location near to the Menkaure Mortuary Temple, the settlement was devoted to providing food offerings for that Temple.[38]

1. Clayton, *Chronicle of the Pharaohs, p 56.*
2. Reisner, *The Temples of the Third Pyramid at Giza.,* pp 15,31,278, plate 19b.
3. The cattle count was usually every two years. Depending on when the cattle count fell, the year after would be either year 2 or 3 of Shepseskaf's reign.
4. Maragioglio and Rinaldi, *L'Architettura Delle Piramidi Menfite, Parte VI*, p 140. Except for a few secondary rooms, all the walls and ceilings were made of granite.
5. Reisner, *History of the Giza Necropolis, Volume I*, p 24. Oddly the listing of excavations in his 1931 book on Menkaure is slightly different. Since he included a more detailed Giza excavation list in the 1942 reference cited, we used that list. We should note that Reisner gives credit to multiple people for leading individual parts of the excavations.
6. Reisner, *The Temples of the Third Pyramid at Giza,.* p 25. Except where otherwise indicated, reconstructions of the temples described in this chapter are based on the work of Reisner.
7. Maragioglio and Rinaldi, *L'Architettura Delle Piramidi Menfite, Parte VI*, p 50. The largest block is identified as 130 cubic meters. This is equivalent to 4,587 cubic feet and at 155 pounds per cubic foot equals 355 tons. These blocks were moved only a few hundred feet from the local quarry.
8. The walls were first coated with a mud plaster, then with a layer of finer gypsum plaster, the final whitewash was also made from gypsum.
9. Maragioglio and Rinaldi, *op. cit.,* TAV 9.
10. Reisner, *op. cit.,* pp 15, 31, 280.
11. Reisner, op. cit., pp 19-20.
12. Reisner, *op. cit.* pp 8-9, 33.
13. Reisner, op. cit., pp 29-33.
14. Saleh, "Excavations Around Mycerinus Pyramid Complex", *MDAIK* 30 1974, pp 153-154. Saleh notes that Vyse and Petrie (possibly he means Perring) searched to the north of the subsidiary pyramids and Reisner to the east, so he (Saleh) searched to the south and west. He made some clearings and dug some trenches but apparently this work was preliminary since he says future work is required to define the results.
15. Maragioglio and Rinaldi, *op. cit.,* p 78.
16. Reisner, *op. cit.*, p 34.
17. Maragioglio and Rinaldi, *op. cit.,* pp64, 120, 150.
18. Reisner, *op. cit.*, pp 34-35.
19. Maragioglio and Rinaldi, *op. cit.,* TAV 10.
20. Reisner, *op. cit.*, p 40.
21. Though likely some minimal provision under the Causeway was made for drainage, the Causeway and Valley Temple rerouted the flow of water down the Plateau.
22. Reisner, *op. cit.* pp 39-50, 280-281.
23. Woods, "A reconstruction of the triads of King Mycerinus," *JEA* 60:82-93, 1974.
24. Reisner, op. cit., pp 56-58, Plate 74, Plan IV.
25. Hawass, *The Funerary Establishments of Khufu, Khafra, and Menkaure During the Old Kingdom* Vol II, pp 757 – 768. Hawass provides a summary of Reisner's detail list provided in op. cit., pp 108-115.
26. Maragioglio and Rinaldi, *op. cit.,* TAV 11
27. We note that this is the only example of pyramids in an east – west line.
28. Maragioglio and Rinaldi, *op. cit.,* TAV 12, 13, 14.
29. Vyse *Operations Carried on at the Pyramids of Gizeh in 1837*, Vol II, pp 38-45. He identifies the material found in the sarcophagus as pieces of burnt reed, charcoal, earthenware with a green glaze, and pieces of red pottery.
30. Reisner, *op. cit.*, pp 55-62.
31. Hawass, "The Discovery of a Pair-Statue near the Pyramid of Menkaure at Giza," *MDAIK*, 53:289-293. 1997
32. Vyse, *op. cit.*, Vol II, p 11. When I entered the passage in 1995, I found it free of debris and high enough to walk through upright. The entrance was later closed by a metal gate.
33. Vyse, *op. cit.,* Vol II, pp. 46-49.

34. Hawass, op. cit., p 271.

35. Perring, *Pyramids of Gizeh From Actual Survey and Admeasurements,* Part II, Menkaure Plate IX.

36. Vyse, *op. cit.*, pp 66-67.

37. Reisner, op cit., pp66-68.

38. Saleh, op. cit. pp131-142.

Appendix: The Tuthmosis IV Stele Between the Sphinx Paws

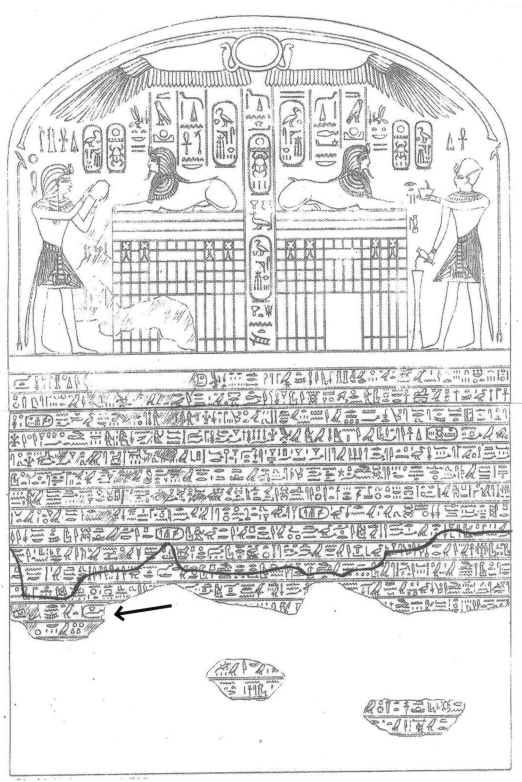

The Stele as drawn by H. Salt about 1818. The partial Khafre cartouche is at the arrow. The stele has continued to erode. In May 2002 all of the hieroglyphics below the line, including Khafre's cartouche, had disappeared.

Translated Stelle Text

Regnal year 1, month 3 of the Inundation, day 9 under the Majesty of Horus, "Mighty bull, perfect-of-diadems", Two Ladies, "Stable in kingship like Atum", "Golden Horus", the strong of might, who fends off the Nine Bows", king of Upper and Lower Egypt, Menkheperure', son of Re', Tuthmosis, gleaming-of-diadems, beloved of Harmachis, given life, stability and dominion like Re', forever.

(Long) live the good god, the son of Atum protector of Harakhty, the living image of the lord of all, a sovereign created by Re', potent heir of Khepery beautiful of countenance like his father, who came forth perfect equipped with his Horus form as his firstborn, king of Upper and Lower Egypt, beloved of the gods, possessor of graciousness among the Ennead, who purifies Heliopolis and propitiates Re', who rehabilitates the temple of Ptah, who offers (the image of) Ma'et to Atum and presents her to the one South of his Wall, who erects monuments as a daily offering to Horus who made all that exists, who seeks out things of benefit for the gods of Upper and Lower Egypt who builds their temples of limestone and renews their offering loaves, the son of Atum of his body, Tuthmosis, gleaming-of-diadems, like Re', heir of Horus upon his throne, Menkheperure', given life.

Now his Majesty was a royal child like the child Horus on Chemmis, his beauty being like the protector of his father- Men regarded him as they did the god himself, one for the love of whom the army rejoiced, whilst all the royal children and officials were under the sway of his might and subject to his youthful vigor when he underwent his rebirth, his strength being like that of the son of Nut.

It was in the desert of Memphite nome on its southern and northern side that he would pursue his leisure taking recreation, shooting at a target of copper and hunting lions and game whilst traveling on his chariot, his horses being fleeter than the wind, together with one of his retainers, without any man being aware of it.

Now the time came for granting rest to his attendant near to the outstanding monument of Harmchis which is near to (the cult place) of Sokar in Rosetau, to Renenutet in Ta-Mut in the pyramid plateau, to Mut, the lady of the northern wall and the southern wall, to Sekhmet, pre-eminent in the desert, Seth, the oldest magician of the hallowed place of the first time in the neighbourhood of the lord of Kher'aha, and of the sacred way of the gods of the horizon west of Heliopolis.

Now the image of Khepery, the most great, rested in this place, the great of power and holy in awe, the shade of Re having alighted on it. The estates of Memphis and every town which is near to it come to him, their arms (raised) in adoration before him, bearing a large pile of offerings for his ka.

One of these days it so happened that the king's son, Tuthmosis, came along in order to travel around at the time of midday. He sat down in the shadow of this great god and sleep took him at the moment when the sun was at its zenith. He found the Majesty of this august god speaking with his own mouth as a father speaks to his son saying, "Look at me, regard me, my son, Tuthmosis, I am your father, Harmachis-Re-Atum who has given you kingship upon earth at the head of the living. You shall wear the White Crown and the Red Crown on the throne of Geb, the prince. You own the land in its length and breadth, (all) that which the Eye of the Lord of All illumines, the sustenance from within the earth is in your keeping and the abundant tribute of all foreign lands and a lifetime consisting of a great span of years."

"My face is turned towards you, even my heart (also). You are mine. See my condition resembles that of someone in extremity for every limb of mine is dismembered. The desert sand on which I am is

encroaching on me (yet) I have waited in order to let you do that which is in my heart for I know that you are my son and my protector. Come nearer; see, I am with you.' I am your guide!" (Thus) be brought his words to end.

Thereupon this king's son stared astonished when he heard these words.................he understood the words of this god, but he put silence in his heart, saying: Come, let us go to our house in the city that we may set aside offerings for this god and that we may bring to him oxen, herbage, and all (kinds of) plants, and that we may give praise to those who were aforetime.................. the august goddess........... Khafre, the perfect one whom Atum and Re-Harakhty created, Re'Harmachis.......... ....at the festivals of...............all.........being numerous.......................for my Majesty for causing to live who..................... for Khepery in the western horizon of Heliopolis in........................(the rest has broken away.) [2]

---

1. Vyse, Pyramids of Gizeh, Plate B.
2. Cumming, *Egyptian Historical Records of the Later Eighteenth Dynasty*, pp 248-250. Other translations differ in the choice of words and phraseology, but the story remains the same.

Photo Credits

All photos, drawings, and tables are the author's except as identified below.

Apollo Mapping and DigitalGlobe (Copyright 2014), Pages 11,13,25,105,112,134,161,193 top, 202

John and Morton Edgar, *The Great Pyramid Passages and Chambers*, Glasgow 1910, Pages 42 top left, 43 center right, 53 left, 62 top, 63 top left/right and bottom, 64 top left/right, 65 right, 72 right, 98 top, 100 left

W. M. Flinders Petrie, *Pyramids and Temples of Gizeh*, London, 1883, Page 36

Howard Vyse, *Operations Carried Out at the Pyramids of Gizeh in 1837 Vol 1, II, III*, London, 1840, Pages 35 top left, 154, 173, 175 bottom, 183 top left and bottom, 184 top right, 205

Description de L'EGYPTE, Paris, MDCCCXXIII (1823), Plate Volume 5, Page 12 (see http://descegy.bibalex.org/index1.html), Page 72 left

Henri Bechard, "Le Sphinx Armachis, Caire (The Sphinx Amachis, Cairo) about 1880, Page 154 top

Suggested Reading and References
(The following were either used as background
or are specifically referenced in the text.)

Abubaker, Abdel Monein and Mustafa, Ahmed Youssef. *Aufsatze Zum to Geburtsag von Herbert Ricke*, "The Funerary Boat of Khufu". Wiesbaden. 1971.

Armour, Robert A. *Gods and Myths of Ancient Egypt*, American University in Cairo Press, Cairo, 1986.

Arnold, Dieter. *Building in Egypt: Pharaonic Stone Masonry.* Oxford University Press, Oxford and New York. 1991.

Arnold, Dieter. "Royal cult complexes of the Old and Middle Kingdoms," in *Temples of Ancient Egypt.* Byron E. Shafer, ed. Cornell University Press, Ithaca. 1997

Aldred, Cyril. *Egypt to the end of the Old Kingdom.* Thames and Hudson, London, 1965. (1982 edition)

Aldred, Cyril. *The Egyptians.* Thames and Hudson, London, 1992.

Anderson, James. M. and Edward M. Mikhail. *Introduction to Surveying.* McGraw-Hill Book Company, New York. 1985.

Anthes, Rudolf. "Egyptian Theology in the Third Millennium B.C.," *Journal of Near Eastern Studies,* 18/3(1959)169-212.

Badawy, Alexander. "Brick vaults and domes in the Giza necropolis," pp 129-143 in *Excavations at Giza 1949-1950* by Abdel-Moneim Abu-Bakr. Government Press, Cairo. 1953.

Badawy, Alexander. "A Monumental Gateway for a Temple of King Sety I: an Ancient Model Restored." in *Miscellanea Wilbouriana*, The Brooklyn Museum, Brooklyn NY. 1972.

Badawy, Alexander. "The Periodic System of Building a Pyramid," *JEA* 63:52-58. 1977.

Baines, John and Jaromir Malek. *Atlas of Ancient Egypt.* Facts on File. New York and Oxford. 1980.

Baines, John. "Society, Morality, and Religious Practice." in *Religion in Ancient Egypt.* Byron E. Shafer (ed). Cornell University Press, Ithaca, 1991

Bauval, Robert G. "A master-plan for the three pyramids of Giza based on the configuration of the three stars of the belt of Orion." *Discussions in Egyptology* 13:7-18. 1989.

Bauval, Robert and Adrian Gilbert. *The Orion Mystery.* Crown Publishers, Inc. New York, 1994.

Bell, Frederic G. "Engineering Geology and building stones of historical monuments: Construction materials; geological Origins: Quarries" p 1867-1874 in *The Engineering Geology of Ancient Works, Monuments and Historical Sites. Volume 4.* Paul G. Marinos and George C. Koukis (eds.), A. A. Balkema, Rotterdam, 1990.

Belzoni, G. *Narrative of the Operations and Recent Discoveries within the Pyramids, Temples, Tombs, and Excavations, in Egypt and Nubia..* H. Remy, Printer to the King. Brussels. 1835.

Bleeker, C. J. *Egyptian Festivals*, E. J. Brill, Leiden, 1967.

Brinker, Russell C. and Paul R. Wolf. *Elementary Surveying, Seventh Edition.* Harper and Row, New York, 1984.

Brock, Lyla. "New Pyramid Revealed at Giza." *KMT* 4(1):10-11. 1993.

Burton, Anne. *Diodorus Siculus Book I: A commentary.* E. J. Brill, Leiden, 1972.

Butzer, Karl W. *Early Hydraulic Civilization in Egypt.* University of Chicago Press, Chicago 1976.

Campbell, Donald H. and Robert L. Folk. The Ancient Egyptian Pyramids - Concrete or Rock?" *Concrete International* 13:28-39. 1991. (*Concrete International* is published by American Concrete Institute, Detroit, MI.).

Campbell, Donald H. and Robert L. Folk. "Letter: Pyramid debate." *Concrete International* 14:18-21, 1992.

Chadwick, Robert. "A Rebuttal to the SO-CALLED 'ORION MYSTERY' " *KMT* 7(3):74-83. 1996.

Clagett, Marshall. *Anceint Egyptian Science: a Source Book, (Volume One, in two parts),* American Philosophical Society, Philadelphia, 1989.

Clarke, Somers and R. Engelbach. *Ancient Egyptian Masonry*. Oxford University Press, London, 1930. Unabridged republication as *Ancient Egyptian Construction and Architecture* by Dover Publications, Inc. New York, 1990.

Clayton, Peter A. *Chronicle of the Pharaohs*. Thames and Hudson, London. 1994.

Cole, J. H. *Determination of the Exact Size and Orientation of the Great Pyramid of Giza.*
Survey of Egypt Paper No. 39., Government Press, Cairo, 1925.

Cook, R. J. "The elaboration of the Giza site-plan*." Discussions in Egyptology* 31:35-45. 1995.

Covington, M. Dows. "Mastaba Mount Excavations," *Annales du service des Antiquites de l'Egypte* VI:13-26. Cairo. 1905.

Cummings, Barbara. *Egyptian Historical Records of the Later Eighteenth Dynasty.* Aris & Phillips. LTD, Warminster, England. 1984.

David, Rosalie and E. Antony. *A Biographical Dictionary of Ancient Egypt.* University of Oklahoma Press, Norman. 1992.

Davidovits, J. "X-ray Analysis and X-Ray Diffraction of Casing Stones from the Pyramids of Egypt, and the Limestone of the Associated Quarries." pages 511-520 in *Science in Egyptology* , ed. Rosalie A. David, Manchester University Press, Manchester, England, 1986.

Davidovits, Joseph. "Ancient and Modern Concretes: What is the real Difference?" *Concrete International* 9:23-29, 1987.

Davidovits, Joseph. "Letter: Great Pyramid Debate." *Concrete International* 14:17-18, 1992.

Davidovits, Dr. Joseph and Margie Morris. *The Pyramids: an Enigma Solved.* Dorset Press, New York 1988.

Davies, N. de Garis. "An Apparent Instance of Perspectival Drawing," *Journal of Egyptian Archaeology,* XII(1926):110-112.

Dawson, Warren R. and Eric P. Uphill. *Who was who in Egyptology.* Third edition revised by M.L. Bierbrier. Egyptian Exploration Society, London. 1995.

Department of Antiquities, "Notes on Archeological Activities in Egypt", *American Research Center in Egypt Newsletter,* Vol 66, July 1968.

Derry, D. E. "Mummification II: Methods Practised at Different Periods." *ASAE* 41(1942): 240-265.

Drower, Margaret S. *Flinders Petrie: a Life in Archaeology, Second Edition.* University of Wisconsin Press, Madison. 1995.

Dunham, Dows. "Building an Egyptian Pyramid." *Archaeology* 9 (3):159-165. 1956.

Dunham, Dows and William Kelly Simpson. *The Mastaba of Queen Mersyankh III.* Museum of Fine Arts, Boston, 1974.

Edgar, John and Morton Edgar. *The Great Pyramid Passages and Chambers. Vol. 1.* Bone and Hulley, Glascow, 1910.

Edwards, I. E. S. *The Pyramids of Egypt* The Viking Press, New York. 1972.

Edwards, I. E. S. *The Pyramids of Egypt.* Penguin Books, London. 1993.

Edwards, I. E. S. "The Air-channels of Chephren's Pyramid" in *Studies in Ancient Egypt, the Aegean, and the Sudan.* Editors William K. Simpson and Whitney M. Davis. Museum of Fine Arts, Boston. 1981.

Emery, W. B. *Archaic Egypt: Culture and Civilization in Egypt Five Thousand Yeas Ago.* Penguin Books, London. 1961.

Engelbach, R[eginald]. "Précis of the Survey of Egypt Paper No. 39, by J. H. Cole on the Size and Orientation of the Great Pyramid." *Annales du Service* XXV (1925):167-173.

Englebach, R[eginald]. "A foundation scene of the second dynasty." *JEA* 20:183-4. 1934

Eyre, Christopher J. "Work and Organization of Work in the Old Kingdom" in *Labor in the Ancient Near East,* Marvin A. Powell (ed). American Oriental Society, New Haven. 1987.

Fakhry, Ahmed. *The Monuments of Sneferu at Dahshur, Vol. I. The Bent Pyramid.* General Organization of Government Printing Offices, Cairo. 1959.

Fakhry, Ahmed. *The Pyramids* University of Chicago Press, Chicago. 1974. (Published 1961, second edition 1969, third impression 1974.)

Folk, Robert L. "Letter: Folk's Response to Morris' Discussion" *Journal of Geological Education* 40(1992):344 (*Journal of Geological Education* published by Association of Geology teachers, Appleton, WI.).

Folk, Robert Louis and Donald Harvey Campbell. "Are the Pyramids of Egypt Built of Poured Concrete Blocks?" *Journal of Geological Education* 40(1992):25-34.

Frankfort, H[enri]. *Ancient Egyptian Religion.* Columbia University Press, New York, 1948

Frankfort, Henri. *Kingship and the Gods.* University of Chicago Press, Chicago, 1978 edition.

Gaballah, Ali Gaballah, Mustafa El-Zeiri, Gilles Dormion, and Jean-Yves Verd'hurt, "Architectural Survey of the Inner Arrangement of the Pyramid of Meidum: Discovery of Two Corridors and Two Chambers," *Abstracts of Papers, Eighth International Congress of Egyptologist,* Cairo, March 23-April 3, 2000.

Galvin, Marianne. "The Hereditary Status of the Titles of the Cult of Hathor," *JEA* 70(1984):42-49.

Gardiner, Alan. *Egypt of the Pharaohs.* Oxford University Press, London. 1964.

Gillam, Robyn A. "Priestesses of Hathor: Their Function, Decline, and Disappearance," *JARCE* 32(1995) 211-237.

Goedicke, Hans. *Re-Used Blocks from the Pyramid of Amenemhet I at Lisht,* Metropotan Museum of Art. 1971."

Goneim. M. Zakaria. *The Buried Pyramid.* Longmans, Green, and Co., London. 1956.

Griffith, F. Ll. "The Inscriptions," in *Medum* by W. M. Flinders Petrie, David Nutt, London, 1892

Griffiths, J. Gwyn. *The Origins of Osiris and his Cult,* E. J. Brill, Leiden, 1980.

Grimal,. Nicolas. *A History of Ancient Egypt.* Basil Blackwell Ltd., Oxford. 1995.

Grinsell, Leslie. *Egyptian Pyramids.* John Bellows Limited, Gloucester. 1947.

Grinsell, Leslie. *Barrow, Pyramid, and Tomb.* Thames and Hudson, London, 1975

Habachi, Labib. "NE64: Deux Graffiti de May." *Chronique d'Egypte,* 1954.

Hamblin, Dora Jane. "A Unique Approach to Unraveling the Secrets of the Great Pyramids." *SMITHSONIAN* , April 1986. pp 78-93.

Harpur, Yvonne, *Decoration in Egyptian Tombs of the Old Kingdom: Studies in orientation and scene content.* KPI Limited, London, 1987.

Harpur, Yvonne, *Tombs of Nefermaat and Rahotep at Maidum.* Oxford Expedition to Egypt, Prestbury, Great Britian. 2001.

Harrell, James A. "Misuse of the Term 'Alabaster' in Egyptology, *Goettinger Miszellen*, 119(1990)37-42.

Harrell, J. A. "Ancient Egyptian Limestone Quarries: a Petrological Survey" *Archaeometry* 34: 195-211. Oxford. 1992.

Harrell, James A. "Letter: Harrell's Response to Morris' Article." *Journal of Geological Education.* 42:195-198. 1994.

Harrell, James A. and Thomas M. Bown. "An Old Kingdom Basalt Quarry at Widan el-Fara and the Quarry Road to Lake Moeris." *JARCE* XXXII:71-91. 1995.

Harrell, James Anthony and Bret Edward Penrod. "The Great Debate - Evidence from the Lauer Sample," *Journal of Geological Education* 41:358-363 1993.

Hassan, Selim. *Excavations at Giza. 1932-33 Vol. IV.* Government Press, Bulaq. Cairo. 1943.

Hassan, Selim. *Excavations at Giza. 1933-34 Vol. V.* Government Press, Bulaq, Cairo. 1944.

Hassan, Selim. *Excavations at Giza. 1938-39 Vol. X, The Great Pyramid of Khufu and Its Mortuary Chapel.* Government Printing Offices, Cairo. 1960.

Hawass, Zahi. *The Funerary Establishments of Khufu, Khafra, and Menkaura during the Old Kingdom.* Ph. D. Dissertation. University of Pennsylvania, Philadelphia. 1987.

Hawass, Zahi. "The Discovery of the Satellite Pyramid of Khufu," pages 379-398 in *Studies in honor of William Kelly Simpson.* Peter der Manuelian (ed). Museum of Fine Arts, Boston. 1996.

Hawass, Zahi and Mark Lehner. "The Sphinx, Who Built It and Why?" *Archaeology* September/October 1994.

Hawass, Zahi. "Tombs of the Pyramid Builders." *Archaeology*, Jan/Feb 1997, p39-43.

Hawass, Zahi. The Discovery of a Pair-Statue near the Pyramid of Menkaure at Giza," *MDAIK*, 53:289-293. 1997.

Hawass, Zahi. "The Discovery of the Harbors of Khufu and Khafre at Giza," in *Etudes sur l'Anciene Empire et la necropole de Saqqara dediees a Jean-Philippe Lauer.* Catherine Berger and Bernard Mathieu (ed.) Universite Paul Valery, Montpellier, 1997. pp 245-256.

Hawass, Zahi. "Pyramid Construction: New Evidence Discovered in Giza." In *Stationen, Beitrage zur Kulturgeschichte Agyptens, Rainer Stadelmann Gewidmet,* edited by Heike Guksch and Daniel Polz, Philipp Von Zabern, Mainz, 1998, pp 53 - 62.

Hawass, Zahi. "The Programs of the Funerary Complexes of the Fourth Dynasty. " In *Ancient Egyptian Kingship*, edited by David O'Connor and David Silerman, E. J. Brill, Leiden. 1995.

Hawass, Zahi. *The Pyramids and Temples of Gizeh an Update.* Included with the 1990 reprint of Petrie's *The Pyramids and Temples of Gizeh*, Histories and Mysteries of Man, LTD, London, 1990.

Hawass, Zahi. *The Secrets of the Sphinx, Restoration Past and Present.* American University in Cairo Press, Cairo. 1998.

Hawass, Zahi, *Pyramid Discovered at Abu Rowash.* The Plateau – Offical Website of Dr. Zahi Hawass, http://www.guardians. net/new_pyramid_discovered_at_abu_ro.htm. 2002.

214

Herodotus. *The Histories.* Translated by Aubrey de Selincourt. Revised edition by John Marincola. Penguin Books, London. 1996.

Herodotus, *The Histories of Herodotus.* Translated by George Rawlinson.

Hobson, Christine. *The World of the Pharaohs.* Thames and Hudson, New York. 1990.

Hoffmeier, James. "The Use of Basalt in Floors of Old Kingdom Pyramid Temples." *JARCE* XXX:117-123 1993.

Hollis, Susan Tower. "Five Egyptian Goddesses in the Third Millennium BC," *KMT* 5:4 (Winter 1994-95), pp 46-51 and 82-85.

Hsu, Kenneth. . "When the Mediterranean Dried Up," *Scientific American*, December 1972. pp 26-36.

Hsu, Kenneth, J. *The Mediterranean Was a Desert.* Princeton University Press, Princeton, NJ. 1983

Hughes, Richard. "Observations on the recent stone block failure of the great Egyptian Sphinx monument." p 2025-2029 in *The Engineering Geology of Ancient Works, Monuments and Historical Sites. Vol. 4.* Paul G. Marinos and George C. Koukis (eds.), A. A. Balkema, Rotterdam, 1990.

Ikram, Salima. "Unique Structure Revealed in Front of Khafre Temple." *KMT* 7(3):18-19. 1996.

Ingram, Kevin D., Kenneth E. Daughterty, and James L. Marshall. "The pyramids - Cement or Stone?" *Journal of Archaeological Science.* 20:681-687, 1993. Academic Press Ltd.

Isler, Martin. "On Pyramid Building." *JARCE* XXII:129-142. 1985.

Isler, Martin. "On Pyramid Building II," *JARCE* XXIV:95-112. 1987.

Isler, Martin. "An ancient Method of Finding and Extending Direction." *JARCE* XXVI:191-206, 1989.

Jacquet-Gordon, Helen K. *Les Noms des Domaines Funeraires sous l'Ancien Empire Egyptien.* L'Institut Francais d'Archaeologie Orientale, Cairo. 1962.

Jenkins, Nancy, *The Boat Beneath the Pyramid,* Holt, Rinehart, and Winston, New York, 1980.

Jequier, Gustave. *Douze ans de fouilles dans la necropole memphite: 1924-1936.* Neuchatel, 1940.

Johnson, George. "The Pyramid of Meidum, Part Two," *KMT* 5(1):72-82. 1994.

Johnson, George. "The Red Pyramid of Sneferu: Inside and Out." *KMT* 8(3):18-27. 1997.

Kemp, Barry. "Old Kingdom, Middle Kingdom, and Second Intermediate Period c. 2686-1552 B.C." In B. G. Trigger *et al. Ancient Egypt: A Social History.* Cambridge University Press, Cambridge. 1983. pp

Kemp, Barry. *Ancient Egypt: anatomy of a civilization.* Routledge, London and NY. 1989.

Kiely, Edmond R. *Surveying Instruments: their history and classroom use.* National Council of Teachers of Mathematics, Nineteenth Yearbook. Bureau of Publications, Teachers College Columbia University, New York. 1947.

Klemm, Rosemarie and Dietrich D. Klemm. *Steine und Steinbrueche im Alten Aegypten.* Springer-Verlag, Berlin and New York. 1993.

Lally, Michael T. "Engineering a Pyramid," *JARCE* XXVI:207-218. 1989.

Lane, Edward William. *Description of Egypt*, American University in Cairo Press, Cairo, 2000

Lauer, Jean-Philippe. "Sur le choix de l'angle de pente dans les pyramides d'Egypte" *Bulletin de l'Institut d'Egypte* XXXVII p 57- 67. 1956.

Lehner, Mark. "Some Observations on the Layout of the Khufu and Khafre Pyramids," *JARCE* 20:7-25. 1983.

Lehner, Mark. "Giza: A Contextural Approach to the Pyramids." *Archiv fur Orientforschung* 32:136-158. 1985.

Lehner, Mark. "The development of the Giza Necropolis: the Khufu project." *MDAIK* 41:110-143. 1985.

Lehner, Mark. *The Pyramid Tomb of Hetep-heres and the Satellite Pyramid of Khufu.* Mainz, 1985.

Lehner, Mark E. *Archaeology of an Image: the Great Sphinx of Giza.* Ph. D. dissertation. Yale University, New Haven. 1991.

Lehner, Mark. "The Pyramid," in *Secrets of Lost Empires: Reconstructing the Glories of Ages Past.* Sterling Publishing Co., Inc. New York, 1997

Lehner, Mark. *The Complete Pyramids.* Thames and Hudson, Ltd. London. 1997.

Lehner, Mark. "The 1988/1989 Excavation of Petrie's "Workmen's Barracks" at Giza", *Journal of the American Research Center in* Egypt, Volume XXXVIII, 2001.

Lepre, J. P. *The Egyptian Pyramids.* McFarland and Company, Hefferson and London. 1990.

Lepsius, Richar. *Discoveries in Egypt, Ethiopia, and the Peninsula of Sinai in the Years 1842-1845.* London. 1852.

Lepsius, Carl Richard, *Denkmaeler aus Aegypten und Aethiopien.* Nicolaische Buchhandlung, Berlin, 1849.

Lesko, Barbara. *The Great Goddesses of Egypt.* University of Oklahoma Press, Norman. 1999.

Lesko, Leonard. "Ancient Egyptian Cosmogonies and Cosmology" p 88-122 in *Religion in Ancient Egypt,* Byron E. Shafer (ed). Cornell University Press, Ithaca, 1991

Lichtheim, Miriam. *Ancient Egyptian Literature, Volume I: The Old and Middle Kingdom.* University of California Press, Berkeley. 1973

Lloyd, Alan B. *Herodotus Book II: Introduction.* E. J. Brill, Leiden. 1975.

Lloyd, Alan B. *Herodotus Book II: Commentary 1-98.* E. J. Brill, Leiden. 1976.

Lloyd, Alan B. *Herodotus Book II: Commentary 99-182.* E. J. Brill, Leiden. 1988.

Lowdermilk, Robert H. "Re-inventing the Machine Herodotus Said Built the Great Pyramid," *KMT* 2(4):45-53 1991.

Lucas, A. and J. H. Harris. *Ancient Egyptian Materials and Industries. 4th ed.* Edward Arnold (publishers) Ltd. London. 1962.

Malek, Jaromir. "Orion and the Giza pyramids." *Discussions in Egyptology* 30:101-114. 1994.

Maragioglio, Vito and Celeste Rinaldi. *L'Architettura delle Piramidi Menfite.*
Parte II: La Piramide di Sechemkhet, La Layer Pyramid di Zauiet-el-Aryan e le minori piramidi attribuite alla III dinastia, Torino, 1963.
Parte III: Il Complesso di Maydum, la Piramide a Doppia Pendenza e la Piramide Settentriole in Pietra di Dahsciur. Rappalo, 1964.
Parte IV: La Grande Piramide di Cheope , Rapallo,1965.
Parte V: Le Piramidi di Zedefra e di Chefren , Rapallo, 1966.
Parte VI: La Grande Fossa di Zauiet el Aryan, la Piramide di Micerino, il Mastabat Faraun, la Tomba di Khentkaus, Rapallo, 1967.

Parte VII: Le Piramidi di Userkaf, Sahure, Neferirkara. La Piramide Incompiuta e le Piramidi minori di Abu Sir, Rapallo, 1970.
Parte VIII: La Piramide di Neuserra, la "Small Pyramid" di Abu Sir, la "Piramide distrutta" di Saqqara ed il Complesso di Zedkara Isesi e della sua Regina. Rapallo, 1975.

Martin, Geoffrey T. "'Covington's Tomb' and related early monuments at Giza." in *Etudes sur l'Ancien Empire et la necropole de Saqqara dediees a Jean-Philippe Lauer.* Catherine Berger and Bernard Mathieu (ed.) Universite Paul Valery, Montpellier, 1997. pp 279-288.

Mayes, Stanley. *The Great Belzoni.* Walker and Co., New York, 1961.

Mendelssohn, Kurt. *The Riddle of the Pyramids.* Praeger Publishers, New York. 1974.

Mercer, Samuel A. B. *The Religion of Ancient Egypt.* Luzac and Co. Ltd., London, 1949.

Messiha, Hishmat, "The Valley Temple of Khufu (Cheops)." *ASAE* 65 9-18 (1983)

Moores, Robert G., Jr. "Evidence for Use of a Stone-Cutting Drag Saw by the Fourth Dynasty Egyptians." *JARCE* XXVIII :139-148. 1991.

Moores, Bob. "Letter: Pyramid debate" *Concrete International* 14:82-84, 1992.

Morenz, Siegfried. *Egyptian Religion.* Cornell University Press, Ithaca, 1973 English edition. (Published in German 1960.)

Morley, Jacquline. *An Egyptian Pyramid.* Peter Bedrick Books, New York, 1991.

Morris, Margie. "Archaeology and Technology: an interview with Joseph Davidovits" *ConcreteInternational* 9:28-35, 1987.

Morris, Marge. "Letter: Morris Responds to Folk and Campbell." *Journal of Geological Education.* 40:344-346, 1992a.

Morris, Margie. "The Cast-in-Place Theory of Pyramid Construction" *Concrete International* 13:29, 39-44. 1991.

Morris, Margaret. "Geopolymeric Pyramids: A Rebuttal to R. L. Folks and D. H. Campbell" *Journal of Geological Education.* 40:35-46, 1992b.

Morris, Margaret. "How Not to Analyze Pyramid Stone. The Invalid Conclusions of James A. Harrell and Bret E. Penrod." *Journal of Geological Education.* 41:364-369, 1993.

Morris, Margaret. "Letter: Response to Harrell's Letter." *Journal of Geological Education.* 42:198-203, 1994.

Murphy, Edwin. *The Antiquities of Egypt. A Translation with Notes of Book I of the Library of History of Diodorus Siculus.* Transaction Publishers, New Brunswick, NJ. 1990.

Newberry, Percy E. *El Bersheh - part I.* Egypt Exploration Fund, London, 1892.

Perring, J. S. *The Pyramids of Gizeh* (2 volumes). London, 1839-40.

Perring, J. S. *The Pyramids to the Southward of Gizeh and Abou Roash.* London, 1842.

Petrie, W. M. Flinders. *Inductive Metrology; or, the Recovery of Ancient Measurements from the Monuments.* Edward Stanford, London, 1877.

Petrie, W. M. Flinders. *The Pyramids and Temples of Gizeh,* Leadenhall Press, 1883.

Petrie, W. M. Flinders. *The Pyramids and Temples of Gizeh.* Leadenhall Press. London, 1885. New and revised edition. Reprinted in series: Histories and Mysteries of Man Ltd. London, 1990.

Petrie, W. M. Flinders. *Medum.* British School of Archaeology in Egypt, London. 1892.

Petrie, W. M. Flinders, *Ten Years' Digging in Egypt (1881-1891).* Religious Tract Society, London, 189.

Petrie, W. M. Flinders. *Methods and Aims in Archaeology.* 1904, Reissued, Benjamin Blom, Inc. New York. 1972.

Petrie, W. M. Flinders. *Gizeh and Rifeh.* London. 1907.

Petrie, W. M. Flinders, Ernest Mackay, and Gerald Wainwright. *Meydum and Memphis III.* British School of Archaeology in Egypt and Egyptian Research Account, no 18. London, 1910.

Petrie, W. M. Flinders. *Tools and Weapons.* London, 1917.

Petrie, Flinders. *Egyptian Architecture.* Bernard Quaritch Ltd. London. 1938.

Petrie, Flinders. *Seventy Years in Archaeology.* Sampson Low, Marston and Company, Ltd. London.

Porter, Bertha and Rosalind L. B. Moss. *Topographical Bibliography of Ancient Egyptian Hieroglyphic Texts, Reliefs, and Paintings. III Memphis. Part I. Abu Rawash to Abusir.* Second edition with Jaromir Malek. Clarendon Press, Oxford. 1974.

Prentice, John E. *Geology of Construction Materials.* Chapman and Hall, London, 1990.

Quibell, James E. *Excavations at Saqqara. Vol. 5 (1911-1912): The Tomb of Hesy.* Cairo, 1913.

Random House. *The Random House Timetable of History.* Random House. 1993.

Redford, Donald B.. *Pharaonic King-Lists, Annals and Day Books.* Benben Publications, Mississauga, 1986.

Reisner, George. *Mycerinus: the temples of the third pyramid at Giza.* Harvard University Press, Cambridge, MA. 1931.

Reisner, George. *The Development of the Egyptian tomb down to the Accession of Cheops* Harvard University Press, Cambridge, MA. 1936.

Reisner, George. *History of the Giza Necropolis Vol. I.* Harvard University Press, Cambridge, MA. 1942.

Reisner, George and William Stevenson Smith. *History of the Giza Necropolis Vol. II.* Harvard University Press, Cambridge MA. 1955.

Robins, Gay and Charles Shute. *The Rhind Mathematical Papyrus: an ancient Egyptian text.* Dover Publications, NY, 1990. (copyright 1987)

Roth, Ann Macy. *Egyptian Phyles in the Old Kingdom.* Oriental Institute of Chicago, Chicago. 1991.

Rutherford, John B. "Letter: Pyramid debate" *Concrete International* 14: 21,82 , 1992.

Rsepka, Slawomir. "Some Remarks on Two Mycerinus Group Stateus," *Goettinger Miszellen,* 166:77-90. 1998.

Said, Rushdi. *The Geology of Egypt.* Elsevier Pub. Co., Amsterdam and NY. 1962.

Said, Rushdi. *The Geological Evolution of the River Nile.* Springer-Verlag, NY. 1981.

Said, Rushdi (ed). *The Geology of Egypt.* A. A. Balkema, Rotterdam and Brookfield, VT. 1990.

Sakovich, Anthony. 2002. "Counting the Stones." KMT, Fall. San Francisco: KMT Communications.

Saleh, Abdel-Aziz. "Excavations Around Mycerinus Pyramid Complex," *MDAIK,* 30:131-154. 1974

Schoch, Robert M. "Comment" to the article "Are the Pyramids of Egypt Built of Poured Concrete Blocks?" by R. L. Folk and D. H. Campbell. *Journal of Geological Education* 40:34, 1991.

Shadmon, Asher. *Stone: An Introduction.* Intermediate Technology Publications, London. 1989.

Shafer, Byron E. "Temples, priests, and rituals: an overview" in *Temples of Ancient Egypt.* Byron Shafer (ed). Cornell University Press, Ithaca, NY. 1997. pp 1 - 30.

Shaw, Ian and Paul Nicholson, *Dictionary of Ancient Egypt.* British Museum Press, London; Harry N. Abrams, Inc., New York, 1995.

Simpson, William Kelly. *The Mastabas of Qar and Idu.* Museum of Fine Arts, Boston. 1976.

Simpson, William Kelly. *The Mastabas of Kawab, Khafkhufu I, and II.* Museum of Fine Arts,Boston. 1978.

Smith, Harry. S. "Uncharted Saqqara: an essay." in *Etudes sur l'Ancien Empire et la necropole de Saqqara dediees a Jean-Philippe Lauer.* Catherine Berger and Bernard Mathieu (ed.) Universite Paul Valery, Montpellier, 1997. pp 3790393.

Smith, H. S. and D. G. Jeffreys. "A Survey of Memphis, Egypt," *Antiquity* LX:88-95. 1986.

Smyth, C[harles] Piazzi. *Life and Work at the Great Pyramid during the months of January, February, March, and April, A.D. 1865; with a Discussion of the Facts Ascertained.* Three volumes. Edmonston and Douglas, Edinburgh, 1867.

Smyth, Piazzi. *The Great Pyramid.* Gramercy Books, New York. *1994.* (Originally published in 1880 as *Our Inheritance in the Great Pyramid, 4th edition.*).

Spencer, A. J[effrey]. *Brick Architecture in Ancient Egypt* Aris & Phillips Ltd. Warminster, Wilts, England. 1979.

Spencer, A. J[effrey]. *Early Egypt: The Rise of Civilisation in the Nile Valley.* British Museum Press, London, 1993.

Stadlemann, Rainer. "The development of the pyramid temple in the Fourth Dynasty" in *The Temple in ancient Egypt.* Stephen Quirke (ed.) British Museum Press, London, 1997. pp 1-16.

Strudwick, Nigel. *The Administration of Egypt in the Old Kingdom: the highest titles and their holders.* KPI Limited, London. 1985.

Swelim, Nabil. *The Brick Pyramid at Abu Rowash, Number "1" by Lepsius: a preliminary study* Archaeological Society of Alexandria, Alexandria. 1987.

Swelim, Nabil. "The Pyramid Court and Temenos Wall of Khafre," in *Etudes sur l'Ancien Empire et la necropole de Saqqara dediees a Jean-Philippe Lauer.* Catherine Berger and Bernard Mathieu (ed.) Universite Paul Valery, Montpellier, 1997. pp 405-414.

Taylor, John. *The Great Pyramid. Why was it Built? & Who Built it?* Longman, Green, Longman, and Roberts; London. 1859.

Thompkins, Peter. *Secrets of the Great Pyramid.* Harper and Row, 1978.

Trigger, B. G., B. J. Kemp, D. O'Connor and A. B. Lloyd, *Ancient Egypt: a Social History.* Cambridge University Press, Cambridge, 1983.

Uphill, Eric. "The Egyptian Sed-Festival Rites," *JNES* 24(1965):365-383

Verner, Miroslav. *Forgotten Pharaohs, Lost Pyramids, Abusir.* Academia Skodaexport, Prague. 1994.

Verner, Miroslav. "Setting the axis: and ancient *terminus technicus,*" in *Etudes sur l'Anciene Empire et la necropole de Saqqara dediees a Jean-Philippe Lauer.* Catherine Berger and Bernard Mathieu (ed.) Universite Paul Valery, Montpellier, 1997. pp 433-436.

Verner, Miroslav and Gae Callender. "Two Old Kingdom Queens named Khentkaus." *KMT* 8(3):28-35. 1997.

von Bissing, Friedrich Wilhelm Freiherr. *Das Re-Heiligtum des Konigs Ne-Woser-Re (Rathures). Band II: Die Kleine Festdarstellung.* J. C. Hinrichs'sche Buchhandlung, Leipzig, 1923

Vyse, Howard. *Operations carried on at the Pyramids of Gizeh in 1937, Vol I, Vol II, Vol III.* James Fraser, London. 1840.

Week, Kent. R. *Mastaba of Cemetery G 6000,* Museum of Fine Arts, Boston. 1994.

White, K. D. *Greek and Roman Technology.* Cornell University Press, Ithaca, NY, 1984.

Wildung, Dietrich. *Egypt: From Pre-history to the Romans.* Taschen, Koln and New York, 1997.

Winkler, E. M. *Stone in Architecture: properties, durability. 3rd ed.* Springer-Verlag, Berlin and NY. 1994.

Wood, Wendy. "A Reconstructioin of the Triads of King Mycerinus," *JEA,* 60:82-93. 1974.